SUE  jour writ. leading newspapers and magazines. She has also worked in print and TV in the UK and New Zealand and has spent many years travelling extensively around the world.

Her first biography was the best-selling book about controversial NSW Police Commissioner Peter Ryan — *Peter Ryan: The Inside Story* — published in 2002. She has also written a travel book, *Getting There — Journeys of an Accidental Adventurer*, published in 2001, and contributed to a collection of short stories, *Love, Obsession, Secrets & Lies* the same year. She co-authored a motivational women's health guide, *Powering Up*, in 1994.

She lives in Sydney with her partner.

For more information about Sue Williams, visit her website at www.suewilliams.com.au.

Mean Streets

Kind Heart

The Father Chris Riley Story

SUE WILLIAMS

HarperCollins*Publishers*

HarperCollins*Publishers*

First published in Australia in 2003
This edition published in 2004
by HarperCollins*Publishers* Australia Pty Limited
ABN 36 009 913 517
A member of HarperCollins*Publishers* (Australia) Pty Limited Group
www.harpercollins.com.au

HarperCollins*Publishers*
25 Ryde Road, Pymble, Sydney, NSW 2073, Australia
31 View Road, Glenfield, Auckland 10, New Zealand
77–85 Fulham Palace Road, London W6 8JB, United Kingdom
2 Bloor Street East, 20th floor, Toronto, Ontario M4W 1A8, Canada
10 East 53rd Street, New York NY 10022, USA

National Library of Australia Cataloguing-in-Publication data:

Williams, Sue, 1959 Apr. 2– .
   Mean streets, kind heart: the story of Father Chris Riley.
   ISBN 0 7322 7472 9.
   1. Riley, Chris. 2. Catholic Church – Australia – Clergy –
   Biography. 3. Church youth workers – Australia – Biography.
   4. Social work with youth – Australia. I. Title.
282.94092

Cover design by Christa Edmonds, HarperCollins Design Studio
Internal design by Melanie Calabretta, HarperCollins Design Studio
Typeset by HarperCollins in Sabon 11.5/16pt
Printed and bound in Australia by Griffin Press on 79gsm Bulky Paperback White

10 9 8 7 6 5   05 06 07 08

To all streetkids, wherever you may be:

know that you are loved.

"We've got to have the courage to demand greatness from our young people."

FATHER CHRIS RILEY

Contents

FOREWORD

By The Honourable Sir William Deane

FOLLOWING A two-year inquiry by the Human Rights Commissioner Brian Burdekin, the Burdekin Report, *Our Homeless Children*, was released in 1989. It revealed that between 20,000 and 25,000 Australian children, some as young as 12, were homeless. Its findings rightly shocked our nation. Most of these children had fled from adults who were abusing them physically, sexually and emotionally, and were now living on the streets, behind shopping centres, in the bush, under bridges and in clothing bins. At the time, I personally believed that Brian Burdekin's estimate of numbers was, if anything, an understatement. Be that as it may, most experts believe that the number has continued to rise in the years since the release of the report.

Homeless children lack the opportunity to speak for themselves. Weighed down by their disadvantages, they are deprived of self-esteem, motivation and, too often, even hope. Without help, they are usually unable to cope. Many turn to drugs or crime or prostitution in their efforts to survive on the streets of our cities and, increasingly, our towns across Australia. If there is no one there to care, pick them up, dust them down and give them a new chance at life, they are likely to be lost forever.

I met Father Chris Riley in 1995 on the first of the farms he had set up to provide a home for boys he'd found living on the streets. Since then, I've been privileged to be associated with him, his work and his band of wonderful supporters. While I was Governor-General of Australia, I became patron, on a personal basis, of his charity, *Youth Off The Streets (Youth)*. When I left office, my wife, Helen, and I became joint patrons.

Over the years, I've watched the number of homes Father Chris has been able to offer streetkids, and those who've hit troubled periods in their lives, multiply. I've also watched the way he emphasises all that is positive about his charges' lives, concentrates on their strengths and their talents and encourages them to take up the challenge of starting afresh. Sometimes, he has been a tough taskmaster, but always there has been his insistence on hope — and his kindness and understanding. Those of us who've stood by and watched Father Chris, helping where we could, have been constantly surprised, and sometimes immensely touched, by the way the young people have responded to his care and guidance.

His success stories are legendary. The hardbitten survivors of the streets, the broken, damaged girls and boys, even those who've been convicted of the most terrible crimes, have often managed to completely turn around their lives. They've gone back to school. They've gone on to college. They've found jobs. They've had families. They've learned, at last, what it is like to love, and be loved. There have, of course, also been some failures. And they have been heartbreaking ... most of all for Father Chris himself.

The story of Father Chris Riley, through his work with the lost children of Australia, and through his commitment and dedication to their cause, is an inspiration to all caring Australians. It is eloquently told in this absorbing book by Sue Williams, one of our country's leading biographers. The story is an uplifting one of second chances, of survival, of renewal, of hope. Equally important, it is also the story of a truly good man who has shown the way towards a brighter future for our children. In helping him reach out to so many of them to give them a new start in life, we may hope to become better people ourselves.

I have often said that the ultimate test of our worth as individuals and as a community is how we treat our disadvantaged and vulnerable. In his work for the most disadvantaged and vulnerable of our children, Father Chris has made and is making a mighty contribution towards helping our Australian nation pass that test.

William Deane

PROLOGUE

HAVING 45,000 children would be pretty impressive for any man. But when that man's a Catholic priest, it's verging on the miraculous.

They're some of the toughest kids in the country, too. Boys who've hit big trouble with the law — one committing 137 crimes by the age of 11, another stabbing a charity worker to death with a carving knife. Girls who are sickeningly violent. Youngsters addicted to hard drugs. Children as young as nine who sell themselves on the streets.

They're kids who've been abused by everyone they've ever loved, kids who've given up their dreams of having a decent life, and kids on whom everyone else has turned their backs.

Yet Father Chris Riley never turns any child away. "How can you give up on a kid?" he asks, baffled. "You can never give up on them. There's always hope."

The man fondly nicknamed "Farvs" by the tens of thousands of streetkids he's helped throughout Australia has dedicated his life to making sure every one of them gets a second chance. And although the battles can be heartbreaking, every youngster he rescues from misery on the streets, and then teaches the skills to pick themselves up and lead a valued and fulfilling life, means one more person who's learned to trust again.

In the early days, working entirely alone, he rode a horse around the streets of Sydney's Kings Cross, looking for lost kids he could help. Today, his internationally acclaimed *Youth Off The Streets* (*Youth*) organisation runs more than 20 thriving projects.

Initiatives include residential farms in the country where kids learn how to pick themselves up again and live a rewarding life, a remarkable inner-city school for streetkids, a drug abuse program that sets children free from addiction and the now famous cattle drives through wild country, where youngsters can test themselves against the elements and savour some of the first triumphs they've ever experienced.

Each night, 365 days of the year, Father Chris has volunteers patrolling the streets to provide hot meals for children who have made their homes on the pavements, in the parks, and in the cold, dark doorways of the nation.

They're the forgotten children of Australia, the poorest members of one of the wealthiest nations on earth. But they've never been forgotten by their Farvs.

Most of *Youth's* funds come from big-hearted private benefactors, generous corporations and Father Chris's own flair for raising cash. He has gradually gathered together a team of top professional experts to help him, as well as a small army of volunteers who work all hours of the day and night to keep the kids safe. In just 11 years, he's built the largest youth community network in Australia, beguiling all who see the astonishing results he achieves. Little wonder then that *Youth* is the favourite charity of its patron, the former Australian Governor-General Sir William Deane.

Time after time, the children to whom Father Chris reaches out respond with gratitude, respect and love for the man who will stop at nothing to make sure they are given every opportunity to get back on their feet.

"There is no such thing as a bad child," says Father Chris. "There are only bad circumstances, situations, environments and families."

Many of us may believe the same, but Father Chris *lives* his beliefs. Every hour of every day.

This is his story and, since he has dedicated his life 100 percent to his kids, it's their story too. In some ways, it is also the story of modern Australia: sometimes sad and shocking, often heart-warming and uplifting, frequently funny and always incredibly inspiring.

Chapter 1

THE ODD ONE OUT

CHRIS RILEY wasn't like other kids. Everyone noticed it: his parents, his siblings, his aunts and uncles — even the little boy he befriended from the property across the dirt road from his family's small dairy farm in country Victoria.

Chris had a will of iron, even as a toddler. If he didn't want to do something, there was no way anyone could persuade him otherwise. The first signs of his stubborn nature came early. His parents, Kevin and Mavis Riley, were driven to distraction by their son's refusal to give up his bottle and move on to solid foods. When they tried to ease the bottle from his grip, he screamed and only clung onto it tighter, gritting his teeth with determination. Chris wandered around that farm, a few kilometres outside Echuca just across the Murray River from New South Wales, bottle firmly in hand, way past his fourth birthday.

He was also quite fearless. From the age of around one, Chris would climb anything and everything. He once had to be rushed to hospital when he slit both his feet open, from his toes to his ankles, while trying to climb a barbed-wire fence. Mavis held his hand all the way to the operating theatre, but soon had to run outside, feeling faint from the sight of so much blood pouring from the deep gashes. Another time she was forced to sit, heart in mouth, as Chris walked along the horizontal bar of the swings in their garden — a good three metres above the ground. He had once seen his dad do it and decided to try it himself.

Yet there was one quality that singled out Chris Riley most from everyone around him: he was a loner. His chronic shyness didn't help. When anyone came to call at the family farm, his sister and three brothers would race outside to greet them, while Chris would vanish from sight. Quite simply, he preferred his own company — and that of his animals — to spending any time with other people. He knew every single chicken on the farm by name, and spent hours talking to the horses. At country shows he would win prizes for skipping on the back of a pony, crawling between its legs, sliding down round its belly and climbing up on the other side. At school he was popular, but while the other kids would love to come on sleep-overs to his place, he would usually tire of their company quickly and disappear to one of his myriad secret places, leaving his visitors baffled and bewildered.

Kevin and Mavis Riley were constantly perplexed by the behaviour of their middle child, Christopher Keith, born on 24 November 1954 in Echuca Hospital in a cloud of chloroform. After the birth, Mavis was unable to recall a single thing about it as the matron liked to knock out women just as they went into labour, to make the whole experience less painful for both the mothers and the midwives. Chris was given the middle name of Keith after Kevin's older brother, who was killed in World War II at the age of 19. It was obvious from an early age that Chris was unlike his siblings. Of the five Riley children — Helen, the eldest, followed by Peter, Chris, Wayne and Greg — Chris was the only one who wasn't outgoing and sociable.

"He was quite different from the other children," says Kevin today. "He was so shy it was shocking. He just didn't seem to want to mix with people. He made friends easily, but he didn't want friends. He much preferred being on his own."

In a tight-knit, easy-going family in a small farming community, Chris's behaviour struck an odd note of discord. Mavis worried about him constantly. "He was just so shy," she says. "I wondered how he'd ever be able to cope with anything. As a teenager, I was terribly shy and wouldn't even go to a dance unless my mother came with me. So I could see a little bit of myself in him, and I knew he'd be given a tough time."

The Rileys were a down-to-earth couple unused to having to deal with difference; they were at a loss as to how to deal with their quiet, sensitive son. They were tough, practical people, eager to make a decent living for their kids, and impatient with distractions. Through the generations, their own families had never been any different.

Mavis's father, Thomas Edward Caine, known as TE or Ted, was born on 17 November 1890 on the Isle of Man in the British Isles. He came over to Australia at the age of 13 with two friends. He fought in World War I with the

Australian Army, and when he returned, worked as a dairy farmer on the rich pastoral plains surrounding Echuca, 217 km north of Melbourne.

Echuca began life in 1854 as a 26-person settlement of rough huts built on the peninsula formed by the Murray and the Campaspe Rivers at the junction of the Goulburn River, and was officially named the following year "Echuca", an Aboriginal word meaning "the meeting of the waters". An enterprising former convict, Henry Hopwood, built a pontoon bridge across the Murray, the river which formed the state border, linking Echuca with its NSW neighbour Moama, located a kilometre and a half away on the opposite bank. Hopwood went on to erect a toll bridge over the Campaspe, and establish a number of stores, gardens, vineyards and hotels.

By the time Ted Caine settled there in 1918, Echuca was a thriving small town of more than 3700 people, with a church, a post office, two banks, four hotels, a school, a community hall and a bustling cluster of tradesmen's workshops and stores. Farmers would ride into town once a week to stock up on supplies, then go straight back out to their farms. The town, by then covering $11 \, \text{km}^2$, continued to grow as the fertile river district — with its population of around 15,000 — became a prime source of wheat, wool, dairy products, citrus fruits and vegetables for the whole of Australia. It was also the crossing place for travellers over the Murray. With the discovery of gold in the Victorian Ranges, great herds of cattle and flocks of sheep were brought south to feed the miners and their families. Echuca, at one point, was Australia's greatest inland port, the hub of a vast supply system that connected 6400 km of navigable river to its wharf and rail terminus, while paddle steamers constantly plied up and down the Murray, bringing supplies 1600 km upriver to the goldfield towns.

The flavour of life during that period was successfully re-created in 1983, when the A$3 million television mini-series *All the Rivers Run*, starring Sigrid Thornton and John Waters, was filmed in Echuca. The sequel, *All the Rivers Run II*, was filmed there in 1989 and proved just as popular, airing in nearly 70 countries. Echuca is today known as the paddle steamer capital of Australia, with the historic boats now proving a popular tourist attraction, along with the faithfully restored port area and its massive red-gum wharf.

In its early days, Echuca's population was incredibly diverse — from overseas sailors who had jumped ship to try their luck looking for gold, and later, as disillusionment set in, moved north to operate the riverboats, to Irish immigrants who came to run hotels and work as tradesmen. When Ted Caine arrived he was simply in search of a better life elsewhere. And he found it. He met local girl Adeline Height (Ada), probably at a neighbourhood dance. She was pretty and quiet — and 10 years younger. They married and she bore him five children. The eldest, Phyllis, died at just 10 days old. Thankfully, all the others were born healthy: daughter Kit, the eldest, then Ed, Mavis (born on 24 January 1931) and Doug.

Mavis, quiet and shy like her mother, met Kevin Riley when she was 16. Kevin was a popular lad in the town, a fine sportsman with a wry sense of humour. He was a good cricketer and the star of the local Aussie Rules football team. Mavis had always loved footy and usually attended the local games. But it wasn't until a regular Saturday night dance in the community hall behind the local Catholic church, St Mary's, that the couple first got together. "She wasn't a bad dancer," says Kevin today. "I used to go to the dances and have a bit of a dance with her. I thought she wasn't a bad old stick at all. We got on very well. I remember the first time I went out with her, I sang 'Sweet Sixteen' to her, but I only knew the first two lines."

Kevin's cheerful outlook and jocular manner hid a troubled family life. His mother Alice, born on 10 January 1900, married a mechanic, Philip, 10 years older. It was a turbulent relationship. She bore him seven children: Roy (born in 1918), followed by Jean, Keith, Clare, Kevin (born in July 1930), Doug and Geoff, born 17 years after his eldest brother. But the couple argued often.

Even today, those bitter rows live on vividly in the memories of their children. Geoff, now 68, says he can still recall the raised voices. "I must only have been two or three, but I can still remember the argument when she finally told him to go and never come back," he says, quietly. "With seven kids to bring up she had to work hard to make ends meet after he left." Philip never did come back to the family home. He went to Melbourne, but later returned, settling just 40 km from Echuca. The two eldest children, Roy and Jean, visited their father occasionally, but the others had nothing to do with him. Kevin prefers to think of him as having died just after he was born. Philip Riley died 35 years ago, alone. His children only attended the funeral at the urging of their mother.

Alice's children grew up absolutely devoted to their mother, and with good reason. She worked long hours in a variety of menial jobs to support them all, scrubbing, cleaning, taking in the local bank manager's washing and doing the neighbours' ironing, with Geoff, as the youngest, usually staying home to help. She also regularly cleaned the Moama and Echuca town halls, two dentists, and the local doctor's surgery. "She was a pretty strong woman," says Geoff. "It was her strength of will that kept her going, and her faith."

Alice was a devout Catholic, and she raised her children in the same faith. Geoff grew up wanting to be a priest but couldn't handle the Latin the church then demanded for all the services, the study and the vows. Kevin never considered becoming a priest. He did, however, serve as an altar boy, and he's been a staunch believer and dedicated church-goer all his life.

When Kevin met Mavis, the pair courted for 18 months before deciding to marry. The only hurdle was that Mavis wasn't a Catholic. She was a baptised Anglican like her mother, Ada, while her father, Ted, was High Church of England. Finally, the priest at St Mary's agreed to marry the couple as long as Mavis promised to bring up their children as good Catholics. Mavis, aged 20, and Kevin, 21, took their vows on 14 July 1951, becoming the first mixed-religion couple ever to be married in front of St Mary's altar rather than hidden away in the vestry. Probably at the back of Kevin's mind was the hope that he would be able to convert his wife. He never did.

Together with Kevin's mother and youngest brother Geoff, the newly married couple ran a fruit shop in the middle of Echuca's High Street. The shop sat among tall, gracious old buildings with wide verandahs and a jumble of new modern stores. The area had gone through a period of decline when the river trade died as a result of the arrival of the railway from Melbourne in 1864 and the increasing popularity of the car. The town began to flourish again 20 years later with the building of better roads, the development of irrigation, advances in farming practices, the establishment of secondary industries and more efficient agriculture supply distribution systems. Big local businesses included the flourmill, sawmills, foundries, shipbuilding, a butter factory, cordial factories, ice works and, from 1959, a large ball-bearing factory. The town itself was, by then, home to around 5000 people.

After a few years Mavis and Kevin moved from town to an 8 hectare orchard 5 km away, where they grew apples, pears and oranges. Six years later, they quit the orchard to run a dairy farm — 93 hectares with 130 head of cattle — in partnership with the owner.

The farm was 18 km south-east of Koyuga, on the road to Tongala, past a seemingly endless expanse of flat, treeless fields that stretched as far as the point at which the horizon touched the wide blue sky. During dry summers, the windswept fields lay yellow and withered, full of spinifex. In good summers, when there had been plenty of rain, the pastures were rich, and the cows fat.

The farm itself was a small cluster of buildings off a dirt road, with a big shed out front, a muddy yard and no power. Soon after moving there, Kevin paid to bring electricity to the property. It was still a hard life, however, for a young couple who by then had five children.

Kevin quickly discovered that he wasn't cut out for dairy farming: he hated cows. "I never liked them," he says. "I always used to think, 'Bugger them!' I enjoyed a lot of things around the farm — weeding and making hay ... everything, really, about farming bar the milking. I never really learned to milk cows. But still I think it was the greatest thing we did for the kids, coming out to the farm. They loved the horses, and it was a great place for them to grow up."

Certainly, all the children say today that they had a happy childhood, although they all knew how tough those times were for their parents. "Life was really hard," says Chris today. "Mum was up at 6 a.m. every day milking cows. They never had holidays, they couldn't afford that, and they had to do all that milking all the time. Then Mum went into town and stacked shelves halfway through the night. Dad's other job was working on an assembly line in a factory.

"That had a great significance in my life — no matter what job they had, they saw it as a worthwhile one. Dad was working in his factory, always making sure there was a good atmosphere there, taking a leadership role, and joking around rather than being depressed about having to do the job. Tragically, he was sacked from the factory because he was the oldest there. Mum, who devoted her life to stacking those shelves, was also called in and sacked when she turned 55. It was terrible to see that happen to a woman who'd worked really hard. But then she started cleaning hotel rooms."

Watching his parents tackle each new setback, each new challenge, with energy and cheerful enthusiasm taught Chris to do exactly the same thing.

"I guess I ended up with the attitude that no matter what you do, it's really important," he says. "It might be teaching kids in a class, it might be negotiating deals. Whatever I do, I see even the very small things as important. Also, I work hard and have an incredible capacity for work. I don't burn out or get worn out easily."

Because they could see that their parents were working hard, the kids all pitched in and helped. The two eldest were particularly useful. Helen did her share of the housework, and she and Peter often used to help Mavis milk the cows. No one ever asked Chris to help in that task. They recognised that he wouldn't be much good at it. "He would have been too slapdash at it," says Kevin. "He would have always been saying, 'Hurry up!' He was always in such a rush about everything."

Chris was small for his age, skinny, quiet and thoughtful. "He looked like if you picked him up, he might break," says youngest brother Greg. Chris's sister and brothers accepted his silences and his need to be either alone or with the animals. From the age of three he always had a dog. His first one was a Pekinese. When she died, Chris, then seven, asked for another dog for Christmas. Getting up early on Christmas morning, he was devastated to find no trace of a dog in the house. Despite feeling gloomy, he tried to smile through the day's ritual of lunch with one grandmother and tea with the other. When the family arrived at Ada's house, however, he was delighted to find a tiny Corgi pup waiting for him. "Rosie" followed him everywhere for years. These days, his dogs have grown a little larger. Now he rarely goes anywhere without his giant Great Dane, Woods, lolloping at his heels.

Every morning on the farm, Chris would get up and help Mavis feed the calves, then feed and play with his dog before feeding the chickens, horses, birds and pet rabbits. "That was heaven for me," he says now. The chickens were a particular favourite. Kevin used to despair of his son's attachment to them. When he was very young, Chris loved putting his favourite chickens in his pram and taking them for a ride. When visitors came, he'd sneak out the door and spend the afternoon chatting to the chickens. "He was mad on chooks," says Kevin. "Every time we moved, I had to build another chookhouse. Even when we moved to town, I had to build a bloody chookhouse. He'd insist on sitting and watching me while I did it. Once, he was sitting so close that I hit him accidentally with a crowbar while I was making the thing, and had to rush him to hospital for stitches. Every chook would have a name, and he'd even go off playing football with a chook under his arm."

Chris also loved horses, and would spend every spare moment in the stables. He and Helen could perform tricks with the horses and, every fortnight, they would ride 18 km into Echuca to attend pony club, then ride all the way back again. Later, Wayne would go too, but Chris would quickly lose patience with his little brother, who was never as passionate about horses as his older siblings. Wayne remembers clearly a time when Chris exploded at him when they were out riding. Chris wanted Wayne to ride behind him, in order to calm down Wayne's skittish mount, but Wayne refused. Fuming, but absolutely determined to have his way, Chris eventually crossed the road and backed up his horse to force his younger brother to follow him. "He was just so stubborn," says Wayne. "And he still is."

It was Chris's love of horses that cemented his first close friendship too, with the boy who lived on the farm next door, Denny Oliver.

"What we had in common was always the horses," says Denny, who went into farming when he finished school. "He loved animals, and was a good, and very capable, rider. We'd just ride horses and talk about them all the time. We used to jump on a horse and say, 'We'll be back later!' When we played around, it was on horses, playing at cowboys and indians like normal kids.

"But there was something about him that made him different. It's hard to explain what. All the other kids always did something stupid, or something wrong, but he never seemed to do those things. If it wasn't me getting into strife, it was someone else, but he never did. With Chris, that was unheard of. He just wasn't like the rest of us."

Chapter 2

HARD LESSONS

WHEN IT was time for Chris Riley to start school, Mavis grew anxious, fearing he wouldn't cope. His sister Helen also worried how her kid brother would manage, but at least she knew he could brawl with the best of them. As children, the pair were constantly fighting, and even though Helen, as the eldest, always won, Chris could certainly hold his own.

Mavis and Helen also wondered how Chris would cope with sitting still at a desk all day — he seemed to have so much energy, and did everything at such a fast pace. "He was always really skinny," says Helen. "I think that was because he was always on the move, always doing five things at once. I remember the doctor saying that most people are like the cow, they just plod along, but that Chris was like a deer, always on the move. Of course there was no such thing as Attention Deficit Hyperactivity Disorder (ADHD) then, but nowadays I wonder if Chris's hyperactivity was something to do with that."

School made a huge impression on the young Chris Riley but he didn't really make much of an impression on school.

Chris began his education in 1959 at St Joseph's, a Catholic school just out of Echuca. The school had started in Henry Hopwood's handsome old red-and-cream brick two-storey mansion, which was bought by the church in 1885, 16 years after his death, and renovated as a convent for the Brigidine nuns. The first lessons were held in the convent parlour the following year. As the number of pupils enrolling at the school increased, buildings were added, and the stables were demolished to make way for extra classrooms and a beautiful chapel with a marble altar.

In 1963, Chris was transferred back into town to St Mary's, a school at the rear of the stately old church, which had been newly taken over by St Joseph's and established as the main Catholic primary school. It had begun in the 1870s with classes for 30 children held in the chapel by a husband and wife who were both teachers. At the time local Catholics petitioned both Houses of Parliament for education grants, without success. In 1886, however, the local bishop, the Most Rev Dr Martin Crane, went to Europe for an eye operation. He happened to meet a bishop from Ireland, and he told him of the school's problems. The Irish bishop, keen to help, sent four young nuns from the Brigidine Sisters in southern Ireland over to Australia to take charge of the school. They achieved immediate results. By December the following year, the cornerstone of a new primary school at the site was blessed. By 1919 the long, low red-brick building that still stands today had been put in place, with its five classrooms all run by the four nuns and the occasional lay teacher.

By the time Chris joined the school, it had grown to over 300 pupils, and there were up to 70 children in each classroom. To keep everything rolling along smoothly there had to be a strict system of discipline, and the Brigidine nuns — renowned for their dedication to teaching and training the young — were experts. They swept through the corridors in their long black robes and white linen headdresses, using a strap to punish children when they didn't behave. They allowed no nonsense. "We really did require discipline, because it was the only way you could control the kids in such huge classes," says Sister Rosa Bourke, who taught at the school at the time. "It was quite different then. You taught, and you expected the kids to sit up and listen."

The children sat in rows in the large, airy classrooms with their high, arched windows and walls with cracks forever appearing due to ground movements caused by the subterranean river. There were so many students that if every pupil were present on any given day, they had to sit three to a seat. Funds were tight. The school received no money from the government; it was paid for entirely by the parish and by fees paid by the parents. These fees had to be kept low to ensure that most Catholic kids could attend, for their parents were taught that if they didn't send their children to a Catholic school, they would go to hell, says Noela Hickey, the one lay teacher at St Mary's during that time. "We used to have one storybook for the whole year," she says. "For the year, we'd read one page a day. There was no such thing as a library. When I came in 1962, they said they couldn't afford to pay me the full wage, so could I take less? Often, they wouldn't pay me at all for weeks. They said I was living at home, so I'd be all right."

Chris arrived, keen, quick to learn, and eager to please. He was always fairly near the top of his class, but never quite at the top — that position might have attracted more attention than he would have been happy with. He wasn't a brilliant pupil, but he was diligent, focused and worked hard for his marks. "He was a bit of a bookworm, and while I don't believe he was that good at school, he would always tackle it head-on," says his youngest brother Greg. Often, Chris worked equally hard at not standing out. When one of the nuns told him off for not finishing a sewing project, he stayed up until 2 a.m. at home trying to finish it. When Mavis discovered him sitting up, bleary-eyed, on the side of his bed, she snatched the project from her son and ordered him to get to sleep. Then she finished it off, leaving it on the bed for him. Chris remembers vividly the relief he felt when he saw it there.

Chris was so quiet that the principal when he first started, Mother Marie Anne O'Brien, doesn't even remember him at primary school. Hickey, however, has a vague memory. "I remember Chris as a little blond fellow playing footy with all the other kids," says Hickey. "He was always a good little boy who did as he was told. The whole family were nice kids. Sometimes, they'd say, 'My mum's not a Catholic, you know.'"

Church played a major role in the pupils' daily routine, with attendance at regular masses and confession compulsory. If anyone didn't attend mass on Sunday, they'd be lined up at school on Monday and asked where they had been. All the children were well aware that in every large family there was at least the hope that one boy would become a priest, and the school encouraged that desire among its pupils. The church elders were always stressing Catholics' duty to stand up for justice wherever it was under threat in the world. Today, the board in the nave of the church reminds visitors, in the adapted words of British statesman and philosopher Edmund Burke, that, "It's necessary only for the good man to do nothing for evil to triumph." It's easy to see where Chris, an impressionable young boy, first encountered the idea that helping others in a wider world outside his own experience was a worthy mission.

The nuns also had a significant impact on Chris. Among most of the pupils, they were regarded with a mixture of awe and respect. In the corner of the school building was the nuns' room, where pupils had to knock sharply on the door for attention. Even Hickey wasn't allowed in; she had to eat her lunch with the children. Chris was fascinated by those nuns, and their dedication to teaching. "I enjoyed all the lessons and I thought the nuns were very good teachers," he says. "I think a lot of my ability to teach comes from them."

Every weekday, after he caught the bus home from school, Chris climbed into the rafters of the old farm shed, where Kevin had built an attic room. There he would dress up in an old frock of his mother's and arrange a scarf on his head to look like a nun. Then he'd order his two younger brothers, Wayne and Greg, and his friend

Denny, who was a year below him at school, to be his pupils, and try to teach them what he had learned that day.

"He wasn't playing," says Helen. "He was deadly serious about it. If they mucked around, they'd get a clip round the ear or get told off." Denny also recalls those lessons well. "I remember him trying to teach me, but he never had much luck with me," he says. "I wasn't a good student — I ended up failing abysmally. I think he started wanting to be a teacher from that time. He'd only have been six or seven, but he always wanted to be a teacher."

Wayne didn't enjoy his brother's lessons much either. He longed instead to be out playing football or cricket. "I don't know why he did it," says Wayne. "He may well have been born to teach, or it may have been about his own desire to learn. But he was so shy and almost reclusive that I think it was his way of communicating." Greg proved only a marginally more willing pupil. "I went up there for the lollies and smokes he'd give us," he says. "He reckons today he didn't give us smokes, but I know he did."

Chris's influence over his younger brothers wasn't as strong as he might have hoped. Another of the nuns from that period, Mother Cletus Dullard, arrived at St Mary's just as Chris left, and ended up teaching Wayne and Greg. The behaviour of these two was in stark contrast to what she'd heard about Chris. "They were the complete opposites of him," she says. "They weren't the teacher's best friend at all! They were nothing like Chris."

While Chris was seen by his teachers as reserved, his iron will showed no sign of softening when he was within the safety of his family. His sister Helen talks about his fiery temper when anyone tried to thwart him which, although it didn't appear too often, could be explosive. These days, his temper is usually only evident when his work or any of the kids he has in his care are under threat; back then it used to fire up whenever he felt he was in the right and others weren't. Helen remembers clearly an altercation at the dinner table between Chris, then aged seven, and their dad — whom most of them call by his first name. "Chris would *never* back down," she says. "This day, Kevin was sitting beside him, and because Chris wouldn't back down, Kev gave him a whack. Chris turned to him and said, 'Hit me again.' We're all sitting there going, 'Oh noooo ...' In the end, Kev did give him another hit, but Chris would not back down. He would *not* cry until he was safe in the privacy of his own room. He didn't care what the consequences were; he just would never back down. He knew how far to push Kev. They used to argue. It could be like the meeting of two bulls."

Greg also remembers those arguments across the dinner table. "He always stood up for his beliefs, even as a kid," he says. "Then there'd be a row between Mum and Dad, and he'd step in to defend Mum. He got a lot of spoons thrown at him over the table, and a few hits and bumps along the way. They didn't perturb him. He'd never give in."

Chris wasn't averse to the odd piece of mischief either — and he rarely got caught. His mate Denny, for example, remembers Chris at the age of eight or nine stealing a packet of cigarettes. "He may have bought them, but I doubt it since we never had any money," he says. "We smoked them, and then, after about an hour we were really sick! That's about the only time I remember him doing anything wrong." Wayne too remembers sharing a cigarette with Chris behind the bike shed at school. "He'd do those normal things that all kids do, but he was always his own person."

Despite being a good student and liking his lessons, Chris never really enjoyed the total experience of school. He found much of it boring, and felt overwhelmed by the presence of so many other children for so much of the day. "I was a loner," he says. "I didn't make friends very easily. I didn't know the words 'introvert' and 'extrovert' in those days, but I just knew I couldn't have people around me 24 hours a day. I couldn't cope. I suppose 'introvert' was a bad word then, but it's just that I got my energy from being alone, rather than from being with other people." Nearly every day he'd slope off when no one was looking and visit his grandmother, Alice, for lunch. Sitting in that house, surrounded by holy pictures and religious icons, she'd serve him up his favourite meal: fish fingers, mashed potatoes and peas. "She would have my special lunch there ready for me every day," says Chris. "She was quite a spiritual lady, and her faith was important to her. She had a great influence on my life. I loved being there. At school I didn't fit in with anyone. I felt so alone." This early sense of isolation perhaps offers a clue as to why he relates so well today to young people who feel alienated and lost.

At the age of around eight, Chris first saw the 1938 American movie *Boys' Town* on the family's TV. In the film, a host of troubled kids are saved by Father Flanagan

— played by a splendidly handsome Spencer Tracy — a Catholic priest who sets up a school for juvenile delinquents, the toughest of whom is a boy brought to life by Mickey Rooney. Chris was spellbound by the tale. Flanagan seemed a true hero for the modern age, thanks partly to an inspired piece of casting in the Oscar-winning Tracy, who was himself educated by the Jesuits, and had considered studying for the priesthood before quitting to join the navy. Every time the film ran on TV Chris was there, enchanted and stirred. Nowadays, he believes seeing that film for the first time was a defining moment. It gave him the idea that he too could do that kind of work, and that he might be eminently suited to it.

In 1967, at the age of 12, Chris transferred back to St Joseph's, which was now functioning as the high school only. There were around 270 children at the school at the time, more than two-thirds of them girls, since many of the boys, particularly the sons of the wealthy farmers, were sent to Rupertswood College, a boarding school at Sunbury, a school with a particularly good reputation, especially in agriculture. St Joseph's then was both a very female and a very traditional environment, with classes of 40-plus pupils taught by one of the eight nuns or six lay teachers — five of them women — standing on the platform that ran along the front of every room. With only one male teacher on the staff and the boy pupils so heavily outnumbered by the girls, the boys attracted much more attention than they would in other schools. This made Chris even more uncomfortable. "The girls idolised the boys because there were so few of them," says Margaret Kennedy, who has been teaching at the school since 1972.

"They'd open the doors for the boys and let them enter the classrooms first. I know Chris would have hated all that attention."

He certainly did, and occasionally he took his revenge — although well out of sight of his teachers. The Riley family moved to another farm, at Nanneella, 12 km out of town, and every day he travelled on the school bus to and from St Joseph's. On that bus, when the older boys would sometimes run riot, pelting the more easy-going drivers with apple cores and jabbing the girls with straightened bale hooks, Chris would often join in teasing the girls. Eileen McQuillen, one of the first lay teachers at the school, was shocked some years later when her youngest daughter told her how Chris used to taunt her. "He was so meek and mild at school, I couldn't imagine him being like that, but apparently he was," she says. "He'd call her names and tease her mercilessly. He may be carrying the cudgels for everyone now, but he certainly wasn't then. He'd bully her."

In the classroom, Chris tried to concentrate on his lessons for the first two years. His school reports from that time say he was consistently an "excellent" pupil, hardworking, co-operative and pleasant. The Brigidine order placed emphasis on the belief that every single child had potential, and that education was a way of helping them realise that promise. This conviction had a profound influence on Chris. By the start of his second year at the school, he seemed to have shaken off, a little, his determination to stay in the background: he was top of his class, and came second in the scholarship exam.

Undoubtedly, the nuns' strictness with their pupils also

left a lasting impression on Chris. He too can be strict with his own students, setting them limits and insisting that they stick to them. "I was a strict teacher," says his former primary principal, Mother O'Brien, who also served at St Joseph's. "I ask the Lord to make straight what I made crooked from being too strict. I worry that my strictness may sometimes have turned them off religion. But in those days the classes were so big, and parents had to dig so deep to pay for their children's education that you wanted to do your best by them."

She recalls Chris as being very unobtrusive. "He came from a very good family, with a standing in the parish," she says. "A good home life was important. He was one of those students you liked to have in your class. He was interested in the work, did well and didn't cause problems. But he was so quiet, I'm surprised at the initiatives he has taken in his priesthood." Mother Canisius Larkin, the Mother Superior or principal at the time, also remembers Chris as a hardworking young lad who was terribly quiet. "I'm constantly amazed at how he joined the Salesians and ended up being so wonderful with young people," she says. "He was just so shy and retiring in those days, I've watched with great interest his progress ever since school. It's amazing to think how he must have come out of himself and realised how he had a gift with young people. He certainly didn't have it in those days."

From the second term of his second year at the school, however, Chris's teachers noticed he didn't seem quite as keen as he had once been, and his exam marks began to show a slight decline. In truth, he'd begun thinking about the possibility of going over to Rupertswood College. At

St Joseph's in Year 9 there were only seven other boys in the class; in Year 10 there would only be one other. Even though he was popular with the girls — "They were always chasing him!" says Helen — and he often went out with the best-looking girls in his class, the idea of studying in a room full of girls made him feel uncomfortable. The movie *Boys' Town* played regularly on TV and Chris still sat and watched it, spellbound, every time. He daydreamed about being taught by priests instead of nuns. He wondered if any of them might be like Spencer Tracy. Little did he know that lying in wait for him was a priest more like a movie villain than a Hollywood hero.

Chapter 3

A BAPTISM OF FIRE

CHRIS WAS the only one of the Riley children who wanted to go to Rupertswood College. Indeed, his elder brother Peter had even left St Joseph's in favour of the local non-denominational Echuca High School for the last two years of his education, and his younger brother Wayne had refused to go to St Joseph's in the first place. Wayne and Greg both went to the same school as Peter for their entire secondary education.

When Chris suggested to his parents that he move to the Salesian boys' boarding school in Sunbury, 35 km north west of Melbourne, they agreed, much to his surprise. He'd assumed that they wouldn't be able to afford it, but they were determined to do their best for their second son. They travelled down from Echuca to the college and asked if Chris could enrol. The principal politely thanked them for their interest, but said there was no room for Chris that year. Showing the kind of stubbornness that they had despaired of so often in their son, Kevin and Mavis simply hung around outside the college, waiting. Finally, the principal walked back out to see them.

"Aha!" Kevin whispered to Mavis, "We've got him now!" He was right. A few days later, at the age of 14, Chris was formally admitted as a pupil. It was an experience that was to change his life forever.

The school buildings were set around an elegant two-storey, 50-room Victorian mansion built in 1874 by landowner, stud-breeder and philanthropist Sir William Clarke. Clarke's father, the pastoralist Sir William Clarke Snr, was thought to be the richest man in the country at that time. With its 30-metre tower adorned with Gothic detail, its stained-glass windows, courtyard and ballroom, the school mansion, reached via a winding road from the gatehouse and lodge at the entrance through 360 hectares of magnificent landscaped gardens and a lake bubbling with ducks, is a well-known landmark in the state.

Close to the mansion is the cricket oval that has become world-famous for its claim to be the birthplace of the Ashes. In 1882, with the odds against them, Australia beat England in London and Britain's *Sporting Times* newspaper printed an obituary to English cricket, declaring, "The body will be cremated, and the ashes taken to Australia." Shortly afterwards, the English team toured Australia and played a friendly match at Rupertswood, since Clarke was president of the Melbourne Cricket Club at the time. Legend then has it that Lady Clarke presented England's captain with a small urn that contained the ashes of a bail from the match — which ended up giving the series of England–Australia fixtures their name.

The Salesians, a teaching order of Catholic priests and brothers based in Turin, Italy, arrived in Australia in 1927 and bought the property the same year to set up a school. They erected buildings next to the mansion to provide classrooms and boarding facilities for boys, opened the chapel and set up the dining room in the mansion, and started attracting students from all over Victoria and southern NSW. By the time Chris went there in 1970, the school had 250 day students as well as 250 boarders, a fine reputation for both academic and agricultural subjects, a good record in sport, and a strong tradition of religious instruction.

Chris was excited about the challenges that lay ahead, but also nervous. His parents shared his anxiety. Saying farewell to him that first day after driving the 230 km from Echuca, they reassured their son that they would visit him every month. In the event, they dropped by to see him every week. "Well, he'd never been away from home before," explains Mavis. "He was so shy, we worried about him." Kevin nods. "If I couldn't go one week, Mavis would go." Mavis tried in any way she could to make the separation easier. "We used to take him food too, as he used to be such a faddy eater," she says. "Today, I can hardly believe the kind of things he'll eat with the kids, bearing in mind what little he'd eat when he was younger. He used always to have five sugars in his tea. I kept saying to him, 'You won't get that at college!' But he did."

Chris was still a small, skinny boy who looked much younger than he was. Rupertswood offered a tough life in a pretty spartan environment and, for a kid as introverted as Chris, it could have been a disaster. And it very nearly was.

The kids slept in long dormitories of up to 100 children with bare concrete floors and wooden walls. They studied in their free time in big, impersonal halls under the supervision of priests and brothers — either priests in waiting or seniors who'd decided to stop short of taking their final vows. Each day was divided into lesson periods. The rules were strict. If a pupil misbehaved in the dorm, he'd be made to stand out in the cold, draughty corridor, where he'd be mocked by other students walking past. "That would be seen to be a humiliating and tough punishment," says Father John Papworth, the principal of the school today. "It would have been a tough life for Chris as a shy country boy, there's no doubt about it. As he got over his shyness and homesickness, he would have been tested pretty sorely. It would have been easy for him to have become a victim if he didn't fit in quickly."

No one had any idea, however, just how much of a victim he was actually becoming. Starting at the school in Year 10, when all the other pupils had already been there for two years, meant that Chris had to break into a culture that was already firmly established, and decidedly resistant to outsiders. It left him prime fodder for the bullies both among the older, bigger boys and a few of the brothers. "I felt so isolated and alienated in that first year," he says. "I felt like I was a real victim, and I was picked on." It wasn't just the other children who tormented him, though. There was also one particular brother who helped make Chris's life a misery.

This brother was, at first, extremely friendly towards Chris. He invited Chris into his study for cosy chats, asked him to assist preparing lessons and gave him special jobs to do, such as getting the sports equipment ready. Chris was flattered by his interest, grateful for his friendship and dazzled by the attention. He quickly began to idolise this brother, who was a talented musician and an accomplished sportsman; he had a wonderful way with his students and he was enormously charismatic. Chris would have done anything for him, and frequently did, finding himself marking out the athletics zone on the sportsfield at 3 a.m. or actually setting the Year 7 classwork for the brother in his own free time. Yet while Chris adored this man, the brother was playing cruel games with his young pupil. One day, during a coaching session for the athletics team, the brother screamed at the first runner in the relay team to get a move on. Chris, who was the second runner, piped up, "Brother, he can hear you, you don't need to scream." The brother looked coldly back at him but said nothing. Later, after tea, Chris saw him and said, "Hi". The brother simply pulled back one arm and smashed Chris across the face, knocking him to the ground. Chris was stunned. The brother didn't speak to him for two weeks after that. Then he called Chris to his science room to apologise and ask his student for forgiveness.

"I felt we were really close and I was utterly loyal to him," says Chris. "But there was so much crazy stuff going on. Our relationship was out of control. I'd work for him until late at night, or early into the morning, then he'd get up the next day and refuse to even acknowledge that I existed, which devastated me. He wouldn't talk to me for a week, leaving me feeling miserable and rejected, and wondering what I'd done wrong. Then he'd send for me in the middle of study and off I'd go, with every kid in that study room knowing who had called me out, which was hard enough. When I found him, he'd say, 'Look, I'm really sorry.' I invariably felt so low, I always forgave him, and then he'd win me over as if he was my best friend."

In retrospect, what Chris experienced was common manipulative paedophile behaviour: the earning of a child's friendship, testing his loyalty, and playing with his emotions to the point where he'll do anything to please and earn back that earlier warmth. Luckily for Chris, he's never been someone who was comfortable with physical closeness. "This is a guy who could have come close to sexually assaulting me," he says today. "But my signals have always been clear. So I think he would try to get close to me, he would say, 'Come to my room, you've hurt your leg at football and I'll rub it with liniment.' And I'd say, 'No, please don't rub my leg.' I wasn't thinking of any abuse — of course we knew nothing about that in those days — and this man was a hero to me. But I've always had my personal boundaries. I've never been a touchy-feely person, so I simply wouldn't have wanted him to rub my leg. I just thought sometimes he was a bit mad."

Those doubts intensified over the months of that first year. It was the brother's job to put the flag up on the top of the steeple at the mansion. The steps were steep and narrow, and the climb was hard. Often, he'd send for Chris when he was at the top and, when Chris arrived, he would faint and collapse on him. The boy would sit patiently until his teacher came round. Once the brother told Chris he was suffering from leukaemia and didn't have much longer to live. He'd often then threaten to throw himself from the top of the steeple, and Chris, beside himself with fear, would have to pull him back from the edge, and plead with him to climb down. At the end of that year, the brother was transferred to another school. Chris, who still revered him, was bereft, and wrote to the brother, begging him to stay in touch. He never heard a single word. A few years later, when the brother had left the Salesian order, Chris tried to trace him, but with no luck again. Six years ago, when he was perusing Australia's convicted paedophiles list, Chris was stunned to find that the man was not only still alive, but had been convicted of sexual abuse.

This brother's erratic behaviour, in addition to Chris feeling so isolated among the other pupils, took a terrible toll on the teenager. At the end of every day he would go to the chapel, kneel down and sob with misery and bewilderment, praying to God for help. The symbol of the cross became a source of enormous comfort. "I would say, 'OK Lord, you took on the cross, is that what you want me to do?' I prayed to the cross a great deal. I was certainly suffering, and I wondered if He wanted me to suffer." From the depths of his despair, however, Chris became stronger. "I think from those moments I went from being someone who could easily be stood over to someone who could be attacked and never fazed. Even today, people can attack me at any level — which they have — and I still won't give a damn. I don't get hurt any more. Emotionally, I'm very tough. That all came from that time." It was also the beginning of a real commitment to Jesus, who, at times, Chris felt was his only true friend. He imagined the pair were united in their suffering and their yearning for a better world. Yet even though the brother Chris admired so greatly had turned out to be a terrible role model, his influence remained. "He was my first hero, despite what he'd done to me," says Chris. "He was such a charismatic man. He was the reason, in the end, that I joined the Salesians."

It was fortunate that the brother left when he did, giving the slight boy with the mop of fair hair a second chance to earn the friendship and respect of his fellow students. At this point, playing sport, and playing it well, became his salvation. Chris had enjoyed mucking around with a basketball at home, and now he took the game up with a vengeance. Despite being short, he soon developed a certain kudos for being able to throw baskets from a long distance. He also played Aussie Rules, where he astonished his opposition with his speed. He continued his horseriding, at one stage becoming president of the school's riding club, and he took up cricket — even though he'd never much cared for the sport. "I wasn't good at it: I couldn't bowl, I couldn't throw, and I always got out batting because I hit the ball up into the air instead of forward," he says. "But I kept it up that year because some of the older kids said I was the gutsiest fielder they'd seen, so at least I could stop a ball, no matter how badly it would hurt my hands."

Very soon, Chris began showing the kind of leadership qualities that startled his family. He started his own basketball team with his mates, acting as both captain and coach, and called his team "The Rebels". It wasn't the greatest of his successes. "We were pretty hopeless," he admits. "We lost by about 50 or 60 points every game, and any score that we got, I would have got it."

Gradually, his popularity grew. Boys would always want to come home to Echuca with him for a weekend. Often he agreed, but always regretted it later. Chris enjoyed their company at first, but would then long to be on his own. Frequently, he'd just vanish halfway through the weekend, leaving his guests to fend for themselves. "I think they were totally baffled, and that's the only trouble I had with my friends," says Chris. "Usually I hung around with the sports kids, and most of them were extroverts. They would have found me very strange."

As Chris grew in confidence, he became increasingly bold. His earlier experiences of being bullied by the older, bigger boys and by some of the brothers had scarred him deeply. "Some of the brothers were absolute maniacs!" he says. "But those guys ended up leaving the order in the end. They weren't suited to religious life at all." By Year 11, he was coming up with plans to make the lives of the younger kids easier. He didn't like, for instance, the way those in Year 7 and 8 were put to bed at 7.30 p.m. simply because the brothers found it convenient to pack their charges off to bed and then enjoy their own free time. He went to the principal, Father Wallace Cornell, and said he and his mate would be happy to take charge of those 80 children for an hour or two so they wouldn't have to go to bed so early. As a result, Chris organised basketball competitions, bingo games and quizzes, and thrived on seeing the younger kids happy. At the end of his HSC year, Chris was voted Boy of the Year by the largest majority of both pupils and teachers ever recorded at the school. From coming so close to being a victim, he'd managed to turn his life at school around completely.

His own studies were going well too. His school reports were littered with As, as well as praise for his hard work, diligence and general aptitude. Only sometimes did his stubbornness come through: one year, when he scored an unheard of D in physics and a rare C in chemistry, his form teacher, Patrick Sheahan, wrote, "Chris is working well in some subjects, but a more flexible attitude and greater willingness to accept advice would lead to improved results in Science and in English."

But he was also enjoying himself. The mix of country and town kids suited him well. "Chris was from a town, but had lived in an agricultural environment," says Father Papworth. "So he and all the others here with a similar background became very involved in activities. On weekends they'd be out chasing rabbits, they'd be building little campfires along the creek on Saturdays and cooking up a few eats, all those sorts of little creative things they could do."

Chris began thinking more and more about becoming a teacher. He enjoyed the company of younger kids — he didn't have to battle to overcome his shyness with them, he related to them well via sport, and he was extremely sensitive to how alone, isolated or anxious they might be feeling. Father Papworth, unaware of how Chris had been tormented by the teaching brother, believes that the kind of empathic quality he developed might have been a result of a couple of the brothers at Rupertswood treating the kids quite roughly: "There were one or two priests here who were a bit heavy-handed, or who would have demanded in a rather cold and insensitive way that the requirements of the regime be met. Now that could have given birth to some of Chris's reaction." Later, he learned too of the brother being convicted of paedophilia after he'd left Rupertswood, and quit the Salesian order. But with the school now co-ed, no longer taking boarders and with a celebrated program of pastoral care, Father Papworth is confident children would no longer face such problems. "That's something today that is very much in the past," he says. "The school is a whole different place to what it was then."

At least one fellow student had also seen how harsh that regime could be at times. Michael Glass, these days the principal of Chris's first school, St Mary's, was three years ahead of Chris at Rupertswood. While he enjoyed the experience overall, he also glimpsed the dark underbelly of the school from time to time. "My dad was quite a strict sort of a man, but even I, when I first went there, thought, 'Oh my God!'" he says. "The first night, I walked into the refectory for tea with 150 other boarders and saw one of the brothers belt a student across the face for talking. I was thinking, '*What's* going on? What sort of nuthouse is this?' I spent all that first night hoping I didn't have that bloke for anything. Then I walked into my first lesson and he was the teacher. Unfortunately, some of the brothers dealt with problems that way; they'd just whack into you. That's the way it was. It was the culture then. I wasn't aware of any sexual abuse, but unfortunately all the orders have had their problems with that, and obviously it could have happened there too.

"I remember the parents of a couple of kids there getting incensed at the rough treatment, so obviously the tide was turning at the time. A lot of kids there really missed their families, too. One of my mates kept running away all the time and going home."

While some brothers had a tendency towards violence or abuse, there were plenty of others who were truly inspirational, and faithful to the spirit of an order that preached equality of all. "They didn't stand apart from the children," says Glass. "They saw themselves as equal. You could flatten them at footy and it didn't worry them, whereas some teachers would have gone absolutely troppo. Some of them were fantastic, and great leaders, where others were just brash young men. It was all pretty tough. I remember Chris when he first started, as someone very quiet and sensitive. I could imagine it would scare someone like him. You were always aware of the odd child who was bullied quite severely."

Chris was inspired by plenty of the brothers, as well as by the principal. Father Cornell, in particular, was a mentor. He was kind, thoughtful and sensitive and, as Chris took initiatives around the school to improve it for the younger pupils, Father Cornell took a keen interest in this plucky lad who had been showing such enterprise and concern. His attention gave Chris a certain amount of protection, too, from some of the worst brothers. One day, Chris passed the school's longest washroom and saw two dozen of the youngest kids lined up as a bunch of brothers took turns to belt them over the backsides with a stick. He was incensed. Chris faced up to the tormentors and shouted, "You can't hit people, you're a Salesian! This isn't the Salesian way!" The brothers couldn't get back at Chris, fearing reprisals from Father Cornell.

While Chris had by now decided he wanted to join the Salesian order and become a teaching priest, witnessing this kind of brutality always stirred doubts. When one of the brothers, hearing that Chris had applied to be accepted as a novice, rounded on him, sneering, "You'll make a hopeless Salesian!" Chris seriously wondered if he shouldn't abandon the idea. He went to Father Cornell. "Look," he said, "I've just had this. I'm not interested. Just take out my application to be accepted in the order." By the next day, Chris had changed his mind again, and he left a message for Father Cornell to put his application back in. Father Cornell had never taken it out. "He knew I was impulsive," says Chris, "but he also had faith in me."

Over the next few years, Chris's faith in himself was to be put to the toughest of tests.

Chapter 4

BREAD, WORK AND PARADISE

THE CHOICE of the Salesians would prove highly significant in terms of Chris Riley's career path. The order was founded in the 19th century by Don (Father) Bosco. As a newly ordained Italian priest, walking the streets of the city of Turin, he was shocked by the conditions endured by so many children flocking to the factories looking for work during the Industrial Revolution, and vowed to help them. "I will give myself to my last breath for poor boys," he promised himself. And he did. He gathered together groups of boys, educated them in the Catholic faith and set to work teaching them a trade. In 1854 he established the Salesian Society, named after St Francis of Sales, whose life had shown how gentleness and kindness could have a huge impact on people. By 1856 the Salesian Society was providing homes, schools and workshops for 156 youths. Don Bosco dedicated his life to helping the young, particularly the poor, the rejected and those at risk and the Pope recognised and blessed his work in 1869.

Today there are almost 17,000 Salesians working in more than 95 countries, in schools, youth centres, camps and refuges. Their constitution enshrines their duty to offer help "first and foremost to the young, especially to those who are poorer". When a new Salesian recruit reportedly asked what he'd get out of the order in return for joining, Don Bosco replied, "Bread, Work and Paradise."

Having been through a Salesian college, and been taught by Salesian brothers and fathers, it was little surprise that this was the order young Chris Riley decided he wanted to join. Chris had wanted to teach from the age of six or seven, the order was all about teaching, and it had, moreover, spawned all his role models. As well, there was the movie *Boys' Town*, based on the original real-life Boys' Town in the American state of Nebraska, founded by the young Irish priest Father Edward Flanagan. The success of the film, as well as the publicity surrounding Spencer Tracy's second Oscar win, gave the concept an extra push. The movie attracted even more attention when the studio's publicist, without speaking to Tracy first, announced the star would be donating his Oscar to the Nebraskan Boys' Town. Behind the scenes, Tracy finally agreed to go along with it — providing the Academy would supply him with a replacement. That copy duly arrived, bearing the words: 'Best Actor — Dick Tracy'. Still, the gesture kept the Boys' Town program in the public eye and the next year, in 1939, the world's second Boys' Town was established, in Sydney's southern suburb of Engadine.

In some ways, however, it was a surprise that Chris had resolved to become a Salesian. At the Riley home, no grace was said at meals, there were no rosaries and Chris had never — and has still never, to this day — had a single conversation with his father about God. However, Chris's decision to become a priest didn't come as a shock to his family. "I think I would have been surprised if he *hadn't* decided to become a priest," says Helen. "I did think he should have taken a break between school and going into the seminary, but he was determined." His younger brother Wayne, too, had expected this move. "I wasn't surprised for a second," he says. "I think when he went to college he enjoyed that lifestyle and the whole concept of what it was all about. He was always going to teach, and having been to a Salesian college, becoming a teaching priest was a logical next step." His grandmother, Alice, had even prayed that he might one day become a priest. She seemed to know that it would happen before anyone else in the family started suspecting that it might.

His mother Mavis, however, the non-Catholic of the family, tried to persuade Chris not to move so hastily; she urged him to take a year off first. "I tried to persuade him to go out to work for 12 months, rather than go straight into it, and think about it," she says. He said no. Kevin agreed with Mavis, but Chris, as stubborn as ever, wouldn't have a bar of it.

In 1973, at the age of 18, Chris moved into the green, wood-trimmed two-storey brick Salesian teaching training complex at Lysterfield, east of Melbourne. Set on 134 hectares of land, tucked beneath the Dandenong Ranges, the college was a little island of tranquillity. But this was no luxury retreat. Chris's small, cell-like room was only just big enough to take a hard single bed, a desk, a chair, and a wardrobe (with a small hand basin hidden inside), but to the young devotee it was enough. Through the big glass door there was the additional bonus of a beautiful view: a pretty, 200-year-old yellow box tree and a sweeping panorama of lush green folds of countryside.

It was a quiet first year. Novices were expected to spend their time exploring their spirituality, with a special focus on studying the Salesian constitution and way of life. Chris quickly found that he had an affinity with the Salesian approach to young people, the so-called "Preventive System". It sounds forbidding in English, but in its native Italian, "sistema preventivo" means standing beside people to speak on their behalf, to be their defender, to encourage them, to have empathy with them, to help them grow. This philosophy was one Chris immediately took to heart. In between study sessions, there was plenty of time for prayer, for introspection and for working around the property, helping with the hay carting, digging, planting, cooking and cleaning.

Chris was one of four novices that year, joining the 24 priests and brothers already in residence. Only two of the four had either the dedication or the academic ability to make it through. Chris was never particularly close to the other novice, but after Lysterfield, the brother would phone him once a month for a chat and to see how he was going. Suddenly the calls ceased, and when Chris phoned the school where the brother worked, they were cagey. They said he had returned to Lysterfield. Chris called him there. "What's going on?" he asked. The priest sighed. "I was overworked and suicidal," he replied. "At one stage, I said I was going to shoot myself, so they sent me back out here." A few months later, Mavis called Chris to say there had been a newspaper article about the priest — he had been charged with sexual assault. Chris was deeply shocked. "We trained together and were ordained and took our vows together, and he was significant in my life," says Chris. "But we'd never been sent to the same schools or worked together. Still, I couldn't believe I'd been the last to know." It said a lot about how predators are able to operate without suspicion. It was a good lesson.

In the year below Chris there was an intake of eight, and among them was a South Australian called Paul Miles, a young man Chris was about to see a great deal of. They studied more or less in tandem for the next eight years, then worked together for four more. "He was a very prayerful young guy," says Paul, now Father Miles, one of only two Salesians from that year still in the priesthood. "I liked him and admired him a lot." Chris spent two years at Lysterfield, studying in preparation for ordination into the priesthood, taking lessons in philosophy and undergoing teaching training, as well as having half an hour of typing lessons a day and going for bushwalks.

Brother Silvio Quaranta, who's been living at Lysterfield since 1964, remembers Chris well. "He was always very enthusiastic about everything, and very caring," he says. "He did his studies very carefully and was very sensitive and kind-hearted. You could always depend on Chris to pitch in and help whenever you needed help."

While it was common for the new intakes, all now referred to as 'brothers', to drop out in horror at the quiet, lonely lifestyle, Chris seemed to thrive on the seclusion and the spartan nature of their lives. That's not to say he didn't have doubts at times. On Saturday nights he would often sit on the top of the hill at Lysterfield, watching the city lights and thinking, "I could be out there partying. What am I doing here?"

"I kept questioning it for years," he admits today. Somehow, though, he managed to find a balance between solitude and sociability; he enjoyed retreating into himself whenever he wanted to and used humour as a way of dealing with the intimacy demanded of him by family and friends. At Lysterfield, they still talk of the day Chris was meeting his sister Helen at the AFL — they're both rabid Collingwood fans — but was late and couldn't find her. He went up to a policeman and asked him to call for Helen over the loudspeaker. The officer could see from Chris's white clerical collar he was a novice priest, so he said he'd help. A few minutes later, the whole stadium knew that Chris was having trouble finding Helen.

The end of Chris's second year at Lysterfield, however, came as a shock to someone thriving on the peace of contemplation and study. On his twenty-first birthday, Chris was sent north to Sydney, to Boys' Town at Engadine, to gain practical experience in teaching, and to see if he could actually hack the reality of what he'd been studying. He could — and he loved it.

Boys' Town at that time was both a residential and a day school, for around 120 Year 7 to Year 10 students who had been proving disruptive in regular schools and within their communities. Most of the students would be at Boys' Town for just one year, then rejoin regular

schools. Within just a few weeks of Chris's arrival for
his two-year stint, it became apparent to everyone
around him that he was a gifted teacher. He could relate
to his students extremely well, he had the knack of
making his lessons interesting, and he was patient with
boys who were having trouble understanding. Father
Bob Bossini was there at the time. "He was very
dynamic, and all the kids liked him. They knew where
they stood with him. He would demand a lot of them,
but the way he did it, they always wanted to give a lot
back." Chris felt, for the first time, in his element.
"That's all I'd ever wanted to do all my life, teach," says
Chris. "That's why I'd taken a teaching degree."

His parents used to visit regularly, and Kevin in
particular was startled by how much responsibility Chris
had at such a young age. "I'd go down and say I reckon
Chris is off his rocker," he says. "He was just 21 but there
were all those kids he had to look after, make sure they're
washed and had cleaned their teeth and put them to bed.
He had 80 kids in a dormitory. If they played up at night,
he never got any sleep. If one went out at night and
disappeared, he'd have to go out and look for him. I told
him that if I were him, I'd walk out, get out, get married
and have five kids with a wife to help me."

Chris's headmaster at Boys' Town, Father John
Papworth, who'd later gone on to be Rupertswood's
principal, was impressed immediately by how well Chris
coped. "He was a very energetic and very committed
young fellow, a bit intense about what he was doing," he
says. "Certainly, he was always very alert and very creative
in trying to engage those kids. He had the energy to carry it

through, too, and he made it work. He took to it like a duck to water. He liked coming up with creative, inventive, thoughtful ways of getting those kids up on their feet. It wasn't always necessarily through classroom teaching; it was through providing them with an experience which they were going to learn by, and find some balance in, and find a way forward. He was good at that, no question about it."

Father Papworth left at the end of Chris's first year, and his replacement, Father John Prest, quickly took up the torch for Chris. Father Prest gave him a glowing report when Chris elected to do the last year of his practical teacher training back at his old school, Rupertswood. "He proved himself to be an excellent teacher," wrote Father Prest. "His discipline and the student interest in his classes were both outstanding. Chris is a very inventive teacher and uses his ability in music and drama to create a climate of pupil involvement. Chris also has a tremendous ability to win over even very difficult students. Chris himself is a man of real character." Even the kids were sad to see him go. One letter Chris has kept is addressed to "The best teacher in the whole world — and I mean that". Another Christmas card was from student Gary, who, although not so good at spelling his message, was certainly sincere. "Hope the gyes in Sunbury are as goode as us," he wrote. "Well mabe a bite beter. Well all the same thael be happy whith a wondefell techer. Yous sinsilly ... "

In 1978 he was back at Sunbury, joined this time by Paul Miles, now also a brother. This time, Chris was teaching Year 12 students, kids not much younger than himself. It was a revelation. "I suddenly discovered that I liked working with the older kids more than the younger ones," he says. "But I only had a primary teacher's degree, so I realised I'd have to go to university to get an area of studies so I could teach the older kids." He was able to laugh and joke with older students, but at the same time was a strict disciplinarian — a balance others, including Paul, struggled with. The pair had adjoining classrooms, and while in Chris's class no one spoke out of turn, the din from the class next door would often be deafening. Frequently, Chris would open the door to see what was happening, assuming that Paul had left the classroom, only to see him standing at the front of another chaotic scene. "Oh, you're here, Brother," Chris would say. "Yes, Brother," would come the stolid reply, "I certainly am."

Yet the two worked together extremely well. Chris still had his own painful memories of seeing other kids being bullied in the dormitories at night when the brothers left to go out together for a drink, and he was determined to make sure the younger kids in his care wouldn't have to endure the same trauma. Chris devised a system whereby he and Paul worked as a tag team: one of them would always be there to supervise the 108 kids in their dorm. Paul would stay in the dorm after lights out, while Chris would have a break, then Chris would come back and do the late shift. "I was just remembering what my days in the dorm were like," he says. "The brothers would go out shooting and we would have talcum powder fights. The place would be wrecked, and some of the other kids were picked on and bullied. Having lived through that, I said 'We are not leaving the dorm at any stage; there will always be one of us here.'"

Only occasionally would their system go awry. Chris, ever the tough but fair disciplinarian, would send a kid outside into the corridor or out onto the verandah if he was disobedient. At least once, he and Miles then fell asleep out of sheer exhaustion, only to be woken a couple of hours later by a timid tapping on the door, and a plaintive voice calling, "Brother, can I come in now? I'm freezing!"

The days were long, and the duties tiring. Chris had to supervise study first thing in the morning, then there was breakfast, followed by prayers, playground duty, lessons, lunch and more lessons. After school, he was involved in a whole range of sports activities, including football, basketball and cricket. Then he had to supervise recreation time, followed by tea, further study and dorm duty.

Chris took an active role in the sports activities of the school, setting up a basketball team, giving everyone a kit and coaching the players. Chris's team ended up winning their first championship. Through both his classes and his extracurricular activities, Chris developed a great rapport with many of his pupils. Ted Baxter was one of them, an agriculture student who later became a financial analyst. Ted was married by Chris and then, a couple of years later, asked Chris to christen his baby daughter. "Chris just seemed to always have time for you, and understood you," says Ted today. "He was always so approachable, and while he was strict and had good control over the kids, he had a nice way about him."

Chris earned his stripes early with the students, even with the most troublesome rebels in the school. One of the teachers, Father Julian Fox, who later became the principal, had started up the Rupertswood Action Groups (RAGs), groups of students from each year who performed helpful tasks around the place, such as repairing the cricket nets. The establishment of the groups caused a certain amount of resentment among the kids who hadn't been chosen to be members, viewing RAGs as elitist groups of top-end students. Ted and friends, in response, formed a rival group, and called it, in an act of deliberate provocation, the Communist Party of Rupertswood (CPR). They had their meetings at midnight, sent spies into RAGs to find out what they were up to, and asked a friendly teacher — Chris — to help them. Naturally, when Father Fox found out, he was none too pleased. "He didn't think it was right what we were doing, but Chris stuck up for us," says Ted. "Chris said, 'Well, it's not right what *you're* doing!' He was always on the side of the underdog. He gave time to kids who needed it, and was all about putting effort into people who were a bit harder to get along with rather than into the top groups. He rarely got offside with the other teachers, though; he was very diplomatic."

Chris also enjoyed having fun with the kids. Late at night, he would sometimes organise a raid on the school tuckshop, then sit around with a group of his students, drinking lemonade and eating chips. Later, quietly, he'd pay for everything they'd had. One of the other brothers, infuriated at the number of raids and baffled as to who might be the mastermind behind them, sprinkled talcum powder on the floor by the tuckshop to try to trap the intruders, but his attempts were never successful. Chris didn't mind making a fool of himself, either. His parents remember once attending a concert the teachers put on at the school, and being startled to see their son appear as Snow White. Chris was batting long black eyelashes as the kids in the audience shrieked with laughter. "It was a real good concert," says Mavis. "He didn't seem to mind a bit."

Of course things at school didn't always run smoothly. In the dining room one day, a fight broke out between two kids, and others piled in. Chris, supervising all 140 students in the room on his own, raced over to try to stop the fight getting out of hand. As he pulled the original pair apart, one took a wild swing and caught him in the face, splitting his lip. It is the only time, to this day, Chris has ever been hit by a kid, and it was by pure accident. "I was only eight and a half stone," says Chris. "He could have flattened me if he'd wanted to. I remember, though, one particularly difficult kid coming up and asking, 'How do you feel?' I replied, 'Do you care?' He shrugged, said 'No', and walked out. Little bugger. I still remember him. But I was determined I wasn't going to be beaten, so I got up and continued with my duties."

During this time, Chris also worked hard at his profession, refining teaching techniques that would stand him in good stead for all the years of teaching to come. He played guitar, and often used music in the classroom. He made sure he kept up with all the latest popular hits so he could converse with the boys about their favourite artists. "He was good at involving kids in the liturgy too," says Paul Miles. "He would get kids acting out the Bible stories. One time, in a story about a blind man, he had three kids volunteer to come to the front of the class. He blindfolded them and had them describe what it was like not to be able to see, and how they wanted to be treated. He was a natural educator and leader.

"The boys all admired him and were really happy to be in his class or his team. Whatever he did, he did well. He demanded a lot from them, whether academically or co-operation or behaviour-wise, but they tended to give it because they wanted to please him. The Salesian philosophy of working is that you love the kids, the kids know that, and, like any good parent, they want to win your approval and not let you down. The kids never wanted to let Chris down."

Those days were indeed so happy for Chris that he actually started to have doubts about returning to his studies to become a priest. As his year at Sunbury drew to a close, and he was inundated with affectionate Christmas cards from the kids, he thought about his move to Oakleigh, the Salesian college in Melbourne's south-east, where he was to live while studying theology for the next four years in preparation for his ordination, with real dread in his heart. "I was so happy. I loved it at Sunbury," he says. "I was the athletics squad coach, I was the swimming squad coach, I coached the under-14 basketball team, I coached the open basketball team, I had a drama group, I taught 34 periods out of 40. I was thriving; it was just a Wonderland for me. I knew I had a choice, to leave there and continue my studies as a priest, or to stay for the rest of my life."

There was also, it has to be said, a woman. Chris met her when he was umpiring basketball in the evenings at

Jordanville. At first, he'd umpired with another brother, but he often did not turn up, so Chris would end up sharing duties with her instead. They fell into an easy, cheerful camaraderie, working efficiently together on the court, and getting on well off it. Their partnership served to remind him that if he went ahead with becoming a priest, the opportunity for an intimate relationship would be gone forever. Chris had always been popular with the opposite sex, ever since he was a kid. One of the mothers who went to the basketball would often tell Chris that all the women were chasing him. "Don't worry, dear," she'd tell him, looking at his stricken face. "They know they won't be able to catch you."

Chris finally decided to write to his old mentor, Father Cornell, who had become the head of the Salesian order in Australia, saying that he had decided not to become a priest, and requesting permission to stay teaching at Sunbury. The reply stunned him. "After giving the matter quite a deal of thought," wrote Father Cornell, "I'm convinced that it could be in your best interests to spend a year at Oakleigh, either commencing your theology or preparing yourself to live out the rest of your life as a brother and as a teacher–educator. At the end of 1979, if you feel the Lord is calling you to be a brother rather than a priest, then you would be posted to a school in 1980."

Chris had no alternative but to accept the decision, and sadly left Sunbury for Oakleigh. It was a tough call. After teaching kids for the past three years, he found the dark, silent corridors of Oakleigh — and being back in the company only of brothers and priests — stifling. Chris's withdrawal symptoms were acute. Between theology lectures at the Catholic Theological College in Clayton, which has since become part of the Catholic University at Fitzroy, he tried to look outwards and started becoming involved in community groups outside the complex to fill the void in his life. But it didn't work. After four months, Chris went to see Father Cornell to announce that he was leaving. He then stayed with his sister Helen. "He was having doubts about whether he was going to go through with leaving," she recalls. "But after that, he was fine. He never faltered after that."

The turning point had been a chat with a priest who had heard that he was leaving. "Did you ever love being a Salesian?" he asked. "Yes," replied Chris. "I lived for it, that's all I ever wanted." The priest smiled. "Well, recapture the love," he said. Chris was taken aback, but thought it over. "And I did," he says today. "That was it, so I walked back into Father Cornell's office four days later and said, 'I think I'll stay.' He said, 'OK', and that was it."

Chapter 5

THAT CHRIS RILEY'S A BASTARD

IF THE Riley family had any remaining doubts over Chris's decision to become a priest, they were finally dispelled on the day of his ordination on 8 May 1982. Geoff Riley, Chris's uncle and very close friend, had been eagerly anticipating the ceremony. Although Geoff's mother Alice, Chris's grandmother, who'd been so influential in encouraging Chris to find his faith, had died three years before to the day, Geoff felt sure she'd be looking on approvingly from above.

As Bishop John Kelly laid his hands on Chris's head in the act of ordination at Oakleigh's Sacred Heart Church, Geoff felt a hand on his shoulder. He turned around to see who it was, but there were only the heads of the brothers, bowed in prayer, behind him. Today, he can't speak of the moment without tears pouring down his face. "It was my mother, I am quite sure," he says. "It was her way of saying, 'I'm here' and telling us that this was right for Chris. The pair had always had such a great rapport, so she was saying this was what had to be."

Chris had been feeling very relaxed and mellow throughout the ceremony, having been out drinking with friends until 3 a.m. that morning, instead of sitting at home and stressing about the solemn vows to come. He was just as laid back at the party following his ordination. Only 45 minutes into the celebrations Chris suddenly stood up and announced he had to go: he had a football team to coach. His family were taken aback by his departure — especially his father Kevin, who was still stunned that Chris had now become a priest. That morning, he'd asked Mavis, "He's going to be a priest?" "Yes," she replied, "he told us that." Kevin frowned. "I never heard that part," he protested. "I thought he was going to be a brother." Mavis shook her head. "No, there's never been any half measures with Chris," she said. "There's nothing that he does that he doesn't do properly." His team that afternoon won their match by an unprecedented 50 goals.

The next day, when Chris's family walked into the church to hear him say his first thanksgiving mass, they were startled to find that it was filled with balloons, banners and kids. "We nearly died," says Mavis. "It was like a big party. They let him have his head completely. He's always had his own ideas about how things should be done." On every seat was a program for the service with a drawing of a candle on the front, and Chris's prophetic pledge, in the words of Brazilian bishop Helder Camara: "God permit that the symbol of my life be a candle that burns itself, spends itself, consumes itself while there is still wax to burn ... "

"That was such a good choice," says Father John Prest. "He just never stops working. He never stops."

The ceremony marked the end of a long road for the newly annointed Father Chris Riley, and the start of another. By the time of his ordination, he had made sure that he was as well equipped for the time ahead as he possibly could be. In addition to his theology degree at the Catholic Theological College, Chris had also taken a second degree, at the same time, in English and Sociology at Monash University, to enable him to teach older kids as well as the young. The years living in the re-erected ex-army huts that served as quarters for the budding priests at Oakleigh had proved very amenable to study. Chris had also obtained a diploma in abuse counselling, a diploma in psychology and a residential care diploma, all by correspondence through the University of Queensland.

"You can see from the way he did two degrees his capacity to handle many things at the same time," says the current head of the Australasian Salesians, Father Ian Murdoch. "Knowing Chris, he would have also been pretty active in community work too."

Father Chris's first appointment was as Religious Education (RE) coordinator at the nearby Chadstone Salesian College, a school for Years 7 to 12 students. It was a comparatively well-off school in a middle-class area, but it offered him exciting possibilities of working also with kids beyond the school. "I didn't join to work amongst middle-class kids," he told his order. "I'd been yelling from the moment I joined that I'm here for the poor, and that's what the Salesians were founded for. If I'm not doing that, why wouldn't I go and get married and have my own family? I'm really sacrificing my life for the poor, that's what I'm about." He thus won some important concessions; he was given permission to take on other work and responsibilities at the same time.

Satisfied by this agreement, Father Chris started at Chadstone in January 1983, teaching and serving as a part-time probation officer in his spare hours. He was most thrilled at the prospect of doing some work in the neighbouring suburb of Jordanville, a much poorer area of Melbourne with a predominance of Housing Commission homes. "I thought, 'If I go to Chadstone, at least I could do some work in Jordanville', and it would be an amazing contrast," says Father Chris. "Given my background, and the fact that I was always shy and introverted, I always felt very at home with marginalised people." It was his first chance, as a priest and away from the direct control of the order, that he would have to start practising what he saw as his life work: not only helping young people, but helping those young people who were poor, dispossessed, angry, unloved, heavily into drugs or alcohol, or simply running wild.

In some ways, the places he saw and the people he met came as a shock to the unworldly young priest who'd spent so much time cloistered with his fellow Salesians. Yet it felt, at last, like liberation. "I was free and out in the open," says Father Chris. "People would call me up and I would go to this house at night or that house in the morning. Sometimes, I was their son's probation officer as well. Sometimes, I was also coaching the other son in football or basketball. I'd go into their houses and there'd be a 70-year-old grandmother saying f...ing this and f...ing that, and she would have a beer in her hand at nine in the morning. The whole family was drunk, the kids were out of control, and I loved it. They were so nice to me and I loved working with them.

"They'd always be swearing in front of me, but I would never ask them not to. They'd start out calling me Chris, and I never asked them not to. But within a month, they'd started calling me Brother or Father, and they'd stopped swearing in my presence. I loved them."

The feeling was mutual. One woman, Betty Johns, a mother of six children, has very fond memories of the young priest who tried to do all he could to help her family. "I thought he was fantastic," she says today. "No one in this area would have a single bad word to say about him. You could talk to him about anything. He'd always have a laugh and a joke with you. One of the girls said, 'Can I come to you for confession?' and he replied, 'I don't think I'll have that much time'. We all cracked up. All the women would think, what a waste, a man like that in the priesthood."

Father Chris talked to kids in trouble about how to get out of it and chatted to others about how never to get into it, as well as coaching their local basketball and footy teams. The football team won their first, and last ever, local grand final shortly afterwards, turning him into an instant neighbourhood hero. He would also frequently serve as the kids' character witness in the courts. His appearances in his clerical collar, speaking passionately about the good in a wayward lad or a girl who'd got into trouble invariably carried huge weight with the magistrates. "He was more of a friend than a priest," says Johns. "If anyone needed him for anything, he'd be there. I think he had a calming influence on all the kids around the area. This place used to be a pretty rough area, although it's quietened down a lot just recently."

Father Chris insisted on seeing the good in everyone; an approach that often paid huge dividends. Kids who had been written off by their parents and teachers, and become used to being regarded only with fear and loathing by everyone else, regularly blossomed after being treated as an equal by Father Chris. He reassured them about their value as human beings. Treat a kid with dignity, and they'll start believing in themselves too, he urged. It was a simple philosophy, but it was surprising how effective it was. "There's no such thing as a bad child," was his mantra, echoing the words of Father Flanagan in that favourite film *Boys' Town*. "There are only bad circumstances, situations, environments and families."

When John Jolly, one of Betty Johns' sons, met Father Chris, he was on probation for a number of offences, and was an extremely angry young man. Father Chris, he has no doubt at all, helped him turn his life around. "He made me realise that there were good people out there," says Jolly, who, at 36, is now working as an electrician's mate and has a happy family of his own, with a partner and two children, aged two and three. "When I met him, I was hard and I didn't have any faith in society. He saw the good side of me that a lot of people don't get to know. He made me realise I'm not too bad a person. Back then, I suppose he guided me in the right way. My father wasn't around, but Father Chris was always there to help or to take me anywhere I needed to go. He was there for you. He was a big part of my life. He made me who I am today. If he hadn't have been around, who knows what would have happened?"

Naturally, there were failures along with the successes. One of his former charges could only, by luck, be tracked down today because a teacher at the school had his home burgled by him the previous year. He's now in prison. Another notorious young local still won't hear a bad word said against Father Chris. "He was a really good bloke," he says. "You could talk to him about anything and he really listened. You could trust him not to yap off to everyone else." Sadly, this young man's hands won't stop shaking these days, obviously suffering from either drug or alcohol withdrawal, and he is unemployed. "But still," says a neighbour, "he might have been in the clink, or dead now, if he hadn't had Father Chris."

Another of his experiments while teaching at Chadstone was his attempt to bring together the Jordanville kids and the students from Chadstone in a couple of football games he organised between the two sides. It wasn't always successful. "The second match was a big disaster," says Tim Cox, the school captain at the time, who's now a teacher. "It disintegrated into a big fight. It was a bloodbath."

Father Chris's work at Chadstone College was usually far more orderly and structured — usually. Paul Miles talks about the day Father Chris caused an uproar when he rode a motorcycle into a classroom and then asked students to write an essay on what he had just done. For he always liked to have fun with the kids, and make his lessons memorable. He enjoyed, for instance, engaging classes in discussions on topics more regularly avoided by the RE teacher, subjects such as abortion, pre-marital sex and contraception. Father Chris had persuaded other staff members to teach religion because he thought the subject was far too boring, even though one of the college's aims was, and still is, "to provide a thoughtfully planned and implemented program that places religious education at the centre of students' attention". Instead, he taught maths and English, as well as creating his own class about issues that he felt would be really relevant to Year 11 kids. "But I only won one battle and got the kids to agree with me, and that was the abortion issue," he says. "I never won pre-marital sex, or contraception, I lost all those battles with the kids. But I enjoyed that, all the arguing and dialogue with that age group. I didn't care if I lost; it was a challenge."

Father Chris proved extraordinarily inventive in the way he managed to connect with kids. Past pupils remember a toy monkey with velcro on its tummy which he gave to younger children to hug — Father Chris, like all the priests, was trained never to touch a child, so the monkey proved a handy substitute. Others remember the chocolate frogs he dispensed to students who gave correct answers to the questions he asked them while walking up and down the classroom, and his use of music. "He would bring pieces of popular music into English class and analyse the lyrics," says Mick Busscher, one of his former students who's now teaching at Chadstone. "He was interested in what interested you, and then played with it in a way to make you look at things more closely." He held mass on a variety of special themes and brought his guitar while encouraging the kids to bang away on a set of drums. He also took great care with the preparation of all his lessons.

"He believed very much that you don't direct from the top, you direct from within. We did things like leadership camp and you'd set a game up and you'd be encouraging the kids. He'd then pull you aside and say, 'That's great!' and you'd get involved as well. If it wasn't for Chris, I probably would've chucked it all in," says Busscher.

As well as teaching and roaming Jordanville, Father Chris also coached three basketball teams, coached the under-16 football team and finally took on the under-12s so he'd be able to connect with the younger ones too. "He was all about reaching kids, and that was a 24-hour job," says Chris Hellyer, who became the school nurse and Father Chris's secretary. "He was always out there in the playground, he organised games at lunchtime, and things with the kids. It really shone through that he had a vocation." In addition, he was a prime mover in arranging the annual Don Bosco summer and leaders' camps, which were held at Dromana, at the foot of Arthurs Seat on the Mornington Peninsula. The kids were always thrilled to go whenever Father Chris was involved, responding warmly to the direct way he seemed to speak to them, as well as his gently jocular manner. A girl called Margaret, from one of the church youth groups who joined in, for instance, wrote in a card: "Thanks for helping to give me the best camp I've ever been on. I really gained so much from it. It was an experience I will never forget. Every word you said was so appropriate to me and I think it was really great the way you gave yourself so honestly and openly. It gave the camp such a beautiful feeling. Thanks a million. Love from Margaret. P.S. Thanks for being a great stir!" It was one of 19 personal messages written in the card from Father Chris's students.

Of all Father Chris's work, dearest to his heart was a special project for which he managed to win support from his order. He wanted to set up a refuge at the back of the school for kids at risk, especially the ones he had come into contact with as a probation officer. The Salesians finally agreed to buy a five-bedroom house, on the condition that he managed to keep all his other jobs going at the same time. It was a huge concession for such a young and inexperienced priest. The order had faith, however, that if anyone could handle such a challenge, it was Father Chris.

Thrilled that at last he was being given the chance to fulfil his dreams of helping kids on the very bottom rung of life, Father Chris set up the house and moved in, together with varying numbers of kids — anywhere from five to 10 at any one time, from the ages of seven to 18. All had difficult home lives and had been in trouble with the law. Without Father Chris, most would have been sent to institutions; he was their last chance. The refuge enabled the kids to attend school next door during the day, then often play sport, and come back to a homely, safe environment to eat dinner, talk, receive counselling and sleep. It also meant that they were close to home, so they could visit their parents once a month. It became the prototype for all Father Chris's projects to follow.

To help Father Chris with his immense workload, he was allowed to employ Chris Hellyer, a woman who has only recently retired from full-time work at the school. She had warmed to the young priest immediately. "He was a very shy, very quiet, very thin bloke, who was very affable and popular," she says. "He was very studious. When he said he was purchasing a house out the back for kids at risk, I don't think people at Chadstone were terribly keen, mainly because it meant Father Chris wouldn't be living in residence at the school, he was going to live in the house. They liked to keep the new priests under their wing."

Family, friends, students and teachers all pitched in to help with this daring new venture, with varying degrees of enthusiasm. Mavis knitted jumpers for the boys, Helen came to visit, and Chris Hellyer organised dental and doctor's appointments for the kids, looked after their general health and went to afternoon tea at the house a couple of times a week just to keep in touch with how they were and provide a female presence from time to time. Other staff members were persuaded to help, and students were asked to volunteer to lend a hand.

It was a bold experiment, and one which took a tremendous toll on everyone involved. "One of the main difficulties was that the kids all had records, and they didn't fit into the mainstream of the school. They didn't assimilate," says Hellyer. "It was a shock to everyone's system when they arrived, and a lot of the students found it hard to associate with kids who had so many problems. Teachers weren't allowed to chastise them very much if they hadn't done their homework or anything, because they were Father Chris's kids. Only he could discipline them. It made it very difficult."

There was also a little resentment from the regular school students towards the newcomers for the attention they received from Father Chris — and animosity when they caused trouble. Mark Donoghue, who joined the staff in 1985, says, "He really had all these ideas about helping people who needed a second chance. He gravitated towards those kids who needed to be guided so they could get moral strength from him. I guess he got that from his religion." Yet that favouritism sometimes created problems. In sporting matches, Father Chris caused difficulties for umpires by always insisting his "house" kids were in the right, and he would do everything he could to prove it. Naturally, he didn't like to see any injustice, but he often gave umpires a much harder time than they deserved. Hellyer remembers her husband Rob saying, at one stage, that Father Chris should be banned from matches. "That Chris Riley's a bastard," was his verdict one day.

Father Chris still struggled, personally, with his natural shyness, but if a downtrodden kid wasn't being treated right, he was prepared to fight — and fight dirty if need be — to make sure his kids would always get a fair go. Some saw Father Chris as soft, an easy target for kids who they assumed would only take advantage of his determination to help. They underestimated him. Certainly plenty did throw his help back in his face. But he was fast developing a tough hide. If it came to fighting the authorities on their behalf, speaking up in court, arguing their case, or hitting back at their critics, he could be intimidatingly blunt, outspoken and dogged. He'd had to battle to get the house in the first place, and he was happy to push every step of the way to keep it open against steadily mounting opposition from both inside and outside the school.

No doubt at times a few of the Salesians were taken aback by how driven and ruthless he could be. But to those who knew him best, it came as no surprise. His younger brother Wayne, who works in corporate insolvency, smiles when he thinks about his brother's determination. "In my kind of work, you've got to be a bastard," he says. "But in Chris's work, you've got to be a bit of a bastard too. To do what he does, you've got to have compassion, but if you don't have a bit of mongrel in you, you won't get anywhere. He sometimes must shit himself, the situations he's in. But if you show weakness you'll be lost."

It was a struggle for Father Chris to keep going all the time. Chadstone teacher Ian Riddock was sometimes amazed how he managed. "He tended to trust people, take massive risks," he says. "Kids would be in and out of court and he'd be there, helping them out, holding their hand, getting character witnesses. He was always pulling one boy out of scrapes all the time." Tim Cox sometimes couldn't understand how he coped. "There were kids who would just crap in his face, basically. He would do everything he could for them and at the last dying hour they would do something else that would tip him over the edge. They had reasons for it, I'm not judging them for that, but he would just keep fighting. A lot of people would have given up."

While Father Chris's conviction about the essential goodness of all young people certainly pushed him through the disappointments, he was also assisted by his faith. Surprisingly, however, he rarely talked about his religious beliefs. Even though he wore his white priest's collar all the time, and debated life and its big issues regularly with both students and teachers, generally he didn't mention God at all. No doubt his pupils liked him even more for it.

Yet Father Chris wasn't averse to putting pressure on them to help in the refuge too. Sometimes, that could cause a certain amount of friction. Cox worked with him often on the youth camps he organised but, when Father Chris asked him to help out with his kids' house, Cox declined. He was stunned at Father Chris's response.

"He was trying to recruit a number of boys to help him out, but I said to him 'I'm really sorry, but I can't do this,'" recalls Cox. "I said I had too many other things on, and that it was beyond me. 'I come from a different background and I don't think I can help you. I can do whatever else you want, not a problem, but I can't help at the house.' At that, he pretty much went through me like a dose of salts. He said I was caught between one place and another, and that I should make up my mind. He was a little abrasive towards me, but only because he was so driven, so intense. And I admired him for that. He was too intense for his own good at times. He had hand-picked people who he thought could help him, but not everyone would go along with what he wanted. Those kids were from dysfunctional families and different environments from us. One was six foot two with missing teeth. How could I control him? It was a side of life I'd never seen before.

"He was a hard taskmaster with his own agenda, and if you crossed him, you could easily find yourself on the other side of the track. It's just that he wanted so much to help. He was so passionate about it. I have always been full of admiration for him, but I struggled, myself, over getting involved." Paul Clohesy, another of Father Chris's former pupils, agrees. "He had a goal, and he was driven towards it," he says. "He didn't have time to waste on people who got in his way."

Despite the strength of Father Chris's drive that everyone else had trouble matching, no one harboured any grudges against him. Even Cox, with the memory of that blasting remaining fresh 18 years on, still sometimes wonders if he was right to refuse. "I've had a few regrets since," he says, sadly. "I wouldn't have minded being involved in that sort of work, working with young people. I suppose it was because of Chris's influence that I became a teacher. I loved working with him. He inspired us all."

There were a few clashes, too, with the other Salesians. Some of them would have preferred Father Chris to toe the line a little more; others didn't like the way he played his own game. He rarely asked for advice. He didn't call for guidance. Yet his devotion to his calling and to the Salesian cause was unquestionable.

"There really is a lot of correlation between the work he did here, and the work of Don Bosco — walking the streets, taking risks and bringing back children," says Cox. "He really is a great Australian. He inspires people in so many different ways."

Life was working out just the way Father Chris hoped it might. He had his own house, he had a bunch of kids he was caring for and who had come to trust him, he had the young people in Jordanville whose lives he was managing, hopefully, to turn around, he was teaching HSC English and he had sports teams filled with enthusiastic youngsters. "I was in Heaven," he says simply. "It was wonderful."

But, on 5 September 1985, suddenly his world came crashing down around his ears. He received a letter from the Provincial, Father Frank Bertagnolli, telling him he was being sent back to Boys' Town in Sydney. Father Chris was hurt, angry and absolutely devastated.

Chapter 6

Boys' Town: Living the Movie

"**B**UT WHY me?" pleaded Father Chris. "Everything is going so well here. Why move me now?" The Salesian Provincial Father Frank Bertagnolli sighed heavily. "Well, you've been yelling about working with the poor," he said. "Boys' Town needs you. They *are* the poor."

Father Chris knew when he was beaten. But he was anxious that the kids he had worked so hard to help at the house at Chadstone shouldn't be turfed out, abandoned once more to fend for themselves. If that happened, it would be disastrous. They might never trust anyone again. Father Chris knew he had no real alternative but to obey the directive to move to Sydney, but he asked for one concession: that the house continue to operate after he left. Father Bertagnolli accepted. "I would hope that the community at Chadstone would accept the responsibility to maintain this service for boys in need," he wrote, reassuringly, to Father Chris. "I shall advise the Rector and the community to this effect."

Reluctantly, Father Chris packed his bags, said his farewells and set off to face his next test. He left behind five boys in the care of one of the school's priests, an exceptionally kind and gentle man. That priest moved on soon after. A brother then took over. He found it impossible to cope with the kids. About eight months after Father Chris's departure, the house finally closed down. Chris Hellyer looked on sadly. "It took an exceptional person to run that house," she says. "The Salesians couldn't carry it on. Chris had that ability to relate to the kids, he'd been the ideal person to run it as he had so much get-up-and-go. It had been his baby. But no one else could manage it."

Father Chris was disappointed, but it was never his way to waste energy moping. Once, Hellyer phoned him and asked if he missed them back at Chadstone. "No," said Father Chris bluntly. "I've moved on." At times, he seems brutally unsentimental, rarely taking the time, or care, to keep in touch with old friends, students, colleagues or even family. They always know where he is, he reasons, so they can get in touch with him if they need to. His younger brother Wayne has become used to it over time. "Sometimes I don't see him for two or three years," he says. "But even if I only saw him every six years, we'd still talk as if we'd only seen each other the day before." In some ways, that's how the Salesians are, explains Hellyer. Because they move their people on so regularly, they often don't have time to form strong attachments. That's also a form of protection, to make sure they can still concentrate on their vocation. In Father Chris's case, it goes even further. He throws everything into the work he's doing at the time, and his focus is so total, he just has no time or energy left over for anything that doesn't immediately require his urgent attention. Nostalgia is a luxury he's never been able to afford, nor seen the worth of.

The idea of Boys' Town in Australia had been born when the movie came out, and it was first established in 1939 by the Irish priest Father Thomas Dunlea, in Sydney's southern suburb of Sutherland. He said he had been aching to do something to help the poor children of Sydney ever since 1921 when, as the assistant to the city centre Haymarket parish, his office window looked over the children's court. One night, he heard a small child, who couldn't have been any older than five, singing in one of the cells. When he strained his ears to hear the words of the song, one refrain stabbed at his heart. "I wish I had someone to love me," the little kid sang. "Someone to call me their own." Later appointed to the Sutherland parish during the depression, Father Dunlea was saddened by the sight of so many homeless children living on the streets — unwanted, uncared for and unloved. Very soon, every space of the Sutherland presbytery, even the bath, was filled with sleeping kids.

Father Dunlea set up a special house close to the presbytery and, in August 1939, he and seven lads, ranging in age from eight upwards, moved in. By December, the children numbered 18, the house was hopelessly overcrowded, the garbage was piling up in the backyard, and the neighbours were complaining. "For heaven's sake," was his reply. "I wasn't trying to build a beautiful street, only citizens worthy of living in a beautiful street." The next year, the local council evicted them.

Yet Father Dunlea was nothing if not resourceful. On 17 July 1940, he marched through Sutherland, followed by 27 boys carrying banners, 25 uniformed soldiers of the second Garrison Battalion Band, two horses, two pigs and two goats, towards the Royal National Park. The priest, the children and the animals all spent that winter camping in the bush at Loftus. He'd successfully drawn attention, however, to the plight of kids who had nothing, those who'd been kicked out of home by their families and who now, he felt, were being rejected by society too. Dispossessed kids had found their champion. "Every unwanted boy must be wanted so badly that we will give him a chance to prove he is worth wanting," he said. "He must be given a home, not an institution. Boys put into institutions are hampered unless these institutions are really homes, homes in which each boy can expect sympathy, can share in love, can expand naturally in the gracious atmosphere and can prove that he is worth being wanted. People who save the unwanted boys, who give them back their self-respect, are among the greatest of our people." It was the clarion call for Boys' Town: the articulation of the same belief that Don Bosco had expressed nearly a century before, and the central tenet of the philosophy behind Father Chris's work. The new Boys' Town was established that September at Engadine, in Southern Sydney, after Father Dunlea accepted an offer of a house and land. In 1953 it was taken over by the Salesians, who raised money for a series of extra buildings on the site.

For Father Chris, returning to Boys' Town at the beginning of 1986 as headmaster after an absence of seven years since his teacher training days, proved to be the seminal experience of his life. He was under no illusion as to why he was being sent back: no other young priest would go, it was too tough a call to manage so many out-of-control boys. But Father Chris concentrated on the positive. He was at last going to have his chance to put his theories about what constituted good education and the best care to the ultimate test. It was also the beginning of the rest of his life working with the poorest of kids. It was his chance to live out the role of Father Flanagan from the movie that had influenced him so greatly. Father Chris relished the challenge.

Boys' Town still today comprises a number of buildings on both sides of Waratah Road. The old red-brick building on one side was donated by the Australian Meat Industry and Allied Trades, and was at first used as a hospital to examine and, if necessary, treat kids before they were brought into the residential units and school. On the other side of the road is a series of long, two-storey buildings clustered around a playground. The kids sleep upstairs, while downstairs are the classrooms, a long dining room capable of sitting 120 kids at once, and a massive kitchen. Nearby is a plain, functional chapel with stained-glass windows, and two more squat red-brick buildings where the kids were once taught trades: baking or butchery. The idea of Boys' Town was to educate "problem" kids aged between 12 and 15 in a warm and caring environment while also providing life skills and opportunities to engender change. Students either lived-in during the week in school terms, or participated in the day program, for about a year. All the kids were referred by their schools, by parents or by government departments, because they were having behavioural difficulties at their regular schools — usually a surefire indicator of problems at home.

On his arrival, however, Father Chris saw a place crying out for change. It was being run in an easy-going, relaxed way, with its 42 kids doing pretty much as they liked. Staff were often so anxious to "relate" to the youngsters that they demanded little from them in return. It was an approach Father Chris had no time for. He introduced a rigorous curriculum, a much more formal style of teaching, a system of writing notes about everything he did, and a regime of appropriate discipline. "People saw me as really demanding," says Father Chris today. "But I wanted these kids to be taught, instead of being able to watch videos all day. They shouldn't be treated as kids who are useless or worthless. I was really tough on people. I believed those kids could achieve. It was a real culture shock for everyone there." It certainly was. In place of a laidback headmaster who dressed in casual clothes, they had a whirlwind who was never out of black shirt, black jeans and a clerical collar. He asked and expected more of his staff, and hoped for far more from their charges. Everything about the atmosphere of Boys' Town shifted a gear.

"He was running a very good ship," says Father Paul Miles, his old colleague at Sunbury who later joined him down at Boys' Town. "The kids responded well to his ideas of order and discipline. They knew the system and they knew what was coming next, so they felt very secure in that environment. They all knew the boundaries and expectations and they either responded to it or challenged it. Chris was always very efficient and organised. All the kids would be on their own level of programs, and he would set them up on courses at TAFE and programs outside to help them prepare for life once they'd left the school. They had a lot of respect for him, and a healthy fear of letting him down. They also came to care for him a great deal. One day, a car turned up at school, it was all smashed up, and some of the kids thought it might be his. They were all so worried that he might have been hurt or injured. I'll never forget that."

Running Boys' Town, teaching at the school and having his own dorm of boys — he would always end up looking after more of the boys than any of the other carers — was an intense learning experience for Father Chris. Unlike the movie, in which the boys had been little more than a bunch of lovable rogues, he often found the easy violence between the boys shocking, depressing and even, occasionally, frightening. In some cases, everything about particular boys, including their appearance, the way they walked, even the music they listened to, carried undertones of violence. Father Chris soon realised, however, that they tended to create this image so they could use it as a shield. "They're always ready to defy, to challenge, to stomp around the house like caged animals; but really, deep down, they're seeking acceptance and understanding," he says. "They're infuriated that all their signals are missed and overlooked. They get power from the fear they create, yet they never really understand the fear that lives within."

Violence can become a way of life for many of the kids. To bruise, to punch, to inflict pain can result in a dizzying high, or be used as a form of relaxation. The kids would also use violence against themselves, systematically

burning themselves with cigarettes, slashing their arms
with knives, and other forms of self-mutilation. Father
Chris often felt a shiver run down his spine when he saw,
or heard about, the brutality of some of the kids who
ended up at Boys' Town: the evening a group of boys
laughed as they burned another's arm with lit cigarettes;
the time he had to pick up a young boy who'd been kicked
unconscious after being labelled a "faggot"; and the
morning the whole school rushed into the playground
when a fight was underway, all eager to join in.

Father Chris refused to believe that any child was born
violent. He reasoned that, usually, they had lived with so
much violence that it became the only way they knew how
to deal with life. Often, it was simply the drama of
revenge, or the need to lash out when feeling cornered. It
generally also accompanied a real sense of self-loathing and
a complete lack of self-esteem. One young man at Boys'
Town, Kim, was frequently violent towards the other boys.
One evening, he careened completely out of control. He
tried to strangle a younger boy, hit another and then
threatened to punch Father Chris. Later that evening,
however, he asked a friend to stab him with a knife and,
when he refused, disappeared into the bushes wth a rope.
Staff members went hunting for him, convinced he would
try to hang himself. They found him just in time.

It was difficult to turn boys away from violence after it
had become an ingrained pattern in their lives, but Father
Chris was always determined to try. He believed that even
the toughest boy had a soft spot. It was his task to find
that vulnerability, locate that responsive chord, and hone
in on it. He'd talk to them about alternative ways of

dealing with conflict and, while he let them know he understood they may have been treated that way from childhood, he challenged them to change.

When Kim arrived at Boys' Town at the age of 13, he was often impossible to deal with — going on wild rampages across the recreational area, lunging at other boys, and screaming at the top of his voice that he was going to kill them. Staff would rush to put themselves between him and his targets, forever fearful of how far he might go. His background was well known. His mother was a heavy drinker who frequently yelled at him for no reason, and often beat him. Worse, however, was the emotional cruelty. She constantly told him that he was responsible for her problems, that he drove her to drink and that she hated the very sight of him. Such treatment often bruises a kid far more than any physical torture. Kim had deep gashes on his arms and hands from where he had repeatedly cut himself with knives, and he was always threatening to kill himself. "I'll go and jump in front of a train, then it'll all be finished," he'd say. His self-loathing often spilled over into hating the world and everyone in it. After all, no one had given him a break; he sure as hell wasn't going to give one to anyone else.

Father Chris encouraged Kim to talk about how he felt and kept urging him to let go of the hate before it destroyed him. "Blame is the ultimate guilt trip, one which paralyses understanding, compassion and love," says Father Chris. "A history of hostility can make each of us hard-hearted, but reaching out with forgiveness and love releases goodness and power. We need to become aware that we do not have to become slaves to history, prisoners of our own smallness, overwhelmed by our own hate, smothered by fear or by our own sense of inadequacy. We have to believe we can break the vicious cycle of pain and broken dreams. Going down into the deepest pit of depression allows us to realise our greatest strength is to be found within. Our greatest destroyers are the conditions and tripwires that entrap our hearts and freeze our emotions. Dealing with the anger is a matter of identifying it, discovering where its energy comes from and gaining a perspective on it. It may mean a scary trip down inside oneself, opening doors that may have been locked for years. It might mean a lot of turbulence. It does mean risking trust, and allowing ourselves to believe that the darkness within doesn't make us untouchable or unlovable." Father Chris was fond of quoting to the boys the line from the U2 song "God Part II", "Kick the darkness until it bleeds sunlight".

Many boys understood what Father Chris was saying, and responded to what he was trying to teach them. Of course, some boys did not, and in some of these cases, as a last resort, he told them that if they didn't try, there was no place for them at Boys' Town and they'd probably meet a violent end somewhere outside. They were harsh words, but he felt they sometimes needed to be said in the hope of shocking the boys into trying. It was an approach he used once with one called Pat, who seemed to use violence indiscriminately. When Father Chris told him he might have to leave as a result, he was taken aback, however, to see tears in the boy's eyes. "I went on to say that he needed to make a choice between the violence in him and the strong gentleness that can be so outstanding," says Father Chris. "Boys' Town could work with the gentleness and help him overcome the

TOP: Chris at age 18 months, posing with his spinning top.
BOTTOM: Chris, standing in front of a fence at his home in Echuca, aged four. As a toddler, he used to throw his bottle over this fence.

Chris in his Sunday best — holding his prayer book and rosary close to his heart — about to make his first Holy Communion at age seven.

TOP: Chris at age 10 on his first horse, Bonnie, at the family farm near Echuca. Chris won prizes at country shows for doing tricks with Bonnie. He would skip on her back, slide around the horse's belly and climb up the other side. MIDDLE: At 14 Chris started at the Salesian boys' boarding school, Rupertswood College. BOTTOM: At age 17, being presented with the prize for Boy of the Year at Rupertswood College, by the Principal, Father William Cornell.

ABOVE: Chris's grandfather on his mum's side, Ted, worked as a dairy farmer on the rich pastoral plains surrounding Echuca.
RIGHT: Grandmother Ada, his mother's mother. The family had a Christmas ritual of having lunch with one grandmother and then tea with the other.
BELOW: Chris and Grandmother Alice, his father's mother — she had prayed that Chris might one day become a priest.

ABOVE: Chris, aged 21, with his mum and dad, Mavis and Kevin, on his graduation day from the Catholic University. Chris is holding his teacher's training diploma. RIGHT: At 18, while other boys his age were buying their first cars, taking their first jobs and having their first serious relationships, Chris was preparing to enter the Salesian Order's teacher training college, at Lysterfield, east of Melbourne. BELOW: Father Chris cuts his 21st birthday cake with his mum and dad in November 1975.

RIGHT: In his second year of teacher training at Rupertswood, Chris continued coaching the boys in all sports, including athletics. He loved the work so much that he hesitated about leaving the school to become a priest. BELOW: Chris took his final vows in 1977, three years after entering the Salesian Order. It was a year later than scheduled because of his doubts about joining the priesthood.

TOP: The Rupertswood basketball team had one of its best years ever in 1978 with Chris as their coach. BOTTOM: Chris was also a popular coach with the Rupertswood under-14 football team — although they rarely won a match.

ABOVE: Chris was made a deacon in 1981, 12 months before his ordination. One of Chris's first communion recipients was his own dad, Kevin.

LEFT: As a deacon, Chris officiated at the 1982 marriage of his brother Greg to Kerri.

pattern of violence. On the other hand, if he didn't make the decision now, maybe I'd have the chance to break the cycle of violence with his son and, if his son wouldn't accept the challenge, then maybe his grandson would."

Many of the kids at Boys' Town had upbringings scarred by violence from parents who might have been lashing out in anger — in frustration at life not treating them well, in misery at not being able to have satisfactory relationships, or in tough times like their businesses failing, unemployment or losing partners or loved ones. Sometimes, the process was slow and insidious, with anger building gradually over years to culminate in rejection and violence. The results were always the same: kids feeling unwanted, alienated and utterly alone. Boys' Town started working more and more with the families of the boys, as well as with the boys themselves, to intervene in the family dynamics rather than simply trying to build up the characters of the kids alone. One of Father Chris's fellow priests, a social worker and a Boys' Town director, Father Denis Halliday, was a particular inspiration. Father Halliday was also studying the students, their needs, their families and the philosophy of the school. "He was probably the most influential guy in my life from a religious point of view," says Father Chris. "He was one of our greatest intellects." At the age of 52, Father Halliday was diagnosed with motor neurone disease but Father Chris visited him just before he died. He was stunned to find the priest in his bedroom surrounded by nothing but positive messages, pictures and cards. "He'd decided he wasn't going to reflect on anything negative at all," says Father Chris. "He was an amazing man."

Twelve years on, the current principal of Boys' Town, Geoff George, who only has around 24 kids at the school at any one time, says it can still be just as hard today caring for such difficult children. He says the kids are brought to Boys' Town often as a result of family breakdown, sometimes when parents split up and bring new partners into the home or when they leave the children with grandparents who can't cope. The increasing fragmentation of society, poverty and a general lack of hope that life will improve also takes a toll. "The strain, stresses and pace of society have all contributed to a more dysfunctional young person," he says. "In the past these young people might have found an uncle or caring neighbour to help out, but that doesn't happen much these days. They have trouble at home, then have behavioural problems which mean they can't fit into traditional schools."

Father Chris always believed that communication was the real key to unlocking the pain of his students and starting the healing process. Kids would often want to talk about what was troubling them, but they found it difficult to start. Mack was a good example. One evening, he paced in and out of his room, asking a staff member every 10 minutes when Father Chris would be back. When the priest did return, he went into Mack's room, but the boy ignored him. "You wanted to talk to me?" asked Father Chris. "No," said Mack curtly. "So why have you been asking for me for the last hour?" "It doesn't matter now," said Mack. Father Chris knew that he had to persist. He sat there patiently for another 10 minutes. Finally, Mack quietly announced that one of his best friends had been killed, and he'd only just found out about it. Suddenly, through the process of sharing his misery with another human being, Mack went from being a twisted coil of emotion to someone starting, at last, to relax.

"In many ways, we are just beginning to understand how our kids ask for help," says Father Chris. "We must be honest and admit that in many ways kids are frightened to talk to adults, in case we see them as failures or crazy. Very few young people talk to adults, and often that silence can make them desperate." Adults, by the same token, are often afraid to talk to young people. They fear their response to questions, they find honesty confronting, they're scared they won't be able to cope with the answers, or they're too busy to seriously listen.

During his time at Boys' Town, Father Chris came to the conclusion that there is often a great deal of love within families, but many have trouble expressing it, appreciating it and letting kids know how much they're cherished. Kids like Justin, a 15 year old at Boys' Town, obviously felt unloved. He spent all his time buzzing around from one person to another just like a mosquito, nagging, talking, badgering and annoying them. "A life that has to keep buzzing to deal with the roar of rejection hidden within," was Father Chris's verdict. Abandoned by his family and shunted from refuge to refuge, Justin survived by wandering around, hoping that someone might want him. "We all long for the person close to us to ask the right question and give us space and support to answer," says Father Chris. "How often do we hit rock bottom and listen for a footstep heading in our direction, or listen for the phone to ring so we can reach out to someone for help?"

Sometimes, Father Chris was angry with parents for ignoring their kids, refusing to listen to them, or not placing importance on the kind of things they held most dear. One presentation night, which marked the leaving of nine of his boys, had gone fabulously well, and they all seemed happy and relaxed. Later that evening, when he was walking back to the living unit, however, he came across one of the students, Jack, who was due to leave the next day. Throughout the evening, he'd been loud and outrageous, but Father Chris knew that had been an act to hide his misery at the fact his mother had not bothered to turn up for this big event in his life.

"Hi Jack, how are you feeling?" Father Chris asked him, casually. The boy immediately burst into tears. "I'm not angry that she didn't come," he stammered, "but I just can't understand it." Moments like this always affected Father Chris. While he accepts that it's easy for parents to forget how much they mean to their kids, he says it's also far too easy for them to fall into the trap of believing that their children don't actually want their parents around. Maybe it's convenient for them, too: parenting can be thankless, exhausting work. But, as parents, Father Chris believes they have a duty to take notice of their kids, to pay attention to what's important to them, and that they should never wash their hands of their children, even when it all gets too hard. Father Chris was always taken aback by how many parents kicked their children out of home when they seemed to require too much effort. "When commitment and forgiveness are withdrawn, then the whole bottom so often falls out of a young person's existence," he says.

Using these kinds of experiences, Father Chris then

started to try to articulate the real purpose of Boys' Town. He made notes about the kids who passed through, he wrote down thoughts that occurred to him at odd times of the day and night, and he referred back to the teachings of Don Bosco, and Father Dunlea's belief that "Every unwanted boy must be wanted so badly that we will give him a chance to prove he is worth being wanted."

Slowly, Father Chris came to his own understanding of the essential problems of dealing with the kids at Boys' Town, and the kind of solutions the problems demanded. He sat at his desk and wrote what he believed the mission statement of Boys' Town should be. "Our challenge at Boys' Town is, and always will be, to highlight the value of each boy," he wrote. "To bring out the goodness and enable them to live with the sadness that often haunts the paths of the young. To create the silence so that the messages are truly heard and understood. People have an incredible potential to love, but so often never communicate that love. Ours is the duty to scream it from the bottom of our lungs that we love, to say it even when we feel ridiculous doing so. Declare it before it is too late."

Sometimes, sadly, it was too late. Every time a kid he knew died, often through suicide, Father Chris felt a deep sadness, a terrible frustration that he hadn't been able to prevent their death, and a gnawing sense of failure. But, one day, something more terrible than anything he had previously experienced happened. And Father Chris sat with the other staff at Boys' Town, tears pouring down his cheeks.

Chapter 7

THE RIGHT TO DREAM

THE ABDUCTION, rape and murder of Sydney nurse Anita Cobby in 1986 was an event that shocked the nation. Father Chris Riley was no exception. Yet, for him, there was also intense personal sorrow. One of her killers, 18-year-old John Travers, had passed through Boys' Town.

As Father Chris sat with his staff in June 1987, watching Travers' family being interviewed on TV, he felt desolate. Anita Cobby, dragged from a well-lit Blacktown street into a stolen car containing five men, had lived through an horrific ordeal of beatings, torture and sexual assault before her throat was cut through to her spinal cord by Travers. Tears welled in Father Chris's eyes. Travers had been the only one of the five to plead guilty at the trial and was, along with the others, gaoled for life. There was applause from the packed courtroom when the judge recommended their files be stamped "Never to be released".

Father Chris was devastated that Boys' Town had evidently done so little for Travers. "John Travers had been at Boys' Town for only a short period and really, no one even remembered him," he says. "We searched his file, but it said nothing. We searched the past year books and found a photo of him. A couple remembered him vaguely: no trouble, took no energy, left soon.

"While I didn't know John Travers, I have kept the thought of him with me as a reminder of all that often is left undealt with in the hearts of the young. What a tragedy it is when our young need to act so violently before they are noticed or given time. The atrocity of that crime can never be denied. Punishment is called for. But we must allow John Travers' story to sit with us, so we can work hard not to allow it to happen again. The toll of sexual abuse, gang fights and family trauma is high. Coldness, anger and violence is developed over time. It becomes a learned response to life. I was filled, that afternoon, with new resolutions to give more energy to each boy within our program."

Every failure of Boys' Town cut Father Chris deeply. When a kid simply would not respond and persisted in being violent to everyone else there, sometimes there was no alternative but to tell them to leave. He was well aware, however, that sometimes that person might leave the program just as resentful and confused as when he first arrived, with the bitter taste of anger in their hearts. Joe was one such boy.

One evening, Joe knocked softly on the door of Father Chris's study and looked at him with big, woeful eyes. "Farvs," he said, quietly, using the kids' favourite nickname for the priest. "I made the new kid go bush."

"How?" asked Father Chris.

"I hit him in the stomach," replied Joe. "He cried and ran."

It seemed like a plea for help. Joe was confessing to hurting someone else; he was almost inviting punishment. He had been sexually abused when he was young, and his behaviour was all part of the syndrome that Father Chris was beginning to know so well: the self-loathing, the guilt, the conviction that he was unlovable, the sudden outbursts of violence followed quickly by shame and remorse, and the knowledge that bad behaviour would simply confirm everyone else's low expectations of him. Father Chris tried to talk to him, but Joe closed down and walked outside into the cold night in his dressing gown.

After an hour, Father Chris walked out to where Joe was sitting, shivering, on the front fence. He talked to Joe about the good things about him, and the way he was always far too hard on himself. He reminded him of the way he could be so kind and thoughtful towards others, and how his infectious laugh always made everyone else join in. But, he told the boy, he needed to deal with the pain raging inside before it managed to ruin all the good in his future life. Joe seemed to listen, nodded, and finally said "Good night", and went to bed.

A couple of days later, however, Joe exploded again. Sent outside for being abusive to staff, he stalked the living room with a stick in his hand, tapping it threateningly against the walls. Each time Father Chris tried to approach him, Joe hurled abuse at him. Two hours later, Father Chris tried again. Joe yelled that he should check his horse. "All its brains are hanging from its head!" screamed Joe. Father Chris's heart stopped as he wondered if Joe was really capable of such an act. He dived round to the stables. The horses were fine. When he returned, Joe had disappeared. He never came back.

"We never did get a chance to help him face his darkness," says Father Chris, sadly. "Life was never easy at Boys' Town. No amount of training or experience can give you all the answers. Just when you thought you were on top of things, the whole world seemed to cave in on you. I couldn't get his depression and his violence out of my mind. So many young people choose suicide. I dearly hoped he wouldn't."

Father Chris knew that the most debilitating affliction for a kid was to feel unwanted. It was the start of so many of their problems. Somehow, it was worse when they actually had parents around who had rejected them. Warren was a Boys' Town day pupil who became homeless when his mother and stepfather said they didn't want him any more. He tried his grandparents, but they didn't want to know him either. He spent the weekend living on the streets before it was time to go to school again on Monday. From there, Father Chris called everyone in his family, but found some had moved without leaving a forwarding address, and the others didn't want to get involved. Warren tried all his friends and contacts, but no joy there either. He spent Christmas at a refuge. Father Chris watched helplessly as he gradually drifted away from society, lost and alone. "The greatest dream a person can have is to dream that someone, somewhere cares and is interested in their story," he says. "Dreams are ultimately destroyed by loneliness."

There were many successes, too, and they always fuelled those working at Boys' Town, giving them the energy and dedication to keep going. There was often a good atmosphere among the boys — plenty of laughs, jokes and warmth. Lou Single, who worked as a lay teacher on staff at the time, and later went on to become principal, says Father Chris had a wonderful way with the boys. Suddenly, lessons became interesting. He put lots of effort into creating individualised programs and never stinted on buying the best books, ignoring protestations that the school couldn't really afford them. Mass was one of the highlights of the week. Single fondly recalls Father Chris playing guitar and singing in the chapel, urging the boys, "Bloody sing!"

"He'd walk around, getting everyone enthused and it was the best time," she says. "He would say he didn't care what religion everyone was, it didn't matter, they should just get themselves involved. All the kids participated in the masses. He'd even tape those music video clip shows on a Saturday morning, write out the words of a song he felt had a good message, and bring them in and show them. Some of them that we sat and watched in the chapel were disgusting! Then he'd bung on a religious song. He made the whole service really appeal to the young. I don't know how he did it."

Often, Father Chris would spend his own money on CDs just to keep the kids interested. He also brought a drama teacher to the school — someone, says Single, they *definitely* couldn't afford. Another time, he took a bunch of kids to a circus school and, once they had learnt an act, he took them on a national tour to show off their skills. "I don't know how he learnt as much as he did about how to relate to these kids," says Single. "He was always initiating things, and they thought the world of him. But he wouldn't take any crap from them either. He always told them to treat him how they wanted him to treat them. He was amazing." Fellow teacher Father Bob Bossini was also stirred by Father Chris's dedication. "He was doing his own thing because he was good at it," he says. "He had so much energy. I really admired him and the work he did."

Having grown up with a strong love of animals, Father Chris liked to encourage the boys to care for animals too, with the aim of bringing out a nurturing side in the boys in an unthreatening environment. He bought a Great Dane, Heidi, and she was always by his side being petted by the students until she nipped a toddler and he had to give her away. It was a heartbreaking decision, especially when he saw her again and she looked undernourished and uncared for with her new owner. He replaced her with another Great Dane, an eight-month-old sleek giant called Collingwood — after his much-loved AFL team — who quickly became his devoted shadow. There were also often a number of horses at Boys' Town. Father Chris taught the kids to look after them, as well as to enjoy their company and have fun riding them. Sometimes, it was difficult to keep the horses in top condition, but he always tried his best. At one stage, when the man who looked after the horses was transferred to another post, Father Chris called on the help of an elderly priest, Father Adrian Papworth, the uncle of Father John Papworth, the current head of Rupertswood at Sunbury. Father Adrian Papworth used to be sent by the Salesians to lend a hand everywhere that

Father Chris went, because Father Chris was so young. This time, he was asked to help look after 14 horses.

"He was an amazing man," says Father Chris. "This guy was so devoted. Some days he'd end up spending about six hours raking up manure. But he never seemed to mind. He was great, and amazingly down-to-earth. He related to the kids, and the kids loved him. He was the superior, but he would swear and curse at the kids and they would do the same back to him. It was so refreshing. He had no pretensions at all." Father Adrian Papworth died in 1994, aged 74.

Father Chris believed very much in working side-by-side with the boys in those kinds of tasks. He dearly wanted to relate to them on their own level. The Salesian way is all about trying to inspire a family spirit among their charges: to be friendly, patient, and familiar with their interests. "They must not only be loved," Don Bosco had decreed, "but *know* they are loved." So Father Chris still played sport with them, coaching the under-15 footy team to an unprecedented grand final victory, watched music shows on TV so he'd always be able to chat, on their own terms, about the music they loved, and took an interest in each, and every, boy.

It was often the smallest things that meant a lot to the kids. Sitting writing in the evenings in his residential unit, Father Chris was constantly interrupted by boys asking, "How do you do this maths problem?" or, amid the buzz of computer games, "Hey Farvs, I got 8.5, 8.0, 7.5 and 8.0!" Absent-mindedly, he'd look up and nod, not having a clue what they were talking about. One day, however, he started thinking again about how recognition and communication were so important. He stopped what he was doing to ask one of the boys what his computer game scores meant. Delighted by the attention, the boy explained he was playing a diving game. "Right," said Father Chris, jotting down the scores the boy had managed so far. "So how about getting a 9.0 next time? Wouldn't that be good to aim for?" A few minutes later, the same boy yelled with excitement. "Farvs! I got a 9.0! Can I have your piece of paper so I can write it down?" It taught Father Chris a valuable lesson: it is the sum of little acts of kindness that often work so well to build up a boy's sense of his value as a person. One of Mother Teresa's co-workers had once said, "Good hides itself in littleness", and Father Chris decided always to mind the small stuff as well as the big. Indeed, often he's found that remembering a kid's birthday is as powerful a message for a child as giving them a safe place to stay.

Father John Prest, who had worked with Father Chris at Chadstone, and was then sent to join him at Boys' Town, was astonished by how much Father Chris knew about nearly every single child. It wasn't only their birthdays, it was their background, their favourite hobbies, their academic strengths and weaknesses, and their individual dreams. "He really *knows* kids," he says. "I never knew how he did that. He was often hard on the kids, very tough, but they liked him and would do what he said. It seemed like the kids who were the angriest or most rebellious or most difficult were the ones who responded the best, too. He first gets at them by tackling them head on, then somehow this strong friendship comes out of it. He was such a positive influence on young people. To bring together a group of those kids into a footy team and to get a real commitment out of kids like them was incredible. After the end of two years at Boys' Town, I was moved. I was absolutely exhausted. But he managed to keep up this kind of work year in, year out, for years. It's incredibly draining. I don't know how he manages."

But Father Chris found the work absorbing and often rewarding. High expectations, he quickly discovered, were extremely powerful in ensuring rewards. If he thought the best of a kid, often they'd strive to live up to his belief in them. Too many others in the boys' lives had treated them as though they were bound to be a disappointment. As a result, that often became the one thing they did best. In this, Father Chris had been inspired directly by the example of Boys' Town founder Father Dunlea. At his requiem mass, a priest described him lovingly. "He seemed to wake each morning with a childlike expectation that wonderful things would happen through the day. What's more, they always did. He never met any ordinary people or situations as other people do ... Every homeless caller was an artist or a scholar of some sort."

A feeling of elation passed through Father Chris every time a boy moved on, happily and healthily, into the next phase of his life. For some, the college courses he'd found for them proved their making. Others were offered jobs by the companies Father Chris had persuaded to give them work experience. A number of them ended up going back home to a parent or parents, having worked through their differences, come to terms with their pasts, and having decided they were prepared to give their families another go. It was wonderful to see a kid who'd arrived angry, sullen and beaten, blossom into a young man who was confident, well-adjusted and ready to tackle life head-on. Many stayed in touch with Father Chris, calling him with news, or visiting to ask him for advice.

Often, he felt humbled by their courage, and he used his memories of the fortitude of these boys as a touchstone for his own ongoing work. Michael, for example, had been away from Boys' Town for two years when he phoned Father Chris to ask if he could drop by the next day. Father Chris had always had a soft spot for him. At the age of nine, after being systematically abused by his parents — including being thrown into baths of burning hot water — he began living on the streets, raiding garbage bins for food. Michael had responded well to his time at Boys' Town and left full of hope about the rest of his life. When he arrived the following day to visit Father Chris, he was just as cheerful, and proudly introduced his girlfriend, Chloe. They had a place of their own, but were having huge problems with Chloe's family. She'd recently accused her father of sexually assaulting her. The revelation had split her parents' marriage, and unleashed a cycle of violence within both her immediate and extended family, resulting in one member being stabbed to death.

"Farvs, do you have any contacts interstate so we can move right away from here?" asked Michael, calmly. "We'd be prepared to go anywhere to live — refuges, units, anything. We'll just start all over again. Start from the bottom and work up again." Father Chris was moved by their simple courage in such traumatic circumstances. "They obviously had a strong sense of commitment to each other," he says. "They sat there, these two young people, very aware of their difficulties and pain, but determined to keep things going. They had a dream — the dream of keeping love alive, amid hatred and violence. I thanked God for the gift of Michael to the world. He lived out one of the greatest struggles to keep a dream alive that I have witnessed. His life had been tough, but he had become tough in the best sense of the word. One of the major tasks of any community is to enable dreams to be recognised, pursued, rekindled and made possible. When reality does everything to make dreams cave in, we have to keep them alive against all the odds." It was a simple mantra and one that Father Chris adopted for his own life, too. Whenever he faces obstacles pursuing his own dream of helping kids, he conjures up a picture of Michael and Chloe — or any of the hundreds of others just like them who he has met since — and vows that he will do anything he can to keep his own dreams alive.

At Boys' Town, as Father Chris grew older and wiser, he remained thrilled by a feeling of freedom from the rigours of the conservative Chadstone and the close eye of his order. He celebrated his 34th birthday by having one ear pierced and wearing a small black crucifix earring. While the kids seemed to appreciate it, others weren't so impressed.

Every year, Father Chris would take a group of kids down to Chadstone to play football. When he arrived there this time, the staff were all agog. "One day he turned up in the staffroom and we nearly all had a pink fit!" recalls school nurse Chris Hellyer. "Chris had an earring in his ear! And these kids — they had rings here and there and everywhere. It didn't go down too well. We weren't used to things like that ... "

Former Chadstone school captain Tim Cox also remembers the Boys' Town visits. "We heard one story about him taking up a group of kids to Lysterfield, just to get them away from Sydney," he says. "They ended up looting all the brothers' rooms ... He struggled, at times, winning supporters for his causes."

But it was Father Chris's passion that invariably charmed everyone he met at one time or another. Chadstone student Paul Clohesy even started going up to Boys' Town to help Father Chris. "I spent a fair bit of time with him there," says Clohesy. "He was so passionate and driven, and he always knew where he was going. Chadstone was a middle-class school, which wasn't really his scene at all. He was far better with the kids who needed him."

The philosophy behind looking after "difficult" children was undergoing pretty fundamental changes in the 80s too. In the years before Father Chris arrived, there were around 140 kids at Boys' Town, all sleeping in one of two huge dormitories. The headmaster during that time, Father Peter Monaghan, says the numbers gradually fell from that point on. "I suppose the difference was that there was more individualised care from then on," he says. "That system slowly evolved. Everyone realised the group needed to become smaller so we could give more appropriate care to the kids."

That kind of care was expensive. Father Paul Miles remembers all the Herculean efforts to raise funds to keep

Boys' Town going. "I remember someone saying it costs $50,000 a year to put each kid through the program. That's a lot of money." Indeed, Boys' Town came very close to closing down several times, but Father Chris proved expert at persuading locals to donate for the cause, visiting businesses, churches and Rotary clubs to ask for help. Fired by his obvious enthusiasm and dedication, they rarely refused. Staff shortages were another problem, as priests went off to other postings, and fewer and fewer younger priests came through the system. The staff who remained, however, were usually enthusiastic. "He was a great motivator," says Lou Single. "He expected 110 per cent from you, but by the same token, he'd give 120. At times, he could be difficult to work with because his brain was always six steps ahead of yours. It was hard to keep up. He was such a good leader, though. He inspired by example." At one point, the staff shortage became critical when Father Chris was the only staff member left who was any good at controlling the kids. Instead of the eight kids he was meant to have in his residential unit, he had 35.

Rarely, however, did these kinds of situations get Father Chris down. Always, he was buoyed by the sheer resilience of the boys he was trying to help. Their courage and their will to survive, often against terrible odds, he found inspiring. Sometimes, Father Chris thought about the lives of these boys in terms of the children's book *The Bumblebee Flies Anyway*: a story about the bumblebee, an insect which manages to fly despite its size, shape, weight, and all the laws of aerodynamics. "Boys' Town's story is powerfully the story of the bumblebee as young lives, which seem scarred forever, break through all attempts to call them to anonymity," says Father Chris. "Just when society feels it has suffocated their ability to hope, to change, to be, our young people do the impossible. They break free from all the things which imprison them, and fly freely. It is a story of hope in, and through, failure, a story of courage amid agonising pain, and of meaning, when there is nothing around any of these young people that gives anything meaning.

"We, as a society, need to be reminded that suffering and pain do not necessarily destroy, but can, in fact, bring new meaning and wholeness. Our young people face life against all the odds, and yet they are able to face most days with a smile. They can be crushed by their circumstances, yet still look towards the stars. Once they face the fear that has frozen their lives, with others' help, they so often go on to fulfil their potential, and find real love."

Yet the successes of Boys' Town were never enough for Father Chris; he always wanted to do more. Hearing the kids talk about the misery of their lives before they had come to Boys' Town made him realise just how many young people must slip through the net all the time, and who would now be eking out a miserable existence on the streets of Sydney, surviving on their wits, and sleeping wherever they could.

The Burdekin Report, *Our Homeless Children*, was released in February 1989 following a two-year inquiry by the Human Rights Commissioner Brian Burdekin, revealing that between 20,000 and 25,000 Australian children were homeless. Its findings shocked the nation. These kids, increasingly as young as 12, had, in the vast majority of cases, run away from adults who were abusing them physically and sexually, and were now living on the streets, in parks, in the bush, on beaches, under bridges and in clothing bins. Many were being forced into prostitution. Many were turning to drugs to dull the pain. All were in dire need of help.

Father Chris's mind was in turmoil. He wrote to the Salesian Provincial, sharing his confusion. While he deeply loved his order and his work, he kept feeling drawn to helping others who weren't so comfortable. "The call to work for the poor is so strong within me," he wrote. "When I think of living poorly, of touching the lives of really broken people, I get scared. I know how inadequate I am, but I know I should have enough faith. This fear always leaves me restless as I am always confronted with a God who is always radically open to the most broken people and rejected people. I am left holding a Rule of Life that calls me to be with youth, especially the poorest. Christ and Don Bosco stand as living expressions of men who risked all ... [men] who saw a need and responded to it with every bit of energy they had."

He soon received his reply: Father Chris was needed at Boys' Town. He didn't consider disobeying the order, but the more he thought about it, the more uneasy he felt about living in a safe, secure housing unit, and sleeping in a warm bed every night while there were so many unloved kids out in the cold. And the more he thought about them, the more determined he became to try to do something about the plight of these kids that society seemed so willing to forget. The only problem was, not everyone might agree with his plan. He would have to keep it a secret from those who might want to stop him.

Chapter 8

ON THE STREETS

IT WAS a bitterly cold night in the middle of winter, with rain and wind gusting through Sydney's city centre. On a lonely bench in Sydney Square, just near St Andrew's Cathedral, a figure lay hunched under a threadbare brown coat, her shoulders shaking as she sobbed. Father Chris Riley went over to her, and sat quietly on the end of the bench. Sensing someone was there, she turned her head and looked at him. She wiped her nose on her sleeve and struggled to sit up. Tears continued to course down her face.

"Hey," said Father Chris, gently. "What's the matter? Is there anything I can do to help?" The girl looked at him, her red-rimmed hazel eyes filled with misery and doubt. She shivered. He offered her a styrofoam cup filled with steaming hot soup. She took it from him, and sipped slowly. After a few minutes of silence, she looked as if she had made a sudden decision, and finally spoke. "They told me my daughter died last week," she said, hesitantly. "They've just told me. I can't believe it. My daughter.

Emma. Dead." Father Chris sensed she didn't want him to say anything. Gradually, her story came out.

Her name was Sherry, and she was just 14. Her father had died when she was five, and her mother had gone through a series of boyfriends until finally settling down with the man who would become Sherry's stepdad. At the age of 12, Sherry had his baby. When her mum found out who the father was, she kicked Sherry out of home. They had taken baby Emma from Sherry and were raising her as their own. They wouldn't allow Sherry to see Emma.

Sherry knew nothing of the circumstances of her daughter's death. She only knew that her baby daughter, whom she'd never had the chance to get to know, and now never would, was dead. She broke down in shuddering sobs once again.

Father Chris felt enraged. Sherry's story wasn't unusual; he had met lots of kids with similar tales to tell. The details, of course, always varied, but at their heart was usually the same betrayals of trust, abandonment, rejection and utter hopelessness. Ninety-five per cent of the girls on the street, he'd found, had been sexually assaulted — either in their home or in the local neighbourhood. Ninety per cent of the boys he helped had been sexually assaulted. The streets of Australia, he was fast learning, were cold and mean. And kindness was an extremely rare commodity. Father Chris went back to his car to pick up a blanket. He came back to Sherry and wrapped it around her shoulders. Locked in her own grief, she didn't even notice.

This was just another normal night on the streets, a world Father Chris was just beginning to get to know, yet which still had the power to chill him, anger him and make him feel totally useless. Sometimes, the tide of human misery threatened to overwhelm him. But always, just as darkness closed in, hope would flicker and burn brightly. One evening, for instance, when he was handing out soup and sandwiches to the 80 or so kids amassed in the square, he realised he was getting soaked in the rain. So did some of the others. Barry, a boy he had noticed a few times before, came up to him.

"Farvs," he said, "why don't you go home now? You must be freezing. You're soaking wet." Father Chris turned and smiled at him. "I'm fine," he said. "I haven't finished yet, but I'll be fine. You go and take cover." Barry looked back at him uncertainly. Then, with a quick gesture, he slipped off his coat and handed it to the priest. "Take this," he said, roughly. "Sorry about the smell." And then he slid into the shadows. Father Chris felt his throat grow tight with emotion. These kids had virtually nothing, yet they were willing to do anything for anyone who showed them the faintest kindness. He slipped on the coat — trying to ignore the powerful odour of a kid who obviously hadn't had a shower for weeks — and continued handing out the food.

This had become a regular routine for Father Chris. Every evening, when his duties at Boys' Town were over and he had put the kids to bed, he would be joined by old Father Adrian Papworth. The pair would sit together for a while, in case any of the boys couldn't get to sleep, or woke up suddenly, and then Father Chris would slip away, leaving his colleague in charge.

Father Chris would then steal into Boys' Town's massive kitchen, and prepare food for the night ahead, ladling it into pots and packing it in eskies. He would pick up his first-aid kit and then set out for the city centre 30 km away. He arrived between 8 p.m. and 9 p.m. every night of the week and would return home to Boys' Town, depending on the events of the evening, either just after midnight or any time up till 4 a.m. He would then have only a few hours sleep before having to get up at 6 a.m., often with a splitting migraine, to start his chores again.

It was a gruelling regime, but Father Chris had always managed on minimal sleep, and he felt the needs of the streetkids dwarfed his own. The more he got to know their world, the further he became drawn to it. He felt this was the work that most needed to be done and which, indeed, God had intended him to do. In a strange sort of way, he was happy helping these kids; he took great pleasure in little victories and tried hard not to be dragged down by the daily setbacks. In July 1987, Prime Minister Bob Hawke had sworn that by 1990 no Australian child would live in poverty. Here, however, Father Chris was seeing evidence — nightly — that Hawke's goal was receding further into the distance as the grim truths of the Burdekin Report were acted out. That had revealed between 8000 and 9000 of the homeless kids were aged between 12 and 15, that many were reduced to prostitution after just two weeks to earn money to stay alive, that the vast majority were fleeing abuse, either physical or sexual, at home, and estimated that one in five would never lead a "normal" life. "We can't seem to realise as a community that our most fragile and precious resource is our children," said Burdekin. The heartbreaking words of a 15-year-old boy seemed to sum up the mood of the entire report. "What do I hope for?" he was quoted as asking. "That I die pretty quick."

Father Chris was determined to help those kids. Most nights, he drove up to Darlinghurst's notorious Wall, where young male streetkids, in the hope of earning enough money to live on, prostitute themselves to men who cruise by in cars. Father Chris gave the boys food, made sure they were all right, chatted to them and, if he could, referred them to somewhere they could receive help, so they could move away from the kind of life they were leading. He became a well-known figure in the area, dressed always in black shirt, black jeans, black boots and white dog collar. "It's kind of a form of protection," he says. "It becomes non-threatening, and hopefully a symbol of trust."

Then Father Chris would drive into the city centre, to Sydney Square, where dozens of homeless kids routinely gathered. It was a grim scenario, one which was increasingly being played out in every city of Australia, if not the world.

Some of the kids would show every night for a week, and then disappear for a month at a time. Sometimes they left to go to the country to try for seasonal work on farms. Along the way some were picked up by the police and sent away, or went back to their homes for a while. Other kids would turn up only sporadically. Gradually, Father Chris got to know all the faces, and personalities, working hard to earn their trust.

There was Ginger, a lively young woman of around 18, with a shock of auburn hair and a quick temper. On good nights, she could be funny and smart. On bad nights, she could sink into a terrible depression and become anti-social and violent. Often, that easy violence between the kids disheartened Father Chris but he knew that, when kids are brought up with violence, they see no alternative for solving conflict.

Throughout the first few weeks he was working on the streets, he noticed that Ginger seemed to be getting progressively more sick. Every time he talked to her, he urged her to go to a doctor, often offering to pick her up and drive her there himself. One night she was so bad, he managed to persuade her to go to hospital. She ended up staying four days, with an acute case of tonsillitis.

He liked Ginger; everyone did. But she had developed a hard, brittle shell to protect herself, and it was difficult to lure her out. One of the guys who was around most often, Stuart, was obviously extremely fond of her. His eyes followed Ginger wherever she went, and he tried to talk to her whenever she felt like talking. They had an argument one night, however, and Ginger lashed out at him, punching him in the face. Stuart, with his confidence already at an all-time low, was absolutely crushed. When Father Chris saw him the next night, he had cigarette burns all over his arms, and he had burned himself particularly badly just above the heart. Gently, Father Chris dressed the angry wounds.

"Why do it, mate?" Father Chris asked him. "Why burn someone so valuable?" Stuart scoffed. "I'm nothing," he said. "Why shouldn't I?" It was that same terrible lack of self-esteem that Father Chris had discovered at Boys' Town to be such a destructive, negative force in so many of the kids' lives. When one of the younger kids, TJ, approached him shyly one night and asked for a blanket, Father Chris was struck by how the boy seemed as though he was asking for a huge favour, the way a kid from a loving, affluent home might ask his parents for a car, or for a deposit on a house. A few nights later, another young man, Gary, actually stood and wept when Father Chris presented him with a birthday cake and joined in with the other 20 kids there that night in a hearty rendition of *Happy Birthday*.

One particularly freezing night in the middle of winter, Father Chris tried to wake up another of the young men, Paul, who was lying on a bench, shivering in only a light jacket, to give him a jumper to put on. It was hard to raise him from his alcoholic stupor; he had been drinking heavily all evening. "At 24, I was struck by how he looked like an old drunk," Father Chris wrote in his diary when he returned to Boys' Town that morning. "So much talent, so many lives, so many gifts wasted." He tried to get Paul to drink some soup, but Paul refused. "It doesn't matter," he said. "Help someone else. I'm not worth it." Aching at the sight of a person living like that, shaking from the cold, Father Chris bundled him into his car and insisted on finding him a place to sleep in the city centre for the night. "No, Father," Paul protested on the way there. "Don't waste your money. I'll be OK." Father Chris ignored him, helped him to the hotel and gave him the money for the room for the night. As he left, he could see Paul standing at the glass door, tears pouring down his face.

Every night Father Chris spent with the kids brought its own share of ups, downs and surprises. Ricky turned up one day, a newcomer to the scene. Just 13 years old, he was living on the streets because he didn't want to stay with his mother, a heavy drug-user who was becoming increasingly violent. A few days later, the news filtered through that Ricky had been picked up by the police sleeping in a doorway and was being held in their cells. Father Chris went to see him. He asked the boy for his mother's telephone number, discovering, with surprise, that she lived in one of the most affluent parts of Sydney. He phoned her and asked if Ricky could return home. She hung up on Father Chris. She obviously didn't care at all. With absolutely nowhere for him to go, he ended up remanded to Yasmar Juvenile Justice Centre. It was two months before Father Chris bumped into him again. This time, the boy seemed so much older and harder. He was growing up fast, but in the worst way possible.

Father Chris turned up each night with not only food, warm clothing, blankets and Band Aids but also any little special requests the kids had given him. One longed for a chicken sandwich, another an orange juice, another liked milk, a fourth phoned him from hospital, asking if he could possibly find a way of picking up his clothes and washing them so he could leave hospital in clean clothes. Every night, Father Chris would dress cuts, treat a bruised ankle or provide fresh bandages for ulcers on legs. He tried to find shoes for kids who were walking around barefoot and, as the weather became colder, he would gather any spare coats he could find. The kids asked Father Chris to help them write letters to friends in detention centres, parents, or to the authorities to apply for assistance, with one begging him to bring her some schoolwork and help her study for her HSC. Another called and asked him to pick up her pet rat as she'd been taken to a detention centre and she wasn't allowed to keep the rat there. He did so.

Sometimes, Father Chris organised activities for the kids, such as a game of basketball, or a trip to the fun park Wonderland, in Sydney's west. He couldn't always satisfy their requests, however. Jessie asked him if he could buy her some underwear. "Sorry," he said, firmly. "I can't imagine myself going into a shop and asking for it, can you?" The pair laughed long and hard together. Another night, 14-year-old Flo told Father Chris she'd just discovered she was pregnant and asked, somewhat unrealistically it has to be said, if he could lend her money for an abortion. "No," said Father Chris, "but I will talk to you about helping out if you have the baby."

The winter of 1990 felt like the hardest Father Chris could remember, with growing numbers of homeless kids, and rain and cold weather that seemed set to go on forever. Frequently, he found it hard to leave the kids in such dismal conditions. Often, however, they were cheerful about their plight. Barry would regularly leave shelter to help Father Chris dole out coffee, more than willing to get cold and wet in the process. Father Chris kept thinking more and more about how there needed to be a place for kids such as these to go. It came to a head when he realised just how many of them were living in miserable conditions in squats. Often, the kids would leave their squats for a night, and then go back to find them boarded up by their owners, forcing the kids to spend their nights outside again. They were always coughing and sneezing, with colds and bronchial conditions they seemed never able to shrug off. One evening, the news came through that Ginger had fallen through the floor in her squat and had fractured her skull, broken her collarbone and had to have two screws inserted in her back. She also lost her hearing in her right ear. She was in a lot of pain and would probably be in hospital for five weeks. A couple of the kids asked Father Chris for a lift to the hospital to visit her.

Drink and drugs were both huge dangers for kids. In 1990, drink was perhaps the biggest threat with drugs only beginning to come on to the streets in large quantities. Jimmy was one young guy who was drinking more and more heavily. Every time he had an argument with his girlfriend Sissy, he'd disappear and then come back worse for wear. He looked on the fast slope to ruin.

Alcohol was also taking a heavy toll on Paul, the young man forever grateful to Father Chris for that night in the hotel. One night, another of the homeless girls, Julie, had spurned his advances and hit him in the mouth. Eaten up with rage, Paul strode over to Father Chris's car and punched the windows, blood still pouring from his mouth. He then ran over to another boy and hit him. Father Chris and Gary grabbed Paul and tried to pull him away. He was shouting abuse at everyone he saw. He finally slumped on the ground, and Father Chris knelt down beside him, trying to talk to him. An elderly Aboriginal man walking past shook his head. "Get up, Father," he said. "Don't demean yourself with these people." On hearing this comment, Paul jumped back to his feet and raced over to a pile of beer bottles standing empty on the ground, picked them up, and smashed them one by one. Then he went over to the garbage bins nearby and kicked them over. He continued his rampage for 15 minutes then, realising Father Chris was still watching him, he walked over to the priest threateningly. Father Chris stood his ground. Paul then put his arms around the priest, and burst into tears. Later, when Paul had calmed down, Father Chris tried to talk to him about what had happened, but he couldn't remember a thing about the last hour.

It was never easy, and Father Chris did make mistakes. One night, he returned to his car to find TJ asleep on the backseat. He didn't have the heart to turf him out into the cold night. Instead, he agreed to take him and one other back to Boys' Town to sleep. As soon as he'd told them, the others started clamouring to come back too. When Father Chris refused, they grew angry. After that night, he promised himself he would never again take anyone back to Boys' Town. "Everyone must have an equal deal," he told himself. "I can't afford to have favourites. I really wish I could find a place in the city so everyone would be able to get the same deal."

The streets were dangerous. The kids' heavy drinking and drug taking would often make them the target for passing young people and others who made their contempt clear. Father Chris one day received an hysterical call about three of the streetkids getting stabbed by a madman and arrived in time to see them being put in ambulances. Sometimes, they'd be bashed by gangs of youths who came into town for the evening, looking for sport.

Yet while the nights could be miserable and violent, often the kids were positive and playful. Father Chris loved those evenings. He was heartened when he saw how, despite their situations, the kids still cared for each other. Many were worried about Barry, a 19-year-old who was regularly having alcoholic seizures. They often tried to persuade him to seek help at hospital. He always refused. Some of them took that hard. Father Chris once rang for an ambulance when he was worried that Barry might not come out of a coma. Barry emerged just as the ambulance drove up, and told the ambulance workers to go away, they weren't needed. This particularly disturbed Steve, a young guy who hadn't been on the streets for long, and still had a soft heart. He was distressed that Barry seemed to have a death wish, and frustrated that there appeared to be nothing he could do to stop him. Father Chris took him off for a walk. Steve cried, and quoted American singer the late Janis Joplin, "It doesn't matter, nothing matters." He talked about the purposelessness of his existence, with no one and nothing to live for. "I might as well kill myself," he said brightly. Father Chris's heart sank. He wondered if he'd ever be wise, and strong, enough to help these kids.

Chapter 9

TAKING RISKS

IT HAD seemed such a good idea at the time. Three of the streetkids in particular really enjoyed their games of basketball every week, so Father Chris thought it might be fun to take them to see a proper match at Sydney's Entertainment Centre. They were excited, and so was he. It wasn't until they walked in and took their seats that Father Chris started to have his first misgivings.

People simply wouldn't stop staring at the odd foursome, and then those sitting next to them shuffled away and others close by changed their seats. It was at this point that something dawned on Father Chris: how far outside normal society he'd travelled with these kids. He stole a sideways glance at the boys. The three were in torn ragged jeans, dirty T-shirts and threadbare flannelette shirts. There was something else he'd never noticed about them before too — they stank. Usually, he realised with a sinking feeling, he only met them outside, or inside when they were on the move. He had never actually sat still with them for long enough to really appreciate the powerful odour of unwashed flesh and clothes. He tried hard to ignore the hostile stares and concentrate on the game.

The kids were doing the same, and they took to the task with enthusiasm. They soon became totally absorbed in the action. The only trouble was, the wrong team was winning, and the kids wouldn't stop swearing, extremely loudly, at the referee. Again, Father Chris shifted uncomfortably in his seat as all eyes turned to him and the kids. He smiled back benignly. "I realised that these kids had grown worlds apart from the average Australian," he says. "Opting to live with them and work with them I understood, from that moment on, would bring me a great deal of pain and misunderstanding. Yet while they didn't have good manners — in fact, very few at all — I loved the way they threw themselves so completely into the experience. They giggled and laughed like babies. The whole atmosphere enchanted them. As the crowd interacted with the game, they cheered and yelled out in unison with the crowd, wide-eyed and thrilled. It was probably the first time they had ever been to something like that. Many of the things we take for granted have never been given to these kids. All the normal experiences of childhood have been ripped away from them by violence, sexual abuse and rejection. As I sat there, I was suddenly very proud of them, and proud to be with them."

But, as Father Chris was to find, time and again, there was no simple catch-all formula to working with these kids. A few weeks later, he took another group of boys and girls to the basketball. This time was even harder. As well as swearing — upsetting the mother of an eight-year-old sitting in front of them — they smuggled in drink and tried to smoke. Father Chris was angry with them, and realised he wasn't enjoying their company. It was no reason not to organise trips like that again in future, he reasoned, but he should be better prepared. Next time, he would sit and talk to the kids first, and hammer out some rules about appropriate behaviour.

It was the middle of 1990, and the police were becoming far more active about trying to disperse the streetkids. The number of children living, and congregating, on the streets at night had grown so rapidly, some nights with up to 100 kids in Sydney Square, that some people were beginning to see it as a problem. Sadly, they didn't see it as a problem that could be helped by the provision of more places for the kids to go, or social intervention; they saw the kids as a problem they would have preferred to remain out of sight, and certainly not on their doorsteps. The local community was insisting the police move the kids on, and even churchmen from St Andrew's Cathedral, located on the square, were reported to be complaining about the kids. One claimed hearing profanities from the kids that not even his 15 years in the armed services had taught him. Some locals were even agitating for the kids to be denied food in the square, as that was "obviously" only encouraging them to hang around there.

Regularly, the police would turn out in force to question the kids. Father Chris became exasperated. A few times the police even noted down his name and address and asked him what his business was in being there. It seemed an utterly pointless routine. "They wanted the kids to move on, but to where?" he asks. "Of course, they had their job to do, but where were the proper long-term solutions being proposed?" The routine questioning sometimes scared but more often aggravated the streetkids. One night, two transit officers came over to Father Chris and asked for two cups of coffee. The kids were outraged. "Why should you take our coffee?" they asked. "You have homes to go to! Leave us alone and take nothing from us." The officers hastily exited. Father Chris, however, ticked off the kids. They were incredulous. "The beauty of the streetpeople is that they welcome anyone and everyone," Father Chris told them. "They don't judge. They take everyone as they are." The kids weren't convinced and, in his heart of hearts, he couldn't really blame them. He could understand how they had learned to resent authority, and to regard it with anger and bitterness.

Their mistrust of authority often proved difficult when the kids fell ill. Many refused, point blank, to visit doctors as they always assumed something bad would happen to them in the surgeries. It meant Father Chris was kept busy with his little first-aid kit: doling out cold and flu tablets, bathing infected blisters, buying anti-dandruff shampoo for one kid, a Ventolin inhaler for another and grimacing when a child screamed in agony as he sprayed their feet, red raw from tinea.

Sometimes, though, the kids would need no more than a simple feed. The night he brought in roast chicken and vegetables, he was mobbed. They also loved his vat of hot spaghetti. Most of the time they made do with sandwiches, fruit and Mars Bars.

Father Chris still found the violence he encountered deeply disturbing. One night, Jimmy and Brian had an argument and tempers soon flared. Jimmy hit Brian, and then Brian punched him to the ground before kicking him as he lay there. Father Chris pushed his way in between the pair, pleading for them to stop, but the others intervened and pulled him away, holding him back. "They have to sort this out, once and for all," the kids told him. Brian continued to bash Jimmy, while Father Chris was forced to look on helplessly, feeling sick to his stomach. As soon as the others let go of him, he picked up Jimmy and dragged him to his car. When he drove him back to his squat, however, Jimmy took out his frustration on his girlfriend Sissy, grabbing her and then banging her face against the window. Such violence was nearly always fuelled by alcohol.

Usually, though, the kids were more keen to protect Father Chris than to hold him back. When Paul, still drinking heavily, tried to pick a fight with a passerby, Father Chris tried to intervene. One of the other kids, worried that Father Chris might get hurt, came to his rescue. The end result? A second fight for Father Chris to break up. Often, these clashes were completely unprovoked. A new kid appeared on the square one day and Steve chased him, caught him and decked him. Father Chris dragged the beaten-up boy to his car. Then he made a tragic mistake: he left the doors unlocked. He then went to help someone else but, out of the corner of his eye, suddenly caught sight of Steve climbing into the car and punching the boy brutally in the face. Father Chris took the kid — who was sobbing by then, and cradling his injured head in his hands — straight to hospital. "I was furious at my stupidity, and angry at their manipulation," says Father Chris. "I found that violence heartbreaking. These kids are generally soft and sensitive, caring and loyal. But they can also be so brutal. I resolved that my life must be all about peace. My words, my actions and my thoughts should never be violent. It's a big order, but I will always struggle towards that goal."

Yet Father Chris found there was always scope for optimism. The night three eight-year-olds turned up on the street, the other kids confronted them as one. "Go home," they told them gently. "You're too young to be here. Go home — while you still can." At one point, the kids even began to care enough about their own surroundings to start cleaning up their own mess, picking up the sheets of newspapers fluttering across the square, putting their foam cups and bottles into bins. Father Chris watched in amazement.

For every kid Father Chris made friends with, however, there were always others far less willing to engage. There was one boy he saw every week for three years, but the kid avoided him at every opportunity and never spoke a single word to him in all that time. The priest couldn't directly ask him his name, either: that simple act of asking a boy's surname could undo weeks of trust-building. But he was an exception. Father Chris worked hard at winning the streetkids' confidence even though often it literally cost him dearly. Once he had won the friendship of a boy, he felt obliged to help them out by paying their fines for stealing cars, shoplifting, loitering or for simply failing to pay penalties from previous offences.

Tony was a bright kid, of about 18, who had been living on the streets for a couple of years. He always seemed to be in trouble. The first time Father Chris was asked to pay bail for him, he knew it was a risk, but felt it was worth the $200 to try to buy the boy's trust. Every time Father Chris saw him, he reminded Tony when he was next due in court. Happily, Tony turned up on the morning of the hearing, and the pair drove to Gosford together. They ended up sitting in the courtroom all day, only to be told the police didn't have their paperwork ready, and the hearing would have to be adjourned. A week later, Tony was back in trouble. He was picked up for stealing a car and gave his name as Tony Theft. The police at Macquarie Fields station called Father Chris and asked if he wanted to bail him out. It was $1000. "I knew that was an even greater risk, but the alternative was that he would be sent to Parramatta Gaol," says Father Chris. "I can't see an 18-year-old go to gaol for car theft." When Tony came back, he was emotional and close to tears. "Thank you," he said, grasping Father Chris's hand. "Thank you." He'd been terrified of going to gaol, petrified that the other inmates might seize on his pretty-boy looks and rape him.

It was a huge relief, then, when Tony did turn up to court on that $1000 bail. Father Chris was sure the magistrate would view this in Tony's favour, but instead he focused on other, much more trivial bail conditions that had been broken. The magistrate remanded him in custody overnight. As remand was announced, Tony stared at Father Chris with an expression of total devastation and betrayal. That night, Father Chris wrote an impassioned report on the boy, and attended court the next day to present it. He sat steadfastly in the courtroom from 10 a.m. to 4 p.m., trying to prove to the magistrate that he had faith in the boy, stubbornly refusing a break. When Tony finally appeared in the dock as the last case of the day, he was given a two-year good behaviour bond and a $1000 fine that he couldn't possibly hope to pay within the allotted four months. "The system screws these kids," Father Chris said angrily at the end. "There are plenty of punishments, but no solutions. Tony had already been on remand for five months at the State's main juvenile detention centre, Yasmar. Nothing had ever been done for him. There was never any follow-up or reports written. The system had completely failed him — and so many kids like him."

Father Chris didn't always get his bail money back. He had severe misgivings when he was asked to bail out a boy named Carlos for the second time in as many weeks on theft charges. Father Chris refused at first, but finally relented. Carlos then disappeared for a month and Father Chris lost the bail money. When he eventually turned up again on the square, he avoided Father Chris. He sat on a far bench and stared into the distance. He looked terrible. His jeans were so torn it was a wonder they stayed on, and he was barefoot, carrying a mat. Father Chris casually strolled over and asked him how he was. He was determined not to mention the bail he'd blown on the boy, even though he was tempted to let the 15-year-old know that he had got into trouble because of it. After a while, however, Carlos himself asked, "How much was the bail?" Father Chris, surprised, brushed the question aside.

"I've forgotten about it," he replied. "Don't mention it. Forget it." But it seemed Carlos couldn't. As Father Chris was leaving that night, he came up to the car window. "I've never trusted anyone before," whispered Carlos, tears in his eyes. He made a hopeless motion with his hand and walked off. Father Chris felt full of despair for him, a lost, lone kid wandering around the country permanently, with no one to care. He had to let him go.

Brian, too, stayed out of Father Chris's way after breaking bail. Eventually, the priest sent him a message via his girlfriend, that, *honestly*, it was OK. "The same thing keeps cropping up all the time," says Father Chris. "The kids are so hard on themselves. They feel they stuff up all the time, and have absolutely no hope that they'll ever be forgiven."

Other bail stories had happier endings. Julie turned up in court after Father Chris posted $500 bail, thanking Father Chris for his trust in her. Ginger was bailed on condition that she live with her mum, something her mum was happy to try. Jasmine's experience was quite different. Her mother phoned Father Chris one night, furious that he had posted bail for her as she'd travelled 20 km to visit her, planning to bail Jasmine out herself. It served to remind Father Chris that some kids on the streets do indeed have parents at home, waiting for them, brokenhearted by their absence. "Sadly, though, it's not many," he says. "A lot of people just don't understand streetkids. They seem to think they're just spoilt kids running away from loving homes. In general, the families they're running away from don't give a damn, or they kicked them out in the first place. Most kids don't leave home; home leaves them." Many of the kids' stories were simply heartbreaking. There was the boy who left home at 13 because of his parents' drunken rages. There was the girl who was consistently raped by her mum's new boyfriend. And there was the boy whose father was so violent that once, when he was pulled over his dad's knee for a smack, his father simply snapped the boy's leg, breaking it in three places. To most people, the kind of abuse meted out to these kids by their parents, their step-parents or their uncles or aunts is just unthinkable. To Father Chris, paying out $500 on a kid's bail, knowing it is perhaps the first kind act they have ever known in their lives, seems little sacrifice.

But usually, the things Father Chris helped the kids with cost far less. All Mark wanted was a razor so he could have a shave. Lenny begged for a pen and paper so he could write to a friend. Kerry requested a Panadol to help him cope with a migraine. The delight these small offerings delivered was out of all proportion to their worth. The night Father Chris gave Bob some Elvis tapes for his birthday, the kid was so overwhelmed, and thanked him so much, talking endlessly about the songs, that he almost regretted doing it.

For Father Chris, every night on the streets was an education. He was thrown into a terrible moral dilemma when one young kid confessed he had killed someone; he hoped against hope it was perhaps just the alcohol talking. He was horrified when another described being drugged, raped, then forced to work at The Wall, and resolved, at some point in the future, to start campaigning against the evils of child prostitution. Often, he was given just glimpses into the soul-destroying world of the streetkids. He was enraged, for example, at the story of Stevo. This young man had previously been caught breaking into his former boss's premises after he had been sacked. When the same warehouse was broken into a second time, the boss automatically accused Stevo, and assaulted him. Stevo, however, was with Father Chris at Boys' Town at the time of the second burglary, and when the boss pressed charges against Stevo for the offence, Father Chris urged the boy to file counter charges. He refused. "It's not worth it, Farvs," he said, with a shrug. "I can't win. No one's going to believe me." Father Chris sighed. He knew, in his heart, the kid was right.

One night, everyone sat in silence when they heard 13-year-old Ken had overdosed on heroin and died. Ginger was particularly distraught; she had given him money for the drug, and blamed herself for what happened to him. The spectre of death never seemed far away. TJ was very depressed after his mates accused him of stealing their rent money and, after talking to Father Chris, he told him to examine his face carefully. "You might not see it again," TJ said grimly. Father Chris feared that Julie, who was pregnant, could also well be the next casualty. She'd already overdosed once on pills, leaving hospital without her shoes, she was in such a rush to get away. Two days later, she was back in the square, wild and delusional on more pills and alcohol. Father Chris tried to warn her about the damage she was doing to both herself and her unborn baby. It seemed to make little difference. For, like most of the kids, she didn't particularly value her own life. Julie's closest friend was Amy, who appeared to have a deathwish too. She turned up one evening with a huge bandage on her arm, from elbow to wrist. She said she'd cut herself. It was a long, deep gash that had needed 42 stitches in hospital. When asked why she had done it, she said her boyfriend had just phoned her from England to tell her he had terminal cancer and didn't have long left to live. "Whenever I've needed him, he's been there for me," she mumbled. "Now he needs me, I can't be with him." She had slashed herself in an act of solidarity. It was her way of sharing his pain. "Without him, I've got nothing to live for," she said simply. Father Chris despaired.

"The kids are all so hard on themselves, and I feel powerless and confused as I hear their stories," he says. "While I might be touching the lives of many young people at Town Hall, the problems are so much bigger. Streetkids form an underground population. Many live on the edge of life and death. Who knows what pain is being experienced, who knows how many kids disappear and are never found? I began to realise that many things will be revealed to me, and I won't be able to do much about them."

On nights like those, Father Chris didn't enjoy his time with the streetkids at all. He was determined, however, to keep his routine intact. If he had a bad night, it should make him all the more resolute about coming back the following one, to prove to the kids that he was there for the long haul. He also tried never to complain or be critical in their company. They had enough problems of their own to deal with, he told himself, and were always so quick to pick up on negativity. Many nights, it was tiredness that would drag Father Chris down, combined with frustration that the kids would come and go so often, making casework extremely difficult. There were also those times the kids would turn on him, abusing him, shouting at him, taking out all their aggravation at the hand life had dealt them on the only adult figure around. Nearly always they apologised the next day. "It's important to show that I'm committed to them," says Father Chris. "Night after night, you just have to turn up, good or bad. You can't let the kids down, or let them think you're just another person who gives up on them when the going gets tough."

And then there were those nights when kids came up to him and quietly, hesitantly, asked for his help to get off the streets. At times like these, his heart would truly sing.

Chapter 10

CAST OUT INTO THE WILDERNESS

MANY PEOPLE worried about Father Chris spending so much time on the streets at night with the country's toughest, most broken kids. His parents warned him against taking unnecessary risks. His sister Helen secretly felt sick whenever she thought of the things that might happen to him. But Father Chris was never afraid.

At the age of 32, when he started at Boys' Town as principal, he lost the fear of death that haunts and inhibits so many of us. He doesn't know why; it just seemed to evaporate. From that moment on, he worked steadily and confidently among even the roughest pupils at Boys' Town and then, at night, he walked the streets without hesitation, approaching the most battle-scarred kids without a second thought. And they responded. In droves.

He had a small stroke of luck there, it has to be said. On a dark night in one of the meanest areas of town where the atmosphere was ugly, an aggressive-looking group of young men approached Father Chris. The gang's leader stopped right in front of the priest, towering over him. He leant down and looked him directly in the face, menace glittering in his eyes. Father Chris caught his breath. Then the man threw out his arms and hugged him tight. "Farvs," he yelled. "You're famous 'cos of me!"

Startled, Father Chris simply replied, "Oh, I am, am I?"

"Yes," said the man, "I was your very first streetkid."

Father Chris looked at him more closely. He smiled. "Yes, you were," he answered. "So, how are you doing now, Gary?" That warm welcome meant Father Chris was instantly accepted in that area.

"I'm not scared of going into any place," he says today. "I've been on the streets for a while, literally out with the toughest kids in the State, and I've survived in that environment. It's the safest place because many of those kids would die for me! That's the incredible thing. That's where people misunderstand these kids; if you help them they protect you. Besides, I'm never afraid of death any more, so nothing else really matters."

Father Chris and the devoted dog Collingwood he was still carefully training to accompany him in his street work were increasingly becoming the only constant in the life of the streetkids, and they soon began showing Father Chris how much they appreciated him. Brian, usually so tough and macho, confided to Father Chris one evening that he had split up with his girlfriend. Father Chris gently asked if he was all right. Brian simply hugged him, then walked away. Carlos approached Father Chris to see whether he could find him a job. Father Chris said he'd definitely try to help. Ginger called round on a trip from her parents' home to say hello. Despite still being in a backbrace from her fall, she looked healthy and happy. One of the guys, Bernie, started talking about getting off the streets, and asked Father Chris for help. "I can talk the talk, but I can't walk the walk," he said. He knew what he had to do but with his self-confidence shot to pieces, he didn't feel he had the strength to escape the lifestyle he had become entrenched in alone. Besides, he was getting weaker all the time with Hepatitis B. Father Chris happily agreed to give him a hand.

There were other success stories too. When Barry turned up again for some food, he ate hungrily, dry-retched and then vomited. He had been off heroin for five days, going cold turkey, he told Father Chris proudly. Although he felt terrible, he was thrilled by what he had so far achieved. He smiled weakly at Father Chris, then wandered away, crouched down and sat leaning against a pillar, hands wrapped round his legs, chin resting on knees, willing himself through the pain. Jim was nearly home and dry too. A New Zealander who'd been living on the Sydney streets for two years, Father Chris had just loaned him the fare back to Auckland for a reunion with his family. He couldn't stop grinning at the prospect.

Yet the persistent violence of the streets, particularly the gang violence, was proving much harder to beat than helping individual kids. Many of them had become so used to living on the streets that they saw everyone as the enemy, the world as a warzone and their gang as their family, able to prove their loyalty only through their willingness to fight side-by-side. Father Chris shuddered as one boy told him how he and his mates had approached an old man sitting in a dark alley swigging from a bottle of methylated spirits. They'd grabbed the bottle from him, poured its contents on his hands and thrown a lit match at him. His hands ignited instantly and he screamed in terror and pain. Viv, one of the regular crowd of streetkids, excitedly told of the night a big man had started attacking a member of his gang; almost immediately, the other members of Viv's gang — 13 young men in all — leapt on the attacker and beat him to a pulp. They left him bleeding and badly hurt in the street. On the train home, fired with the scent of blood, drink and drugs, they terrorised all the other passengers.

Father Chris, stunned, asked why he did it. "It's survival," said Viv, evenly. "You need a gang to take care of you. You need to belong." Father Chris sighed. "I understand his need for mateship, and I began to see that, for Viv, this mateship is ultimately tested through loyalty in fights," he says. "He has had no one else for three or four years. He has to survive. He has lived in toilets, and broken into shops just to get food to live on. Each day is a new battle. Parents and other authority figures have come and gone, but he has found acceptance in a gang. He has a support and this quickly merges into a lifestyle." Ironically, however, all Viv dreams about is a car, a house and a family. All he has, is a life sitting around outside pubs downing beer and spirits, filling in time, waiting for a rival gang to turn up and for all hell to break loose. "He knows he needs a job and a more settled lifestyle if he is to live beyond 21, but the attraction of the street life lures him strongly," says Father Chris, "I see more and more that entrenchment in violence is going to be difficult to fight. For Viv, the world is the enemy."

But then again, the streetkids did have a caring side which, particularly when they were so battered and bruised themselves, was always gratifying to see. The girl with the pet rat was now tenderly nursing its babies. A young woman who was pregnant was being looked after by her boyfriend. One night, Father Chris was coughing badly and sneezing, with the beginnings of a bout of flu. The kids gathered round, concerned, and told him to go home. "You shouldn't be here in that state," said one, who didn't sound much better himself. "Go home. Get some rest."

Their acts of kindness were, however, occasionally just a little misdirected. When a group of the kids discovered one of their friends had been locked up for six days for not paying $1000 in outstanding fines, they rang Father Chris to see if he could lend them the cash. Sadly, he said he didn't have that kind of money. But everyone was so determined to help, they hatched a plan. When they confided in Father Chris what they intended to do, he was appalled: they had decided to commit a crime to collect enough money to cover the fines. Gently, he suggested this might not be the best of ideas and managed to raise $250 over the next couple of days, enough to get the boy out. "I hope he pays me back," he said to himself, "but I won't hold my breath."

Often, he received a sharp reminder that even though the streetkids had seen and lived so much, at heart they were still children. Whenever they played with a skateboard, or announced animatedly they were off to Hyde Park to play hide 'n' seek, he realised that beneath their tough exteriors there were still remnants of the childish innocence of youth. "It reminded me that, while these kids have to battle the world alone, they're still kids, and need to do the things other kids do," he says.

Those close to Father Chris, looking on, felt they could discern a real change in him from spending so many nights on the streets. Always kindly but usually a little distant, he seemed to have become gradually much more compassionate and warm. Fellow teacher Lou Single, for instance, was amused by how reserved he was with her own children when he first came to Boys' Town, almost shooing them away when they approached him. After a while working the streets, however, he became a lot more friendly, shaking their hands and chatting to them about how they were. "I think at first he probably hid a little bit behind his collar," says Lou. "He was shy, and a bit reserved. He wasn't sure how to work with the young girls, because they were much more touchy-feely. He still kept his distance from them. But he was learning all the time."

By mid-1990, Father Chris was organising regular meetings with other groups from organisations that also worked the streets, including Sydney City Mission and the St Vincent de Paul Society, to discuss how they could work together to help the kids. Father Chris wrote a proposal that outlined a joint project with St Vincent de Paul for a large residential centre for streetkids and sent it to Robert Fitzgerald, the Society's State President. In a remarkable stroke of luck, a letter from NSW Community Services Minister Virginia Chadwick arrived on Fitzgerald's desk at exactly the same time as Father Chris's proposal. The Minister was offering to fund a large residential centre for chronically homeless kids living on the streets.

"They both arrived at the same time," says Fitzgerald, who's since left the Society to become the NSW Community Services Commissioner. "As it turned out, Chris Riley's proposal, our own thinking and the Government's all came to a similar conclusion." Talks began afresh about the possibility of a joint venture between Father Chris and the Society for some kind of permanent refuge for streetkids, funded by the State Government.

But as the talks dragged on, Father Chris became increasingly impatient for action. A major new study by the Commonwealth Department of Community Studies was underway at the time, and researchers were slowly discovering the extent of teenage prostitution on the streets of Kings Cross. The findings were coming as no surprise to Father Chris. From interviews with a sample group of 103 young streetgirls, the study revealed that many of the girls selling themselves to middle-aged punters had been doing so for years, some since the age of 12, after being forced to leave home. Most had experienced violence, including rape, a number had since contracted AIDS and some spent up to $400 daily on drugs. In the 14 months from February 1990 that it took to finish the study, five girls from the original core group of 12 had died from drug overdoses. Their stories were heart-rending. One girl had gone on the streets at the age of 12 after both her father and stepmother physically abused her; she had started injecting heroin by 14. Another had been kicked out of home at 13, and told never to come back. She never had, and was selling herself to support her huge heroin habit. A 15-year-old boy, Roy, had tried to defend his mum when his dad started beating her up in a drunken rage. His father threw him across the room, then went outside, brought in the boy's pet dog and cut its leg off. Roy had fled from home and, when he tried to go back a couple of months later, was told that his parents had moved, leaving no forwarding address.

Their tales were, in many ways, typical of those of all the kids Father Chris had met and was battling so hard to help. Yet, in reality, his double life was becoming increasingly difficult to sustain. At Boys' Town, his residential unit was taking more and more boys with whom the other priests couldn't cope, he was teaching a full program of classes, and organising as much extracurricular activity as he could fit in. His work at night was proving more and more absorbing. And then Father Frank Bertagnolli, the former head of the Salesians who had ordered him to Boys' Town and then followed him to be director of the school, found out about his secret night-time activities.

One evening, wandering through Father Chris's residential unit, Father Bertagnolli found Father Adrian Papworth watching over the sleeping kids. He was obviously puzzled. "Where is Father Chris?" he demanded. Father Papworth reluctantly confessed. Father Bertagnolli was none too pleased to discover his young headmaster had been roaming around the streets of Sydney with gangs of wild streetkids instead of fulfilling his proper duties at Boys' Town. It was the beginning of the end.

Lou looked on. "Bertagnolli didn't want Chris to burn himself out," she says. "But I don't think you can burn yourself out if you're doing something you love. On the contrary, you draw strength from it, often. You might miss meals and sleep, but if you're doing it for the love of it, there's no way you burn out. Chris was definitely living what he was preaching in the Salesians. He was determined to go out and help wherever he could."

Indeed, Father Chris wasn't going to give those streetkids up for anyone and, more and more, he'd been feeling that he had done his time at Boys' Town anyway. His students mostly had decent homes to go to on school holidays or weekends and when one student, on the insistence of the board, was expelled after being kicked out of home permanently — since staff couldn't therefore work with his family effectively at the same time — Father Chris was enraged. It felt like the last straw.

"I'd spent five very tough years there, and I wanted to leave," says Father Chris. "I had done my job there. I now wanted to be with those kids who literally had no one. I'd been working on the streets for three years and had really grown to love those kids a lot. I got on so well with them. So eventually I felt I had to get out of Boys' Town. It wasn't my life mission. Expelling a kid who was kicked out of home didn't make sense to me. They said, 'We don't take kids who don't have homes'. I thought that was crazy."

His time working in places such as Jordanville and on the Sydney streets had given Father Chris the confidence to know that he could cope in a non-institutional environment. He knew he could leave Boys' Town and manage. He went to the head of the Salesians, Father Julian Fox, and talked to him about his need to go and work full-time with the poorest kids on the streets, the ones who had no one. Father Fox agreed that, at some point in the future, Father Chris could leave Boys' Town, with the consent of the order, and go to work on a project of his own. The only conditions were that he had to be careful to stay in touch with the Salesian community and return to Boys' Town weekly to participate in spiritual and religious duties. Father Chris was delighted. He then went to Father Bertagnolli in December 1990 and told him that he wanted to quit.

If Father Chris had been hoping for sympathy and support, he was disappointed. Father Bertagnolli was angry and, instead of letting him leave just before the beginning of the new term on 14 January, told Father Chris he wanted him out by the end of December. Father Chris was taken aback; the arrangements to set up his new project weren't finished, and the Government funding hadn't yet come through. But Father Bertagnolli was adamant. What's more, he said, he didn't want Father Chris to return for at least a year so he couldn't interfere with the way his replacement would run Boys' Town.

Father Chris was upset and hurt. He'd been working at Boys' Town for five years, he'd given everything to the boys there, and had become very close to the staff. To be forced to leave so quickly seemed terribly unfair, particularly as he had nowhere to go. "His last words were, 'Don't come back here for a year, so the new man can settle down'," says Father Chris, bewildered. "But I'd been there five years, I'd been principal, I'd designed all the programs, the staff were very loyal, and he didn't want my influence around so this new guy would not be impeded? It was crazy. But he needn't have worried. I never go back." Today Father Bertagnolli says he can't remember exactly when Father Chris was asked to leave but, certainly, his anger over the young priest's decision to quit Boys' Town hasn't abated at all. "We are Salesians, we work in communities and that's our vocation," he says. "We don't work individually. That isn't the Salesian way of life. If [Father Chris] doesn't want to work with us, then he's got to make up his mind and he should leave the Salesians."

Father Chris said his sad goodbyes to his colleagues and to the boys, and penned his last report for the end-of-year annual. "I especially would like to thank all the boys I have worked with for showing me their great courage to change," he wrote. "They fight against great odds, at times, to bring some kind of order back into their lives."

Then he packed his cases, called Collingwood to heel, put his black Appaloosa, Sarah, in the horsebox he attached to the back of his car, and drove off towards the city. "I didn't have anywhere to go," he says. "I didn't know what to expect." The irony of his burning desire to go off to work for streetkids actually rendering him homeless himself, was lost on no one. As he drove off, he felt a mixture of elation at his new freedom, and a cold, gnawing fear about what that might bring.

Chapter 11

GIVING REFUGE

LTHOUGH HIS experiences with the streetkids had left Father Chris with no illusions about life among society's rejects, his own temporary homelessness taught him further poignant lessons about the grim realities of life on the streets. Within three months of checking into a Matthew Talbot hostel for homeless men in a particularly rundown part of Sydney, nearly everything Father Chris owned was stolen. Gradually, all his ordination presents disappeared in a series of break-ins into his room, and many of his books, and souvenirs of his time at Sunbury, Chadstone and Boys' Town also slowly vanished. Yet Father Chris didn't waste too much time fretting about what was gone. He was far too busy preparing for what might come.

His first priority was continuing to feed those streetkids with whom he had so painstakingly built up a relationship. Using all his powers of persuasion, he managed to talk another hostel resident, Cecil, into cooking up pots of hot food for him, which he would then take out onto the streets every night. He bought cakes, doughnuts and ice cream with the small subsistence stipend he was still receiving from St Vincent de Paul — after all, these were still children, with children's tastes — and set out every night with Collingwood to feed the kids around Town Hall, The Wall and Kings Cross. Sometimes, Father Chris picked up Sarah from her stable at Centennial Park, and rode around the streets, checking the kids he had got to know were all safe. The sight of a priest looming up on a handsome Appaloosa in the middle of the night, with a black Great Dane trotting along beside them, invariably attracted a crowd, and proved a great way of meeting other kids who were living in the shadows. They'd happily approach Sarah and Collingwood to give them a pat and ask Father Chris about the animals, feeling unthreatened, then, by his presence. The odd trio became a well-known sight around the streets.

Every night Father Chris would leave his single room at the hostel at around 9 p.m., and work the streets until 5 a.m. He'd then sleep until late in the morning, and spend each afternoon trying to push for the NSW Government grant that had been promised to help set up the refuge for young streetkids or to raise money of his own by talking in churches about the kids and their need for help. Eventually, he managed to collect a staggering $200,000 and, together with St Vincent de Paul's State President Robert Fitzgerald, he set up St Vinnies for Youth, their new joint venture, to operate the refuge. After three months, the Government money finally came through.

The first time Father Chris went to look at the property

the Society had bought with the cash, he felt his spirits soar. It was a large freestanding red-brick house behind a low brick wall, right on Marrickville Road, Marrickville, in Sydney's inner west, just a few minutes away from the suburb's main shopping street. Inside, there were large, high-ceilinged rooms he envisaged turning into an office at the front, lounges, recreation areas, a big kitchen and at least five bedrooms with three to four beds in each. Out the back was a yard that would be perfect for chucking around a ball, together with a small swimming pool and a tiny windowless brick shed.

Father Chris immediately returned to his hostel to pack up his belongings. It didn't take long. All he had left were a few papers, a couple of books and Collingwood. As he drove to Marrickville, he was filled with elation. "It was so liberating," he says. "I was out of that community circle, I was out in the world again by myself and I was doing what I'd wanted to all my life: helping the kids that no one else would. I knew it was going to be tough — all the other refuges that had been opened had closed within six or 12 months — but I also knew that this was going to be good."

He settled into the shed out the back, installing an air-conditioner in the tiny, dark, windowless room equipped with only a toilet, a sink, a single, hard bed and a small stool for his challice. But it was all he needed. The lack of light meant he was able to sleep at any time, day or night. The kitchen in the main building was fitted with a large oven and pots and pans that had been either picked up in second-hand shops or donated by well-wishers. Beds were brought into the bedrooms. A TV and some old sofas were carried into the lounge. Five horses and three motorbikes were housed out the back. Phones were installed in the office. Kids were brought in from 4 April and, on 14 July 1991, by which time 146 kids had already passed through, a small ceremony was held, presided over by House of Representatives Speaker The Hon Leo McLeay, to officially open the refuge. It was later renamed Don Bosco House, after the founder of the Salesian order, Father Chris's philosophical and emotional champion.

It was a rocky start. The streetkids had become used to an erratic and destructive lifestyle, and most had already been kicked out of other crisis centres. Father Chris knew he wouldn't be able to achieve miracles overnight. His first priority was to provide a safe place for them to stay, under the care of staff who wouldn't be judgmental or too hard on them, and could be flexible enough to cope with their needs.

"I had to set up a place that wouldn't alienate that group of kids because if I was going to open a house with them, I had to make sure it was structured in such a way that it didn't force them away," he says. "A lot of people set up a program and say, 'OK, this is the program. If you get into it and do it our way, you can come here. If you don't, we'll kick you out.' So I had to try to set up a situation where I wouldn't be kicking out the kids that I wanted to work with. That was the challenge. I had worked with those kids for two or three years, I knew they didn't sleep during the night, so we didn't force them into bed. We didn't have curfews for them. They came and went as they liked. We demanded almost nothing from them as far as chores or jobs were concerned, and we basically just nurtured them. If they were drugged or drunk we still allowed them to come in. They had done that forever, and I knew that I couldn't possibly bring them in and say, 'Right, you've got to change immediately!' The other refuges wouldn't allow kids in if they'd been using or drinking, but that didn't make sense to me: kids are unsafe on the streets when they're drugged or drunk. But the result was absolutely mad. It was a very exciting time, but it was also crazy."

There were nine staff working with Father Chris and all were under 24. None of them had experience in dealing with kids with such overwhelming problems. One youth worker left after just two days. "This is too hard!" he yelled as he walked out the front door. And it was. At any one time, there would be up to 30 youngsters sleeping in the beds and all over the floor. The refuge was in a permanent state of absolute chaos. Father Chris worked there during the day, talking to the kids, trying to help them with their difficulties, and arranging courses for them on subjects they were interested in, whether it be music, sport, horse management or youth work. Three sports teams were set up, and games arranged. At night, Father Chris continued to go onto the streets to feed and check up on those kids who had chosen not to come back to the refuge with him. Building up their trust — showing that he would always be there for them — was the only way he might eventually help them, he reasoned. When he returned to Don Bosco House, however, he often found trouble. There were stolen cars left all around the block by the kids living in the refuge, there were some of his girls working as prostitutes across the road, and his staff reported that there were boxes of pills under all the beds — the haul from nightly break-ins at every chemist shop in the area. Sometimes, he simply despaired.

The neighbours weren't too pleased, either. On one side, Malaka Farag, who had lived in her house for four years with her children, was quite alarmed by the goings-on. "Oh, it was terrible at first," she says. "There were all these needles left all the time at the bus stop and the kids were always jumping the fence into my garden. My bedroom looks onto that fence and sometimes it was quite bad. One time, they lit a fire in the house, and I had to ring the fire brigade."

Father Chris worked hard to woo the neighbours to support his cause. He called round and managed to charm everyone into making allowances. Farag was converted into an instant fan. Still living next door to the refuge, today she smiles and shrugs. "He was always so very nice," she says. "He's a good man. It's very important to have someone like that to look after the children who don't have anyone. Someone's got to live next door to them. And it's much better these days," she adds.

The priority for Father Chris was always the thought that he was making a difference to the kids' lives, however small. When staff argued he should be kicking out a few of the troublemakers, he was passionate in their defence. "But they've been doing this for years," he'd counter. "What we've got to do is offer them positive experiences that will lead them away from those negative experiences. By kicking them out we won't do that..." All of the kids were allowed to stay. The goals Father Chris set were small and achievable. Some of the residents would be taken out for a drive to the beach at 2 a.m. to stop them from using drugs for even three hours, or on a bus ride at 11 p.m. to take their mind off alcohol. Regular camping trips in the bush were organised, well away from any access to drink or drugs. In the daytime, all the kids were encouraged to take a TAFE or some other course in whatever interested them, whether it be first aid, horse management or even song-writing. Gradually, the refuge began to receive national recognition for its trailblazing methods, and a visit by the NSW Governor, Rear Admiral Peter Sinclair, provided a major morale boost.

Father Chris's old friend Father Bob Bossini looked on in amazement at all he was achieving. "People with that kind of dynamism bring all their energies to their work and go on to establish their own work with their own seal," he says. "He threw himself completely into his work, which explains how he was able to achieve so much."

That dynamism sprang both from his anger at how badly so many children were treated, and his burning desire to do right by them. Kids like 17-year-old Jeremy from the NSW South Coast were so plainly needy, that Father Chris couldn't fail to respond. Jeremy's problems started at age 10, when his mother, who completely ignored him, became constantly involved in affairs with other men whenever his stepfather was away. The stepfather would invariably find out about her other men and end up taking out his rage on the little boy, belting him with his fists or a strap. Jeremy started running away from home and became involved in drugs to numb his pain. When he walked out of a drug rehabilitation program at the age of 14, after just two days, his stepfather found out, and sent one of his mates to bash the boy. As Jeremy ate hot chips in the corner of a milk bar, a man whacked him across the head with a cricket bat, leaving him crumpled and unconscious on the floor. The man hit Jeremy several more times, tied his hands with tape, threw him into the boot of his car and drove him to the police station as he was in breach of bail. Doctors found 42 cuts and bruises on his body and kept him in bed for a week. Later, a stay with an uncle resulted in the boy being punched regularly, and kicked unconscious. Father Chris's plea for leniency in the court on Jeremy's behalf saved him from a custodial sentence. Jeremy seemed to be responding to the kindness he was being shown at the refuge, albeit with with some confusion as to why he was being treated so well.

Then there were girls like 17-year-old heroin addict Mel, who turned up at the refuge 32 weeks pregnant. She had just been discharged from hospital, with no place to stay. She'd been on the streets since she was 11. She spoke quietly to staff at the refuge and then, 10 minutes later, wandered out into the backyard. There, she slashed her wrists with a surgical knife she'd stolen from hospital. Staff immediately called for an ambulance and Father Chris visited her in hospital a couple of hours later. He walked into the room just as she was on the phone to her mother. "Mum, I know I've been away, but now I'm pregnant and I've just tried to kill myself. *Please* can I come home?" The answer, apparently, came immediately: "No". Father Chris took her back to the refuge, but Mel seemed to have lost the will to live. She continued to use more and more drugs daily and prostituted herself to earn the money for them, even while heavily pregnant. The very night she had the baby she was picked up by the police for attacking a punter with a knife. Her child was taken away from her, and police refused to release her from their cells.

With kids like those, disarray at the refuge, to some extent, was unavoidable, says Robert Fitzgerald. The residents were some of the most vulnerable kids who had more or less reached the very end of the line. Further problems were inevitable due to the differing philosophies of those setting up Don Bosco House: the Government wanted a large facility, while St Vincent de Paul preferred a smaller, more manageable one. Then there was Father Chris to contend with.

"He's fairly independent," says Fitzgerald, selecting his words with care, "and the Society is fairly conservative. So trying to create a good marriage was always going to be a challenge. We had different approaches. Chris has a very clear view of the way kids' services should be run and he has a very hands-on approach to its operation and to the kids. The Society, however, runs a very large number of homeless services and was doing so well before Marrickville. They were more traditional in flavour. But, in relative terms, it worked well because everyone was thinking of the kids and how we could benefit them, and it did prove very successful."

Father Chris quickly managed to gather together enough volunteers to help him keep the refuge running. Desma Jama had heard Father Chris speak at an Easter mass a few years before and was inspired to volunteer after being horrified by his stories about the backgrounds of some of the kids he'd been looking after. She readily agreed to cook lunches for the kids every day, and also help out delivering food to those still on the streets. She was surprised by how polite and respectful the kids at Marrickville were towards her, and often wondered if she was getting more out of the experience than they were.

"Christmas and Easter there were such special times," she says. "At Easter, I made up a wreath with a candle in the middle and chocolates all around. They had a great time with it. They were so grateful. At Christmas, I took along 20 bonbons and one boy opened 19 of them, he was so excited about reading the jokes inside. It was beautiful to see. Those kids really taught me so much."

Father Chris briefed Jama, and the other volunteers, that they were needed both to help out the regular staff, and to help the kids, who were, after all, everyone's future. In addition, the kids at the refuge needed to know there were people in the world they could trust, that not everyone was going to abuse them and give them a raw deal. Meeting the volunteers, sharing a laugh with them, and being treated as decent human beings, could help the kids learn how to trust again. It sounded a simplistic, hopelessly idealistic notion, but the volunteers found it invariably held true. "Those kids really responded," says Jama. "They became so alive with fresh ideas and rejuvenation. They deserved to be nurtured; they were, and they blossomed.

"Father was a hard taskmaster but they seemed to like that. I came to admire him greatly for his guts, his determination, his foresight and his focus. He's really the

Don Bosco of today. He won't let anyone get in the way of what he wants to do. Number one is the kids and if he loses friends along the way, so be it. I'm sure Don Bosco was the same. He's got to be that way to achieve what he's achieved. If it wasn't for Father Riley, I hate to think what would have happened to so many of our children."

As well as his work at the refuge, Father Chris was still spending large chunks of every night on the streets, making sure the kids were fed, and as safe as he could make them. He soon realised he needed help if he was going to be able to keep supplying food. He started talking at churches, volunteer groups and charity clubs such as Rotary, asking for both financial and physical help. One of the first couples to put their hands up was David and Colleen McIntosh. Devout Catholics, they were both moved by Father Chris's zeal when he spoke at a mass at their church in Sylvania towards the end of 1991. They were inspired by his compassion for the plight of his streetkids and his pledge to those kids that he would feed them every night of the week, all year round. All he needed now was a few people to help. "He impressed us so much, we just wanted to get involved," says David McIntosh. "He was so passionate about those kids. Everything was for the kids. I always heard him saying, 'There's no such thing as a bad kid'."

David signed up for the nightly food van roster with their son Michael, serving up hot meals on the streets once every two weeks. Both found the experience to be a complete revelation. Cooking sausages and boiling vegetables in the big kitchen at the Marrickville refuge before driving out on the rounds at 10 p.m., the pair was shocked one of their first nights when a kid raced down the hallway yelling that his mate had just slashed his wrists. Out on the streets, every night brought a different confrontation. Once the van was attacked by a group of kids who were out of their minds on drugs; they found often that the kids were pushed aside by older people desperate for food; they were even, on occasion, approached by Japanese tourists asking how much the coffee was. But the rewards were frequent.

One time, they had a big tray of sausages and gravy for a bunch of kids living in a squat. When they arrived, however, there was no one there. In the end, they delivered it to the brothel next door and asked them to pass it on when the kids came back. "The two groups of people hadn't got on at all," says David. "The woman in charge was always saying, 'Bloody kids!' But after they passed the food on that night, they all became quite friendly." Another night, a new runaway, a little girl no more than 13, came up to them sobbing, saying she'd lost her only friend, her puppy. Immediately all the other streetkids gathered round and organised a search party. "Don't worry," one of them assured David. "We'll look after her. We won't let her get into prostitution. We'll make sure she's safe until someone arrives for her." Doling out hot food in the teeming rain in the middle of winter to a bunch of around 25 depressed and grumpy kids, they were startled another night when they heard the clippety-clop of hooves and saw Father Chris loom up out of the gloom on his horse, Collingwood trotting along by their side. "It was astonishing," says David. "These kids who'd all been so miserable and cranky just seemed to come alive. They all gathered around, chatting and petting his horse. I thought, 'How does he do it? How can one man do so much?'"

Once freed from food duties, Father Chris would spend his time looking out for the kids: dragging them out of fights, standing around police stations trying to persuade police to let them go after they'd been picked up, and often sitting for long stretches in hospital, at the bedsides of various kids who had accidentally overdosed on drugs, or who had tried to take their own lives.

Those suicide attempts always hit him hard. One boy who Father Chris had grown particularly close to, Luka, was 15. He always had a ready smile and was popular with the other kids for his cheery demeanour and his "cool" appearance, with studded leather bands around his wrists, and chains in his pockets. But Father Chris knew that the boy's smile hid intense hurt. As a baby, he had been given away by his sick mother to another couple to bring up. At 11, those new parents declared that he was simply too much to handle, and they made him a State ward. When Father Chris first met him, he'd been living on the streets for three years: a sad, lonely boy, filled with the misery of rejection, and anger for anyone he saw in authority. As a result, he was always getting into trouble with the police. When he agreed to come back to the refuge, Father Chris hoped this might prove a new beginning. In the end, however, the odds proved just too steep.

One night, Luka called Father Chris from a police station. Earlier in the evening he had become drunk and gone out looking for trouble. He'd eventually found it, and the police had brought him back to the station. He was still drunk, and very angry. Father Chris talked gently to him, but Luka became even angrier and slammed down the phone. Luka didn't return to the refuge that night, or the next. Father Chris looked for him on the streets, and hoped he might show up later. He didn't. He hung himself in a small cell in a youth detention centre. Father Chris was devastated. A sense of guilt and pain that he'd been unable to make life worth living for Luka haunted him for months. "He came into the world a stranger, and left a stranger," he says sadly. "It was that feeling of loneliness that ultimately led to his death. No one can stay alive if there is no place to call home. Everyone wants to tell their story and share their moments of pain and exhilaration with someone who is waiting for them to come back. Luka could share with no one. No one had ever wanted him, or had cared for him, and so he distrusted everyone. Can anyone imagine what it is like to have no one to talk to, to share with? What point would there be to life? We all need to feel the love and warmth of a friend in spite of what we do and who we are. I was too late for him, but I prayed I might not be too late for others."

The kids who responded to Father Chris's care rewarded him by going on to lead normal lives. Tom, a 14-year-old hard drug user who had been on the streets for two years before agreeing to come back to the refuge, is one. He stayed at the refuge for four months in 1992, then moved up the coast and found a job. He's been working ever since, and has never looked at drugs again. Today, he's 25 years old, and living with his dad in Sydney's south west. "It was a hard decision to go to the refuge, but he'd got me out of a lot of trouble," Tom says. "And it turned out pretty good. I liked it there. You spent time in the pool or doing projects Farvs set you around the house. He used to hold lessons there, basic knowledge and stuff. He made a huge difference to my life. It was excellent what he did for me. I really liked him. He was a top man."

Many, of course, couldn't cope with being cared for after being alone so long. Frequently, kids disappeared into the night, but would then return days, or weeks, later for a second, third, fourth or fifth try at cleaning up their act. Those kids, Father Chris knew, would be willing to die for him, so grateful were they that he always seemed to be there for them. And Father Chris continued to be heartened by little victories. One kid who remained using drugs after he left the refuge stumbled from relationship to relationship, fathering five children of his own along the way. But he always rang every week, just to have a chat, and to tell Father Chris how much he cared for him. Father Chris would reply, "And I love you too." Sadly, the boy died recently.

Another young man, John, who had stayed at the refuge often, was killed in a car accident in 1993. His death affected everyone. One of his friends wrote to Father Chris from prison. As he read her letter, he felt a lump in his throat. "I'm still pretty shattered about John," she wrote. "I can't believe it. I keep thinking that when I get out I'll see him again. You want to know something, Father? You gave him something no one ever did, and that was a chance. You made him feel wanted and no one ever gave him that before, not even his family. But then again that refuge and you were his family."

Ironically, the refuge soon became a victim of its own success. Every new intake of kids was influencing the previous bunch of kids with reminders of their old ways and the temptation to return to them. "Farvs, a lot of us have been here for a while now," a girl told him one day. "But every time we come home, you've brought six new kids in and they're all heroin addicts. They'll ask us if we want to have a shot with them, so we go down and do it, and it puts us right back. We need to get away from here." The others agreed. "We need something more than this," said one of the boys. "This isn't enough."

Father Chris knew they were right. He had provided them with a fair start, but he needed to do more to help them long-term. If they were giving up everything about their old lifestyles for him, he at least had to give them something to put in its place. The only question was what on earth that should be.

Chapter 12

DISASTER DOWN ON THE FARM

IT HAD sounded idyllic: a farm in the country where the kids could live, far from the temptations and dangers of the city, looking after themselves and each other. The reality, however, was proving quite different. As soon as Father Chris had put a bunch of kids on a farm he found near Goulburn, some started growing marijuana out the back, one of the girls had fallen pregnant after getting on rather too well with one of the boys, and they were all running rampant across their neighbours' land. And that was even before the fire . . .

Father Chris had heard about the 700-hectare farm on barren land an hour north of Canberra after it had been abandoned by the De La Salle brothers. They had originally set up the farm for deprived children but were forced to quit when they couldn't persuade any of the kids to live there. Father Chris had few doubts about his own powers of persuasion and the farm seemed like the perfect solution. The kids at the Marrickville refuge who were trying hard to make a fresh start could benefit enormously from breaking their ties with the city and spending time in a healthy country environment. Still a country boy at heart himself, he believed it was the best setting to provide the second chance they needed. In June 1993 he took a group of kids, aged 17 to 19, to the farm, set them up in the collection of houses and the barn, and hoped for the best. It never came.

In some ways, Father Chris's new adventure seemed doomed from the word go. He had no money, and he couldn't use any of the Don Bosco House funds, so he couldn't afford to hire any staff for the farm. His solution was to leave the kids there, on their own, promising he would visit them as often as possible. He told them it could be just like his old favourite movie *Boys' Town*, where the youngsters run the place themselves. "The result was really quite chaotic," he admits. "They were into all sorts of things. They were growing their own pot out there, and I became a grandfather when two of the kids had a baby together. It was all quite mad. After that experience, I certainly came to a clear understanding that I couldn't have kids without any staff supervision." There was an even bigger problem on the horizon, however: the farmer who owned the property.

He hadn't much liked the arrangement from the beginning. He looked anxious as the kids started to arrive at the farm, and saw red when Father Chris started bringing horses and cows onto the land. He stated bluntly that this wasn't allowed. Father Chris was incredulous. "Why not?" he asked. "This is a farm!" The farmer grew angry. "But I thought the kids would write poetry and sing songs," he protested. "You're kidding," replied Father

Chris. "They do write poetry, but they don't sit around all day writing it! They need other things to do as well."

Tension between the farmer and his young tenants steadily increased, soon spilling over into outright hostility. At first, he started visiting the farm and making derisory comments about the kids within their earshot. Then he began criticising Father Chris in front of them. That proved the turning point. They could handle being put down themselves — after all, they'd grown up with that — but they couldn't stand by and listen to Father Chris, the man who was working so hard for them, being ridiculed. After about 16 months at the farm, the kids took matters into their own hands and burnt down the farmer's shearing shed.

The farmer ordered them off his land but Father Chris refused to budge until he had somewhere to move them to. For, the shed incident aside, the kids had really responded to living at the farm. Since moving there most had become drug-free and had started living completely without violence; nearly all were taking responsibility for their own lives, as well as helping others who were finding the going tough. The daily routine kept them busy. They'd get up early to work on the farm all day or go to school. They spent time with the horses: feeding, grooming and building stables for them as well as learning how to ride. One boy had even been invited to work with a champion showjumper who'd helped teach him to jump, and then discovered he had enormous potential. The kids cooked and cleaned for themselves and were looking healthier and happier than they ever had.

The couple who were having the baby married and had a beautiful daughter, Karissa, and were living happily as a family on the farm. Of course, life wasn't easy there, at the end of a 14 km dirt road 35 km from Goulburn, but everyone was finding pleasure in the simplest things in life, like the playful black puppy who'd quickly become a member of their family, and the arrival of the first foal to be born on the property, in September 1993, a little chestnut colt the kids named Rat Bag. "Best of all, they learn to achieve, and that they can achieve," Father Chris had said at the time. "Their triumphs, big and small, give them self-respect and dignity. They become individuals, instead of part of the mass of young people who trudge through the streets, homeless and aimless."

After making so much progress, Father Chris couldn't entertain the thought of leaving the farm and moving the kids back into the city. He applied for a bank loan but considering his only income came from the donations he received, it wasn't looking good. He then called Julia Zaetta, at that time editor of the magazine *Better Homes and Gardens*. She'd been talking to Father Chris for a year about her boss, Matt Handbury, the managing director of Murdoch Magazines, who was interested in supporting a project that was helping the homeless. She and the magazine's marketing manager Mark Kelly had been down to the farm at Goulburn to take a look at what he'd been doing there, but no decision had been made about how they might support Father Chris's work. That day on the phone Father Chris came straight to the point. "Look, if he wants to help us, he's got to help us *now*," he told Julia. "I need him *now*, I need a place for the kids."

Mark Kelly was keen to help. On his trips to the farm, he'd been impressed not only by Father Chris's obvious dedication to his cause, but also by his relationship with the kids. "I thought he was a visionary and incredibly dedicated and giving, and he was putting so much work into it," says Mark. "I was, and still am, in awe of his drive. The farm was always chaotic, but I think there was a bit of chaos theory going on — order through chaos. His relationship with the kids was incredible though. The kids looked up to him so much and wouldn't do the wrong thing by him, they felt so indebted to him. And seeing them in that farm environment with the animals, and how they reacted and opened up, I found it a very emotional thing. A lot of them always said how much they liked being on a farm and, even though it was so far removed from their previous lives in the city, a common theme was how happy they were there and how they never wanted to return to the city."

The American magazine company that had been publishing *Better Homes and Gardens* in the US since 1923 supported a charity for the homeless, and the Australian magazine donated to the Salvation Army every time their cover price went up. Next time, Mark Kelly suggested to Matt Handbury that they donate to Father Chris instead. Julia Zaetta was enthusiastic too. "The first time I went to his farm and met his kids, it seemed like he'd dropped down from Heaven for them," she says. "There was just no bullshit about him. He was facing up to the reality of the extraordinary problems they had, without any of the religious nonsense that usually goes on. He's one of the most grounded human beings I've ever met. You could just see he'd succeed if he was given a bit of help." Now that the kids were about to lose their farm home, the project acquired a fresh urgency, and both Julia and Mark encouraged their boss to visit.

Matt and his wife Fiona came down to the farm the next week to take a look for themselves. They couldn't have picked a worse time. As the Handburys walked into the farm, one of the kids came running towards them with the news that there'd been a bad accident. Some of the kids had been careening around one of the fields on old secondhand motorbikes when a boy had somersaulted off, injuring himself. Father Chris raced down to see the young man, with the Handburys in hot pursuit. "I'm sorry," he gasped when they arrived. "I've got to take him to hospital." "No problem," said Matt, unfazed. "We'll follow you there." They left the boy at the hospital being stitched up, as the three went on to visit an old rundown farm nearby that Father Chris had found for sale.

Just as they began inspecting the property Father Chris's mobile phone rang. It was more bad news. One of his kids was in Melbourne, being charged with armed robbery. Father Chris turned to Matt and Fiona. "Look, I'm so sorry," he said, his heart heavy with the knowledge that he must have blown any hope of a deal. "I'm going to have to leave you. I've got to go to Melbourne." He shook their hands solemnly, then jumped back into his car, raced to the hospital to pick up the injured kid, took him back to the farm, and then set off for Melbourne. A few kilometres down the road, his phone rang again. It was Matt.

"Look, this is silly," came the voice. "We'll pay for a flight for you to go to Melbourne." "Thanks," said Father Chris. "But no. I never take money for me personally. I'm happy for you to give me a farm, but I don't need money to fly anywhere." As he hung up, he felt a wave of depression. There was no way they would help him now.

Matt, however, had been impressed by the concept of taking kids out of the city and putting them on a farm in the country for a fresh start. These were kids who rarely knew the safety or beauty of a good home — something his magazine was all about creating. In addition, from Father Chris's descriptions of his charges, he knew they would have little hope of finding a way out of their predicament without a helping hand. But, more than anything else, he was quite simply taken with the energetic priest who spoke so passionately about "his kids" and was so obviously determined to do everything he possibly could for them, even if it meant racing around the entire country, picking them up from hospitals, police stations and gaols at all times of the day or night.

"His unconditional availability seemed to be exactly what the kids needed," says Matt. "Chris is such a Christ-like figure, such a giving, loving person, and I could see that total commitment to the kids. It would have been far easier for him to stay in the city and keep the kids in a confined, controlled environment, but he wanted to take them to the country, to work with animals and start again away from all distractions, to escape city life and whatever they'd been doing before. It was making his life extraordinarily complicated, but I could feel it was helping the kids. They'd had their faith in human beings totally shattered and had got to the point where they only expected bad things, almost asked for them because that's all they'd ever experienced, and here was this saint-like figure coming in and making a difference." He knew, too, that Father Chris might face a battle to raise funds from more conservative charities or corporations with such an experimental program, helping the kind of hardbitten kids some critics would say would be better off in gaol. There was a certain appeal, he couldn't deny, in helping a program that might not happen if he didn't support it.

Fiona was in complete agreement. "He is so very, very good at what he does," she says. "He's got a great ability to help young people and connect with them. Helping him seemed the classic good thing to do." Later, they phoned Father Chris again. "We're so impressed with what you are doing, we've decided we want to help," said Matt. Father Chris was startled, then overjoyed. "You sort out a few farms for us to come and have a look at, and we'll come down."

A few days later, in June 1994, with the lease on the Goulburn farm already up, Father Chris and the Handburys looked at a few farms dotted around the rugged countryside of NSW's southern highlands. All featured cheap, rundown and bleak old homesteads, that were in urgent need of major renovations. Matt wasn't keen on any. In the end, he decided to take Father Chris over to an 80-hectare stud farm he and Fiona had been thinking of buying for themselves. Tucked off the end of a long dirt road at Canyonleigh, west of Moss Vale, it was a newly built mansion with a tennis court, a swimming pool, heated stables for 20 horses and even a horse arena under lights, with the main house surrounded by a neat white picket fence. "What do you think?" Matt asked, turning to Father Chris. "Would this be appropriate?" To

Father Chris, it looked a palace. "Absolutely," he said quickly. "These kids deserve being somewhere nice and pleasant. This place feels good, and the kids need to know they're worth this."

Fiona Handbury wasn't so sure. "No, I think it's maybe too good for your kids," she said. Father Chris bit his lip and said nothing. The next day, Fiona spoke to her godmother. Fortunately, she happened to work in welfare and told Fiona that those kids deserved the best, that was the thinking in social work these days. Fiona was won over. "We've decided to buy it," she told Father Chris the next day. "My godmother knows what she's talking about. Would you like it?" Father Chris grinned. "Are you kidding?" he exclaimed in delight.

But there was still one last hurdle to clear. The liquidators were auctioning the farm the next day on the Gold Coast. Matt asked Father Chris to go, to remember to wear his collar — "I always do, Matt," he replied patiently — and told him he could bid up to $475,000, nothing more. Father Chris arrived early for the auction, went straight to the auctioneer and told him what bid he wanted to make. The pair got talking. When the man discovered Father Chris was a Salesian, he became animated. "I was taught by the Salesians," he said. Father Chris was overjoyed. "*Yes!*" he shouted inside, suddenly filled with confidence he'd found an ally. "Yes," said the man, thoughtfully, "I was involved in a fight one day and the principal came up and flattened me. He didn't even ask who started the fight, he just hit me."

Disheartened, Father Chris left the bid with him and went to a nearby park and lay in the grass to wait to see what would happen. At 2.05 p.m., his phone rang. "All bids were meant to close at 2 p.m.," came the auctioneer's voice. "But at two minutes past 2 p.m. another bid came in that was much bigger than yours..." He paused for effect. "But it was late, so I'm ignoring it. Congratulations. The farm's yours!"

Father Chris named the place Better Homes Farm, after the title of the Handburys' magazine, and moved in with the kids in August 1994. It was the beginning of his dream. The caretaker of the farm, Dale Ridley, stayed on, so there was a staff member with the kids all the time, and Father Chris travelled there for two days a week. "They were still wild times, but at least there was someone with them," he says. "We didn't have any money, so it was difficult. Matt said very clearly in the beginning that he was giving us this facility, but that we shouldn't come back for more money later from him. I respected that. When other people said go and ask, I would say, 'No, this is our agreement.' Matt would give, but when he wanted to, and in his time. He's always been a very warm and caring man, and he's been very involved from that point on." Fiona too has remained close, despite the couple's subsequent divorce.

Money was always a problem, but Father Chris felt sure that somehow things would work out. Often his supporters worried that he might have been biting off more than he could chew, but there was never any chance of talking him out of it. If he saw a need, then he'd find a way of satisfying it and think about the cost later. Frequently, that kind of blind faith caught others offguard.

One friend remembers walking around Better Homes Farm when Father Chris had first taken possession. "He had no furniture, no money for the upkeep, but he didn't seem to worry about it," he says. "He just went and said a rosary and asked Our Lady for furniture. The next day, he received a donation cheque in the mail for $20,000 — exactly the amount he needed. With faith like that, he doesn't see any obstacles in the way of what he's doing."

With two projects, the farm and the refuge, now underway, Father Chris realised he'd have to adopt some kind of organisational structure to keep things moving, to enable him to expand, if he could, and to raise funds. There was a good management committee at St Vinnies For Youth, but Father Chris felt they didn't understand young people well enough. He didn't believe he would be able to develop under them. That feeling was pretty mutual.

St Vincent de Paul's Robert Fitzgerald says that while he admired Father Chris for his absolute personal commitment to youth, and his tenacity to make things happen against extraordinary odds, they had a "fairly robust" working relationship. "But the youth sector is notorious for that," says Robert. "It's a great thing that it's full of passionate people even though it can sometimes make things difficult. But Chris has achieved things that have been quite remarkable."

Father Chris instead decided to start his own charity, where he wouldn't come under the control of so many outside influences, and he'd be able to pick and choose who he wanted to work with. That stubbornness which had proved such a great asset in getting things done, he was quickly learning, could also make him someone regarded as difficult to work with, because of that quality of uncompromisingly dogged determination and a passion that some saw as bordering on zealotry. Starting his own organisation seemed the only way to go, and he named it plainly after what he now saw as his mission in life: *Youth Off The Streets (Youth)*.

Going into business on his own, however, signalled another step away from the Salesians. They had agreed to the refuge as a joint venture, but *Youth* would mean he would be actually going out on his own, completely independent of his order. Some Salesians were outraged at his audacity. Others felt he should be ploughing his obvious energy and drive into helping revitalise their own projects and plans which focused on helping boys who were having difficulty fitting in with their families and mainstream schools. Back at Boys' Town, Father Chris's input was still regarded as extremely valuable. The priest who had taken over as principal casually remarked to him one day, "Bloody Riley! You've been gone four years, and you were quoted three times in the staff meeting today!" Such things weren't said only in jest.

Allowing one of their best and brightest priests to work more permanently outside the order, the Salesians knew, would be a huge loss. But, in truth, they also realised they were becoming less and less able to stop him. The joint venture with the St Vincent de Paul Society for the refuge had been a good compromise for a Salesian priest determined to work so hard, on a secular level, for youth. After all, one of St Vincent's favourite sayings was that if you were at prayer, and someone needed to be fed and clothed, you left your prayer to feed and clothe them. But Father Chris going it alone was rather less palatable to some. "A lot of people felt a bit of ambivalence towards him," says current Salesian Provincial Father Ian Murdoch, carefully. "On the other hand, when you see how highly others think of Chris, it's a bit hard to quarrel. There's no doubt his heart and his work are intensely Salesian. He's got a heart for the victims, the poor and those treated badly."

At a time when new recruits for all religious orders are falling in Australia, it's also difficult to criticise one of the highest profile members, however wayward he might be. For while Salesian numbers are increasing in Asia and Africa, elsewhere they are falling, probably as a result of a combination of factors, such as an increasing emphasis on materialism, a steady move to a more secular society, and a tendency for Catholic families to have fewer children. Also, there are more options available now for believers to lead a Christian life yet still have a family. The rash of bad publicity for the Catholic church, over scandals about the mistreatment of children and sexual abuse by priests wouldn't have helped.

There's a certain belief in some quarters, says Father Murdoch, that any future regeneration of religious orders, such as the Salesians, may lie with liminal personalities, those figures right on the threshold of change. "The argument would run that that's where the adaptation would take place, right out on the furthest limit," he says. "It's not going to take place where it's predictable and safe. So if you ask me who would I nominate as a liminal figure amongst the Salesians, Chris Riley would have to be one ... He was stepping more and more outside of the established structures and trying to find something a bit

more flexible and open-ended. But, in the end, if what
we're on about is to help young people, it's a bit hard to
quarrel and say Chris is not Salesian. We can't expect
someone like that, an advanced figure of what the future
might look like, to operate if we keep them back at base.
That solution probably wouldn't make anyone happy
ultimately." In the end, the Salesians reluctantly agreed to
Father Chris's new venture.

Father Chris settled happily into Better Homes Farm
with his kids; all delighted at this new level of comparative
luxury. Whenever he was at the farm, he ran classes,
encouraged the kids to play sport, taught them how to
care for the animals on the property and took them out
horseriding. The rest of his time, he spent back at
Marrickville, looking after the refuge, or talking about his
work at any churches that would let him in, or clubs that
were looking for good causes to support. It was all far too
much for one person but, with funds so short, despite help
from Rotary and the Catholic community, Father Chris
simply couldn't afford to employ too many others to share
the burden.

And then, early one Saturday morning in 1995, Sir
William Deane — the man who was about to become
Australia's next Governor-General — came calling.

Chapter 13

THE QUEEN'S MAN

B Y EVERYONE'S account, it was a quick visit. Sir William Deane drove up to the Better Homes Farm early one Saturday morning late in 1995, dropped off a box of his own children's old books for the kids, had a quick chat with Father Chris and a cursory look around the place, and then disappeared in a cloud of orange dust. That visit, however, was one of the most important single events of Father Chris's life. It showed him that people he may previously have considered to be completely inaccessible, weren't. It also taught him that others really do care.

Sir William Deane had been living with his wife, Lady Helen, in nearby Moss Vale when he first heard about the work of Father Chris. He soon became curious. Having served as a Justice of the High Court of Australia, the highest court in the land, since he was appointed by Prime Minister Malcolm Fraser in 1982, he was now about to retire in order to become Governor-General, a posting given by Prime Minister Paul Keating. At that time, he was probably best known for his position in the 1992 Mabo case, and his commitment to reconciliation, Aboriginal rights and the disadvantaged. His visit to Better Homes Farm may have looked casual but, in truth, he'd been intrigued by what he'd been told about Father Chris and his project. He phoned Father Chris before his visit and said he liked the sound of what the priest was doing and, even though he felt certain that his collection of schoolroom classics, such as *Alice in Wonderland*, might not particularly interest the kids, he wanted to take a look.

The following year, as Governor-General, Sir William received a call from Father Chris, asking him if he would become patron of the newly formed *Youth Off The Streets* (*Youth*). Sir William liked the idea but, when his office vetted the charity, they came back with the verdict that it didn't meet the strict requirements of his office, mainly because it hadn't been going for long enough, and wasn't as financially robust as necessary. Reluctant to turn down such a good cause, however, Sir William agreed to become patron in his personal capacity, one of only a handful of charities he was prepared to sponsor personally. "I was essentially drawn to the work *Youth* does," says Sir William today. "If you treat young people as the special category of the most vulnerable people in society because of their age, then *Youth* works with close to *the* most vulnerable and most disadvantaged groups of people in the country.

"When you look at the backgrounds of those kids, most of them have been on drugs, most of them have some background of sexual abuse — commonly by someone they should have been able to trust — and most have fallen into some kind of criminal activity, whether drugs or theft or whatever, to manage. Many of them have escaped from sexual abuse at home to sexual abuse on the streets to survive. When you add these things together, the challenge of turning their lives around isn't only incredibly difficult but, in my mind, it's extremely important if we are going to be a decent society. Chris has a unique program. From the word go he appreciated that the most effective way of dealing with the kids' problems is taking them right away from their environment to a place where they're completely safe from drugs and any kind of manipulation, and where they have the opportunity of getting a regular education and can build up their self-esteem. They can have the chance of human interchange with people they can trust, see as role models to some extent, and who can turn around their distrust and often bitterness at the deal they've been given in life. If you asked me if *Youth* is perfect, my answer would have to be that it's pretty close to being as good as it could be."

Sir William's endorsement of everything *Youth* was working towards came at a critical time for Father Chris. Overnight, public perception of the organisation changed. It went from being viewed as a couple of risky experiments run by a renegade eccentric for a bunch of kids who might be more at home in gaol — leaving everyone else feeling a whole lot safer — to a courageous and inspired new program that dealt with some of society's most downtrodden youngsters, people who really deserved help and support. If the Governor-General was involved, went the thinking, then *Youth must* be doing something right. That seal of approval gave Father Chris an incredible boost.

"It was very important for us when he agreed to be our patron," says Father Chris. "We had been ignoring the normal traditions of networking and talking about what we wanted to do, in favour of just doing what we knew to be best, which meant we were regarded as new and radical. My theory is: I know what I'm doing, the kids need me *now,* so let's do it. Others saw me as a cowboy, and some people do still see me that way. But I don't care about what people say about me, I never have. I knew I was doing the right thing, and Sir William's agreeing to become patron meant that a lot more people took us seriously too."

There's little doubt Sir William's seal of approval and willingness to become Father Chris's mentor was a turning point in the fortunes of *Youth*. Immediately, he had credibility, and a lot more people were willing to come forward and help, even though some of his schemes appeared way out.

To Father Chris, however, it all seemed perfectly reasonable. The philosophy behind the farm was to provide the homeless with a place to call home, so they could find a sense of belonging, and family. The aim was to foster in young people a real belief in themselves and an opportunity to make a contribution to the world. For this, Father Chris impressed on each child a sense of personal responsibility, giving them the power to make decisions about their lives, and hoping they would learn from the process of taking control over how they lived. Immediately, Better Homes Farm started delivering promising results. Some of the kids took apprenticeships to become youth workers. Nearly all, even the ones who'd never before been to the country, adapted quickly and easily to the lifestyle.

Some went to local schools during the day; those who didn't worked a full eight-hour shift on the farm. The cows, many of which had been donated to Father Chris, had to be milked, the eggs from the chickens collected, horses groomed, pasture sown, vegetables tended and all the animals — including a herd of Appaloosas and Angora goats, miniature cows and horses — fed and watered. There were fences to be maintained, outbuildings to be sorted, the garden to be looked after and, in the house, meals to be cooked and cleaning and washing to be done. Often, they were too exhausted at the end of each day to even consider getting into trouble. When they weren't working, the kids tried hard to live as a family, caring for each other, and supporting anyone who was having difficulties.

Dale Ridley, the original caretaker of the farm who had stayed on after its sale, looked on with interest. "In those days, you were allowed an open fire — before DOCS (Department of Community Services) banned them — and Father would sit with the lads in front of the fire, talking to them. He wasn't giving them formal lessons, but he was asking questions and making them give proper answers; it was like he was teaching them social skills. It was amazing to watch them like that. We had murderers, drug addicts, even someone who had stabbed somebody 27 times. And there they'd all be, sitting quietly, talking to this priest."

Certainly, the variety of kids they had through the place was incredible. At one particular time, under his care at the farm, Father Chris had a 16-year-old Vietnamese refugee who had been charged with kidnapping, a 14-year-old who had burgled a house to pay for drugs, and a 10-year-old who, having lived on the streets since the age of eight, had just been in front of the courts for stealing. For many kids like these, it was the farm or the lock-up.

Father Chris believed passionately that detention centres and gaols weren't the right place for these kids. Most of the Juvenile Justice budget was being spent on keeping children in custody, despite studies — both in Australia and overseas — that had shown that the system just didn't work. "If you lock them up in the first instance, then you may as well leave them there for life," he says. "They will come out angrier, more crime-wise, and 85 per cent will reoffend. We need to turn around our thinking." Father Chris never hesitated to go before a magistrate and plead that a kid be given a last chance at his farm. Often, the magistrates agreed and there would be tears of gratitude from the kid.

Father Chris quickly came to the attention of the legal fraternity. Barrister Sue Kluss was often taken aback in court when she read the meticulously detailed reports he wrote on each kid, with information about their background, a full description of their current situation, and an exploration of all of the options for future care. "They were amazing," says Sue, who later became another of Father Chris's supporters, frequently helping out with free legal advice and representation. "They were full of plans about what the kid needed and how they could achieve an end result. He had the clients no one else would take, the ones who had burnt their bridges with everyone else. By pleading that they shouldn't be sent into custody — and often to adult gaol where they could have become rape fodder for other inmates — he made an absolutely significant impact on their lives. And he dealt with each kid as if they were the only one who existed."

Sue Kluss wasn't the only one taking notice of the priest. One evening, former TV current affairs host Derryn Hinch ran a story on Father Chris focusing on the amazing work he was doing with some of the wildest kids in the country. At the end of the story, the program ran a clip of Ben, a heroin-addicted streetkid and former Boys' Town pupil. He was just out of gaol and had a big mohawk hairstyle, a fine selection of tattoos and a mean demeanour. He was sneeringly dismissive of everyone trying to help him. When Father Chris accompanied Ben to court the following day, the magistrate happened to have seen the show and declared that the priest was doing a magnificent job with kids, but that Ben had let him down badly. He then sentenced Ben to a year's gaol. "I couldn't believe they'd put that on TV before I went to court," says Ben today. "I had a bit of a temper in those days, but it wasn't very fair." Father Chris appealed to the Supreme Court and Ben was released to his care after two days.

Back in Canyonleigh, the local community was ambivalent about their new neighbours. One night, Matt and Fiona Handbury were enjoying dinner in Sydney with another couple, good friends of theirs, when the couple announced they had bought a pretty little weekender in the country. They were worried about their daughter hanging out with some wrong types in Sydney and wanted to take her away from the bad influences of the city. Yes, it turned out that their new retreat was next door to Better Homes Farm.

But Father Chris was determined to win over the locals, and bring them onside right from the very beginning. He appealed through the region's newspaper for anyone who was willing to offer help with extra tutoring, horseriding, cooking, supervising cleaning, teaching the kids how to sew and iron, or simply dropping in for a chat. He was also looking for locals who could pick the kids up from the farm and drive them into town so they could get involved in community sporting clubs. Father Chris was keen for the kids to mix with different personalities from the community; he urged locals to "become part of their story". "We can't ghetto them, they need to be involved with the local community," he said.

Just before the farm's official opening on 21 October 1995, presided over by NSW Premier Bob Carr, Father Chris issued an invitation to the community to visit the farm — and its inhabitants. He wrote an open letter to the *Southern Highland News*, begging even more in the community to become involved in the project. "Better Homes Farm is a radical approach to working with streetkids because it takes as its underlying principle that streetkids are capable of making decisions, contributing to and being responsible for their own lives and the lives of others," he wrote. "Australians have a long history of helping their mates when they are down on their luck. When there is a crisis, everyone pitches in to help out. Once crisis situations are dealt with, Australians can have a fall-back position of being critical and judgmental — they are dole bludgers, they should go home to live with their parents. Better Homes Farm is more than an attempt to deal with crises. Hopefully, the crises have been dealt with already and now we are trying to address their lifestyle and future in such a way that they will not be welfare-bound for the rest of their lives. The first step in this journey is to find a community that will give them a place to belong. Come along and be a part of our family. We can no longer say, 'They are not our kids', but rather we are all challenged to say, 'We are all relatives'. Homeless youth call on the community to be their mothers, fathers, brothers, sisters, friends."

That weekend, more than 200 locals piled into a barn on the farm to escape from the rain and listen to Premier Carr encouraging the kids to succeed. "Life has been tougher for you than it has been for most kids your age," he told them. "But the opportunity you've got by meeting the challenge, is to emerge as stronger kids."

Very soon there was a management committee up and running at the farm composed entirely of local people. Neighbours dropped in to play pool or give riding lessons. People from as far afield as Sydney travelled up for a chat. Regular working bees were held at the property. Many of the volunteers were amazed by how strongly the kids responded to positive reinforcement, care, and the interest they expressed in the kids' lives. Most helpers said they found the experience one of the most rewarding of their lives. "It comes from just seeing the happiness on their faces," said one Sydneysider, Jack Spain.

Despite volunteer support, it was still hard work to keep everything running. Ridley was astonished by how much stamina Father Chris displayed. Often, he'd drive more than two hours down to the farm from Sydney in the morning, spend all morning working, then race around all afternoon in a ute, collecting food for the kids and for the animals. Then he might get a call to say he was needed in Melbourne. "He'd leave at 6 p.m., drive for 10 hours, do what he had to do, then drive straight back," he says. "I don't know when he had time to sleep."

Back home, his family was concerned about the phenomenal pace at which he was working. His parents and sister Helen often visited him at the farm while his youngest brother Greg worried from a distance. He didn't like Father Chris doing so much driving and on such bad roads. "He's only got one fault," says Greg. "He's the worst driver I've ever seen. He usually doesn't even wear a seatbelt if he doesn't have kids in the car. He believes God is going to save him. He drives very fast and he's up there in the clouds when he's driving, thinking of 101 other things, or on the phone. It's a worry." He's not alone in that criticism either. Val O'Keefe, receptionist of Murdoch Magazines, says he's very dangerous on the road. "He's driving up and down to Sydney all the time, even when he's tired, and he tends to work all the time he's driving. On the way to the airport once, he wrapped the car around a tree. How he survived, I don't know." Everyone shared a sigh of relief when Father Chris took on a driver, Ken Hill, so he could continue to work in the back of his car, fitted out like a mini-office with a phone, fax, computer, filing cabinet, TV and video, even a small fridge. Doubtless the local police were equally pleased: they often stopped him for speeding down the dark country roads, but rarely had the heart to book him.

When he wasn't driving, working at the farm, staying at the refuge or out on the streets, Father Chris would usually be trying to raise money to keep his programs going. With Sir William as a supporter, he was welcomed even more warmly anywhere he went. He appeared at fundraising talks, lunches, afternoon teas and at the functions of anyone who might be able to help with a donation. The Catholic community was invariably supportive, as were Rotary and various Lions clubs. Father Chris was always happy to talk about his work at schools, and, as a result, many ended up holding events to raise money for his cause. One school even bought him a cow they named Moodonna after hearing that was what he most needed for the farm. He was also beginning to approach corporate sponsors in between saying mass at all the local parishes who would have him. Invariably, everywhere he spoke, he went down a storm.

Frequently, grown men were reduced to tears by Father Chris's descriptions of the misery he'd seen on the streets and the brutalised backgrounds of the kids he had come to know. He held nothing back. He told audiences about a child who'd been stripped and held down by his brothers while being beaten senseless with a stick by his father and then thrown out of home, at the age of seven — all because of something he'd done when he was just three years old. He told them about the four-year-old who saw his mother murdered in front of him, the seven-year-old forced to eat his own faeces, and the 15-year-old held down and burned with a gas stove lighter across his buttocks and down the back of his legs. He described what life was like on the streets for the kids: no family, no friends, often sick, hassled by police and security guards, ripped off, involved in prostitution and crime, hit on by paedophiles, hungry and cold, and taking drugs to kill the pain, emptiness and hurt. He spoke of the kids whose bodies lie in the morgue, when the pain was finally over, unclaimed by their families, then given a pauper's burial.

Even his friends were often shocked by the way Father Chris would talk. "He wouldn't hold anything back," says David McIntosh. "He'd talk about this boy slashing his wrists, or something else terrible someone had done. You could see how he stunned people." Colleen smiles. "With an older priest we knew who was very staid and proper, when Father Chris stood up at mass and talked about the sexual abuse of kids, his eyes nearly popped out of his head. You could see him thinking, 'There's someone in my pulpit talking about sexual abuse!' But afterwards he said, 'I just couldn't believe people do that kind of thing to children'."

Often, whole congregations would be moved to empty the entire contents of their pockets onto the collecting trays. Once, he raised an amazing $80,000 in a single tour of saying mass. In just one collection, he raised $1116. Another time a woman told Father Chris how much she admired his work and then pressed $1000 into his hands. "He talks with such sincerity and from the heart all the time," says Colleen. "You feel *involved*."

Such performances didn't make him universally popular, however. One elderly parish priest, used to collecting $1200 from services over seven days, shook his head miserably when he counted the $5000 put on the tray for

Father Chris after just one mass. "We'll not get any more money from them now for the rest of the year," he complained. Some churches refused, after he'd cleaned them out once, to invite him back.

And that was a pity, because Father Chris had plans. Big plans.

Chapter 14

KICKING DRUGS

S HE WAS pregnant, she was a heroin addict, she lived on the streets. And she was just 12 years old. More and more, the kids coming to Father Chris for help were already deeply embroiled in the world of hard drugs. Often, like that young schoolgirl Avril, not yet into her teens, they had their first hit courtesy of their drug-addled mums or dads, who saw injecting their offspring as a handy means of keeping them quiet and, ultimately, under their control. It meant that their children became willing accomplices in seeking out supplies, and in finding the cash necessary to sustain the habit. And what the kids wouldn't do for their parents out of love or their own addiction, they'd usually do under the threat, or reality, of violence.

Often, it would take tremendous courage for a kid to tear themselves away from those parents but, when they did, they usually found there was nowhere else to go but the streets. With drug programs all the time being started up and then closed down, Father Chris felt there was a real need to set up an emergency program to help kids who were battling to wean themselves off the drugs they knew were destroying them.

Working towards this goal, Father Chris received his big break in April 1994, when he was invited by the World Health Organization (WHO) to be the official representative from Australia at their conference in Geneva on streetchildren and substance abuse. The WHO worker in charge of the conference, Dr Andrew Ball, hailed originally from Australia, and had taken a keen interest in Father Chris's refuge at Marrickville. Dr Ball had been impressed by how it was operated, with the kids having to obey few rules and allowed to stay even when under the influence of drugs or alcohol. He was eager for Father Chris to contribute to the conference. The experts at WHO were alarmed by how many of the estimated 100 million streetkids around the world were rapidly developing a dependence on alcohol or drugs — including heroin, glue in cities where shoe-making was common, solvents in industrial areas, cocaine in coca-producing regions, cannabis and pharmaceutical products — and were anxious to find agreed ways of tackling the problems. WHO was considering adopting the Modified Social Stress Model it had developed from the work of Rhodes and Tasan (1988), which sat very easily with the philosophy behind the Marrickville refuge.

The rationale of the Model is that kids are more likely to use drugs when there's great stress in their lives, caused by factors such as a breakdown in family relationships, the presence of violence at home, and a lack of support and interest from parents and friends. Conversely, if kids have good bonds with their parents and are in a healthy, nurturing environment, they're much less likely to use drugs to cope with any problems that come along. It's thus understandable why streetkids should have so many drug and alcohol problems.

"At least during initial stages, the use of drugs by streetchildren is functional in most circumstances," says Dr Ball. "It is a coping mechanism. Substances may be used by streetchildren to keep awake for work, or alert to possible violence, to get to sleep, to dull physical or emotional pain, or to replace the need for food."

For Father Chris, the invitation signified high-level recognition of his methods which was a major boost, both intellectually and psychologically. "That was pretty significant," he says. "I was the only Australian representative, and most of the other delegates were from the Third World. We agreed, basically, that kids are less likely to use drugs if they're in a protected environment, but are more likely to use if there's a crisis going on, drugs are available and they feel like they can't cope. There are so many important lessons here for parents whose kids are using drugs. They should put protective factors around them rather than alienating them, and they'll probably all survive."

In addition, the conference discussions and findings served to underline his belief that adult drug rehabilitation units were completely wrong for kids; that their needs and psychology were completely different. Whereas adults might comfortably sign up for a month or six-week program, for kids the timeframe had to be much shorter. Even two weeks, through young eyes, could look like a lifetime. Young people wouldn't react positively to the 10-step program that worked so well on older people, either. Adults would respond to having their lives and personalities stripped back to the basics, at being made to feel vulnerable, so they could be built back up. Kids, on the other hand, weren't anywhere near as resilient. The evidence presented to the conference even suggested that this kind of program could lead young people to suicide. Far better that their strengths be shored up, they be reassured about how capable they are, and they be given strategies to cope with stress and the lack of family support.

Buoyed by the acknowledgment he'd been given, and reassured by the way his own theories had been reinforced, Father Chris returned to Australia fired with determination to do something more for the streetkids he'd come to know so well. He drew up his plans for an emergency detox centre and then searched for a sponsor. He got lucky. Business was going well for insurers CE Heath International Holdings, and the head of the company was looking for a good cause to embrace. Father Chris's new benefactor was Ray Williams, in charge of a business that was later to become HIH Insurance, and who, a few years on, was to preside over its 2001 $5 billion collapse, one of Australia's worst corporate disasters. Back then, though, Ray Williams was doing well, and offered to pay for three staff over the next five years.

Finally, the Dunlea Drug and Alcohol Centre for Adolescents opened its doors in April 1995, named after Father Thomas Dunlea, the priest who'd founded Boys'

Town and Alcoholics Anonymous in Australia. Located in Campbelltown in Sydney's south west, the two to four-week residential program for six teenagers at a time aimed not only to get kids off drink or drugs, but also to help them change their lifestyle permanently, and to teach them the skills they'd need for a future beyond the crisis program and refuge. As with all of Father Chris's projects, there was also an element of enabling the kids to give something back. It would give them the presentation skills to later visit schools, if they wanted, to help present a drug and alcohol message to others.

It was an instant success. Suddenly, the kids at the refuge had somewhere to go if they wanted to try to kick their habits, and be supported while they did so, while kids on the street had a quick program they could join that would also make sure they had a bed, and food, for the time they were there. With the number of homeless young people rising every month — a Royal Melbourne Institute of Technology–Monash University study at the time revealed that seven in every 10 NSW schools had students with nowhere to live — and their average age falling, Father Chris was inundated with calls from kids as young as 12 who wanted to make a fresh, drug-free start. A couple of months after the opening of Dunlea, he received a letter from Jo, a young girl who had started injecting heroin at the age of 11, managing to almost destroy her family in the process. After being kicked out of home, she'd gone on to the streets, working as a prostitute to earn enough to keep herself on drugs. One day, when she just couldn't take it any more, she signed up for Dunlea. After successfully completing the program she was now starting a new life, well away from drugs. "Thank you, Farvs," she wrote. "I'd lost all my self-respect and morals, but then I met a man as tuff [sic] as nails, but as kind and caring as possible. Thank you. You showed me who I was, not what I was. So anyone else who cares, take some advice while you still can: don't make your move too late."

Matt, 15, was another grateful participant. His drug problems had started early, at the age of 10, after his mother had sexually molested him. By 11, he was living full-time on the streets. In his first week, he was pack-raped by a gang of men. He couldn't walk for more than a week. He started smoking marijuana and then moved on to using cocaine and heroin. Then he experimented with LSD and speed, and he drank as much alcohol as he could afford. In Dunlea, Matt was encouraged to keep a diary. "All my feelings deep inside are making me feel like it's all happening again," he wrote. "Things nothing like I really wanted to say but if I start I could be writing for years and tears will fall like a big dam or a stream running through. Now I have expressed this is my life, I just want to get on with the rest of it. While at Dunlea, I enjoyed kicking the football around. I feel like I can get some of my problems out. I've learned never to give up hope with anything, and you might just get somewhere if you want to live."

Naturally, there were plenty of kids too who weren't able to make it through the program. Often, however, they'd leave for a few weeks, then plead to be allowed back. "Just a short note to say I'm sorry," wrote 16-year-old heroin addict Lincoln. "I really don't know why I did what I did. I think everything just gets on top of me and when it hits a certain point I just bolt. I just take the easy way out and go back to drugs. But please help me Farvs. Give me another chance. I need help. Please." Father Chris would invariably let them back in again for a second try — sometimes even a third and fourth. After all, some of these kids were struggling to come to terms with such terrible, long-term problems and Father Chris knew that no solution would be quick or easy.

The backgrounds of most of the kids approaching Father Chris constantly shocked and saddened him. He was contacted every day by both kids and welfare services about horrendous cases of abuse and neglect, and he never hesitated to try to help. If there wasn't room for a child on a program, or a boy or girl had needs that couldn't be met by one of his projects, then he'd just start a new one. "Their stories always make me desperate to establish new services," he says. "Kids *must* be fought for. I can never turn a child away." Those kids usually had no one else to turn to, in any case.

There was 12-year-old Zack, a bright little boy with a haunted look in his eyes. Over several years, he and his brothers had been the victims of brutal physical violence, and were also routinely sexually assaulted by their stepfather and his friends. When their mother finally decided to flee with the kids, she was intercepted by her husband and five of his mates. As the boys crouched trembling in a corner, their mother was strangled to death before their eyes. The terrified boys were ordered to bed. The next morning, the stepfather came for Zack. He told him to get up and get dressed and forced him to take his mother breakfast in bed. When the police arrived later that day, Zack was made to pretend to the police that his mother had died in her sleep, and that he had discovered her body when he tried to wake her.

Micky was another boy with a terrible past. At the age of 14, when his dad went to hold his hand as they walked to church on Easter Sunday, Micky pulled away. His dad was furious, but Micky was adamant: he didn't want to be seen holding his father's hand. When they arrived home, Micky paid dearly for an act of rebellion that is seen merely as a rite of passage for most kids. "He belted me so badly," he told Father Chris. "Then he tried to hang me. He pulled me up for about 10 seconds with his belt, then let go and walked away. I remember my mother trying to pull him away from me but all she could do was cry. All my sisters and brothers were yelling." At the end of his story Micky broke down and wept, the first time he had cried in months.

Then there was Billy, a 15-year-old who wouldn't talk about the bruises all over his body when he turned up first at the refuge and then at Dunlea. Many of the kids were encouraged to write stories and poetry about their lives, which Father Chris discovered was far less confronting for them than having to speak about their pasts. It also often tapped into a rich vein of creativity within the child. Billy's poem gave Father Chris all the answers he needed:

My life has been unused with its ups and downs
Me mother left me father, then we moved town
Me mother met a new bloke and he ended up me dad
But she didn't know it was the devil she had
I never had a normal life like the other boys have had

Instead of playing football
I was the football for me dad
And now my mind is in a state of deplore
Wondering, wondering, what is the score . . .
I wish there was someone to share my pain
Then they would know I'm not to blame.

Father Chris found many of the kids' poems so touching,
he collected them over the years and, in 1993, published a
collection in a little book, *Streetlights*, together with some
of the children's artwork and photographs. It was a clever
move. It gave the kids an enormous feeling of achievement
and a real sense of pride to see their work was worth
publishing. Sales of the volume also helped raise some
much-needed funds for the refuge. The poetry not only
showed people from beyond their world the kind of hell
the kids often went through, but also how their
experiences had failed to crush their spirits. Sometimes the
poetry was happy, but often it was sad, telling of lost
families, loneliness and, over and over, a simple burning
desire to belong. The tragedy of suicide often cast
shadows over so many young lives. Melanie, 17, expressed
in her poem how she couldn't get over her brother killing
himself.

You told me never to give up
Why didn't you practise what you preached?
Was it too far out of reality and out of reach?
I didn't see it coming
I didn't have a clue
I always wish it upon someone else, anyone but you . . .

Ever since that day I've never been the same
Who can I take the anger out on?
Who's to blame?

The publication of *Streetlights* was a wonderful way of communicating to the public the pain experienced by these kids. While outsiders acknowledged Father Chris was doing good work — he received the Variety Club Humanitarian of the Year Award in March 1995 — their understanding rarely extended to those young people he was doing it all for. Still the idea persisted that his charges were little more than precocious kids drawn to the bright lights of the city, having a wonderfully irresponsible time, putting their parents through heartache while living off the charity of others. Many still seemed to believe that the problems of these kids would be solved if only they could be made to see sense and return home. While that might be true in a small number of cases, the vast majority, Father Chris knows, have little choice. "It is so frustrating trying to get people to understand," he says. "You can't show photos of these children in the newspapers. You can't name them. You often have no idea what's happening to them until we have to pick up the pieces because it all happens behind the closed doors of home."

Certainly, the brutal truth about the lives led by many of these kids at the hands of their mothers, fathers, step-parents, siblings, uncles, neighbours and family friends usually only surfaces if a child dies and there's a national outcry, sparking investigations into DOCS or asking why neighbours, who heard the screams or saw the child regularly looking withdrawn, shrunken and battered, did nothing. But they're only ever the tiny fraction of cases that hit the press. You never hear about the kids who soldier on, who are beaten into submission, or who escape. "How about the two-year-old who is regularly scalded by her mother with hot water?" asks Father Chris angrily. "Or the three-year-old who is routinely sexually abused by her stepfather? Or the four-year-old boy who has a dog collar locked onto his neck and is then chained to the clothesline for two to three days at a time?"

The problem is that, for most people, such levels of cruelty are simply unimaginable. They like to think the stories that make newspaper headlines are isolated instances of aberrant behaviour, rather than having to concede they are only the few that manage to trickle into the public arena from a vast hidden well of darkness. The nation was appalled when it read about the couple who sold their 11-year-old daughter to an elderly man for sex, and then used the money to buy cigarettes. Similarly, all were horrified by the story of a three-year-old boy who was bashed and burned with a cigarette, then tied up, put in a cardboard box and locked in a cupboard with an untreated broken leg. But while these cases made it to the courts, so many thousands more go undetected forever. Some parents believed they had a right to do anything they wanted to "their" kids, and would go to any lengths to regain control over them.

One day, the father of a 15-year-old boy turned up at the refuge to see his son. He promised he had changed, vowed he would never hurt his son again and begged him to come home. The boy agreed, but within a couple of days the sexual assaults had begun again. The devastated child, his dreams of a normal life again shattered, fled back to the streets. That night, he tried to overdose on heroin. "The only thing attractive about the streets is the use of drugs to kill all the pain of the past abuse and the hope of a quick death," says Father Chris.

Having witnessed so much misery and wanton destruction, it could perhaps be easy to become bitter or cynical. But Father Chris always tried to concentrate on individual kids and their potential, instead of looking back at their pasts. He celebrated success and made the kids focus on their strengths and on their futures. He was thrilled when a 19-year-old graduate of Better Homes Farm found a job selling cars and settled happily into a shared household. He treasured the essay written by 14-year-old Mark: "What *Youth* has meant to me." At the farm for a year, he was in Year 10 at the local school, and doing well. "I thank Farvs for sharing his trust and love with me and the residents at the farm who have specially helped me over the past year and a half. I call Farvs now 'Farther' [sic] as my father wasn't there to give me an understanding to life. Thank you for being there."

Every Father's Day, Father Chris was saddened by the stack of cards all addressed to him in childish handwriting. He knew that so many of the kids had no one else to send those cards to. But at the same time, they were proof of what he was always preaching in churches and telling people at fundraising functions: "Those kids have so much love to give. If you are kind to them, they'll really respond." The cards always contained a similar message. "Thankyou for giving me a life!" wrote Luke. "Thankyou for helping me when I needed it and being there always," wrote Ben. And from David, "Thankyou for everything you don [sic] for me. With love."

Despite the gratitude Father Chris received from the kids, he knew he was far from perfect himself. In this fragile world of broken down kids, it was easy to make mistakes and he would take himself to task for every one of them. Jim, for example, was a kid being held in gaol, facing 82 break-and-enter charges for stealing office fax machines which he then traded for heroin. At the prison, Father Chris was shocked to see bruises on his face and slash marks on his wrists. Father Chris went to court and pleaded with the judge to release Jim because of the bashings and his suicide attempt, saying that his problem was his $700-a-day drug habit, and gaol wouldn't cure that. The judge agreed to let the priest take Jim into drug rehabilitation. As the boy was standing in the dock, a tear trickled down his face before he hastily wiped it away. It was Friday night, however, and there wasn't a place at the centre for Jim until the Monday. Father Chris therefore decided to keep the boy with him all weekend. On the way back to Sydney from giving a Sunday mass at Nowra, however, he was hit by a migraine, and Jim took over the wheel. Then, as he got out of the car at their destination, he nearly collapsed with the pain. Jim rushed to support him, but Father Chris pushed him away, saying he'd be fine. The next day, Jim disappeared back to Kings Cross and ended up back in gaol. Father Chris blamed himself. "I had done everything for Jim, but that wasn't enough to help him," he says. "What he needed me to do was to let him reach out and help me. When he needed power, I kept him powerless. When he needed to give, I turned him away. These kids have a great deal to give and are waiting for the chance. They have so much love that over the years has met with rejection; they are just waiting for the chance to show it. I must let them give and share their love."

But far from being discouraged, failure only ever made Father Chris eager to do more. The refuge was going well, with around 800 young people passing through during the first two years alone. Dunlea was proving incredibly popular and was recognised by WHO as a leading model for helping streetchildren worldwide. Street Outreach, the program responsible for the food van, was serving 180 hot meals every night, and Better Homes Farm didn't have enough beds to satisfy the demand. Yet the number of requests for places in Father Chris's various programs was rising all the time as word of his work spread. Typical was a poignant letter from a boy in gaol, who pleaded with Father Chris to be allowed a place on the farm when he was released. He asked Father Chris in the meantime if he could please send all his worldly possessions to him for safekeeping: a briefcase, a backpack and his pool cue.

With Government funds for only one project, however — it gave $450,000 a year towards the refuge's running costs — money was always the hurdle to setting up more programs. Father Chris's preaching over the year had raised an astonishing $1.3 million and while there was always, of course, the option of asking the Catholic church for funding, Father Chris didn't want to risk being tied in red tape. "It's too bureaucratic," he says. "I can open a house in response to need, but the Catholic church hierarchy will give you 100 reasons not to."

Instead, Father Chris launched two more programs that he knew wouldn't be too expensive to continue: the Job Target Program and the Wilderness Adventure Program. The job program placed kids into work experience or jobs after they'd been through rehabilitation, and the Wilderness program provided a five-day camping experience, including vocational guidance and lifestyle discussion. Run every nine days this helped supplement Dunlea's drug plan. With heroin withdrawal taking three to four days, a chance to go away would at least help take the kids' minds off their addiction.

At the end of 1994, Father Chris decided he would hold a presentation for all the kids who had done so well on each of the programs. He looked around for a venue, but soon decided that because the kids were from the streets, the presentation should be held on the streets too. He set up a band from the refuge at the open-air amphitheatre in Martin Place, in the centre of the city in Sydney, stepped up on to the raised stone steps and read out the kids' names. He asked each kid to come forward and collect their certificates for reading and writing, one by one. "It was incredible," says Sue Kluss. "There were probably a couple of thousand people there from the lunchtime crowds. There were mums and dads, office workers, bankers, everyone. They all really got into it, clapping and cheering. He ended up with not only his kids feeling tremendous, but a whole raft of extra volunteers too."

This experience gave Father Chris the further inspiration he would need to continue his work. For however hard he tried, another new challenge was always just around the corner.

Chapter 15

A PRIEST IN GANGLAND

IN EARLY August 1995, the leader of the notorious 5T
gang, 20-year-old Tri Minh Tran, was assassinated,
together with one of his loyal lieutenants, sparking
fears that the troubled Sydney suburb of Cabramatta
could erupt in bloody gang warfare.

Detective Sergeant Debbie Wallace, who'd been
working in the area since 1990, was appointed head of a
gang squad, specially formed to beat the threat. In an
effort to head off trouble, she was assigned the task of
talking to 5T, a 140-member gang who had established a
fearsome reputation for running extortion rings, heroin-
trafficking and armed robbery. She already had a good
relationship with many of the members and arranged a
meeting with them to discuss the situation. By the end,
they had thrashed out a deal: 5T agreed to call a halt to
violent crime in the area for a trial three-month period on
the condition that she would help the younger members,
aged between 14 and 16, get an education. They shook
hands on the arrangement and, in order to keep her side

of the bargain, she spent the next few weeks approaching all the schools and colleges in the area, trying to find places for the kids. They all refused.

Increasingly desperate to maintain the fragile peace, she listened sceptically when one of her colleagues brought up the name of Father Chris, and described him as a man who was a marvellous teacher who rarely shirked a challenge. Unconvinced that he could help in this situation, she agreed to phone and ask him over. "I thought, 'This'll be interesting'," says Wallace, today a Detective Chief Inspector. "A Catholic priest on the streets with these kids? I thought he'd be horrified."

When Father Chris arrived in Cabramatta, she casually showed him round all the local drug haunts, waiting for a reaction. When finally it came, it wasn't at all what she'd expected. "This is all very interesting," the priest said at last. "But I see drugs every day. I'm here to help you with your street youth. When am I going to meet them?" Wallace was startled, but smiled inwardly. *Street youth*? She was dealing with tough, violent gangs here: murderers, standover men and drug-pushing armed criminals who would do anything to get their way. But she arranged a meeting with 5T members in a local café and then led Father Chris to the rendezvous, wondering what the hell the hardened gang leaders would think of a do-gooder Catholic priest.

She didn't have long to wait to find out. "Oh, hello Father," they said, as Father Chris walked in. "Let's get you a seat." As they scurried to find a chair, and then wipe it down, Wallace stood speechless in the background. The gang then outlined their wish for the young members to get an education, so they would be better equipped to deal with a future where the gang might not be around to protect them. Father Chris listened quietly. "Okay," he said, finally. "Let's run a school here in the café." And he did.

Three mornings a week, from 9 a.m. to midday, between five and 20 young teenagers would sit around a group of the café's outdoor tables in Freedom Plaza and take lessons with Father Chris in preparation for their School Certificate. Wallace watched in amazement. Often a few of the older kids would drop by the class to see what was going on, and occasionally a couple would shyly join in. No one was allowed to approach the area to buy or sell drugs during school, and police agreed to leave them alone during lessons. Outside those three hours, life continued as normal. "It was tough," says Wallace. "Sometimes they'd turn up, some days they wouldn't. But Father said that was fine. He'd say that even one is a success. But I'd get angry with them."

After nine to 10 months of the lessons problems began to intrude. The Wood Royal Commission into police corruption was underway and, unbeknown to Wallace, she was being investigated, suspected, ironically, of being the underground leader of the 5T gang. Later, one of the gang members told her that police investigators had asked him if she gave him orders. "No," he'd replied, puzzled, "but she used to yell at us a lot if we didn't go to school."

Cameras had recently been installed in the streets of Cabramatta in an attempt to prevent crime, and there were jokes that cameras had even been placed inside drains to keep tabs on the gangs. A police officer new to the area one day approached one of the younger kids and told him that he knew the boy had given the wrong answer to question three of an exam. "We see everything you do on the cameras," he said. "You're a dummy." The kids, as a result, demanded the lessons be moved to the nearby snooker hall. Wallace refused. As a police officer, she wouldn't be allowed to work in licensed premises. A few days later, however, the situation came to a head when some of the young guys in the gang were involved in a kidnapping.

A crisis meeting was held between 5T members, Father Chris and Wallace, and a new deal was struck. The gang leaders said that if Wallace and Father Chris were able to get their junior members out on bail, they would allow the boys to go to Better Homes Farm, and wouldn't have any more contact with them. It was a major breakthrough. Whenever Father Chris had previously mentioned going to the farm to any of the gang members they had paled. It was only later he and Wallace discovered that, within 5T, "going to the farm" was a euphemism for making someone disappear, sometimes permanently, and usually after a brutal beating. After pleading with the magistrates for bail, the kids that Father Chris took to the farm did, happily, disappear permanently — but from the streets. They all made great progress and never returned to a life of crime. "It's like they reverted to being normal teenagers, rather than trying to be young criminals," says Wallace.

Back in Cabramatta, a number of the kids not implicated in the kidnapping were given places on a motor mechanic course, and seven were guaranteed apprenticeships. However, there still seemed to be a need for something else to help dissipate youth gang problems. Talking to 5T members one day, a young man made the point to Father Chris that while the local council had spent $1 million on street cameras, they hadn't installed a single basketball hoop in the area. Father Chris was eager to help. In the past, he'd often found a good game of basketball was a wonderful way of forging bonds with young people. The local Police Citizens Youth Club offered him a ground just out of town, but he refused. He wanted a place right in the middle of the action, easily accessible for everyone. In the end, Father Chris was given a $5000 police grant to buy portable hoops, lines were painted in the Arthur Street carpark in the middle of town, and lights were erected. Volunteers from the local Rotary club agreed to cook a barbecue, someone else arranged a disco, and, every Monday and Friday night, up to 70 young people from all over Cabramatta, along with parents, community leaders, and off-duty police officers, would get together for a game of basketball, with Father Chris umpiring. "It was really popular," says Wallace. "The kids would laugh about it and say 'You've finally broken us down. Now we're even eating pizza.' Even today some of those kids are still playing basketball, some in the A grade. It was a huge success."

Once the basketball nights had been established, Father Chris moved on to other projects, and the games lasted for just another year before the original 5T members grew older, began to drift away and the evenings stopped. He regrets that now, as trouble flared up again in Cabramatta over the next three years from 1997. "On reflection, it was bad that I moved out," he says. "Basketball was a very positive thing for the area, and for the young people there. I let it go, personally. I should have stayed but, once you've left, it's hard to go back." Despite this, he believes that initiatives such as the basketball nights show that it's still possible to work with kids in the most difficult of places. Father Chris would get annoyed whenever the media painted a grim picture of Cabramatta, particularly when ABC TV's *Four Corners* ran a program describing the suburb as the "black hole of Australia". Writing off a complete community and its children as a lost cause is the worst possible thing anyone can do, according to Father Chris. "The more we ostracise, marginalise, exclude, the greater power the subculture will have," he says. "Nowhere I go, no matter how difficult the situation or how bad the reputation of the kids, do I find youth resistant to care. We, as a nation, need to look beyond notoriety and reputation to see the light of hope and courage in the eyes of our young. They wait for us to reclaim them."

Father Chris left a strong impression on many people in the suburb, including Wallace. "He seemed to come from nowhere," she says. "He was so compassionate but also very strict. I'm a bit, 'Do the crime, do the time', but he was good because he was tough. I learnt a lot from him. He's very driven and very focused but also very funny. I laughed all the time. He's quite an exceptional person and I'm proud to call him a friend." Later, she even took on the role of chair of the *Youth* board for a while before work commitments forced her to leave.

But Father Chris had plenty of other projects he wanted to pursue too. He longed to do more to help those streetkids who were missing out on schooling because he knew that, without an education, they could be lost forever. A school for these kids, without the same strict rules as other schools, was his dream. Typically, he began to pursue his new goal at the same time as helping in Cabramatta. In January 1996 he placed a recruitment ad in a newspaper for someone to head up a new school. Mignon Bonwick, who'd just finished a special education course, was intrigued, and applied immediately for the job.

Father Chris held the interview in his cluttered office at the front of the Marrickville refuge, with his Great Dane, Collingwood by his side, seeming to fill up half the space. Mignon thought the interview was going well until she started asking questions about the school. "Where is it going to be?" she asked. Father Chris was nonplussed. "I don't know," he replied. "I just only know it will happen, we have to *make* it happen." Mignon, usually called Min, was speechless. "There was this man, employing me at the beginning of the year, and paying me, and he didn't even have a school," she says today. "He has amazing faith." He took on Min and a man fresh out of teaching college, Peter Woolridge. After three or four weeks, Father Chris phoned to say he'd found them a school: the basement of a Catholic church, St Francis de Sales in Surry Hills. They went down and had a look. It had been used as a migration office and was filled with papers, medical supplies and dusty documents. "What do we do for furniture?" Min asked Father Chris. "That's your job," he said, dismissively. When she and Peter went to collect Father Chris's teaching manuals from his office at the

Marrickville refuge, there was a further surprise in store. The first book they pulled out from the massive bookcase was a children's novel entitled *Love Stories For Mignon and Peter*. Father Chris didn't bat an eyelid over the coincidence. "That's just the way He works," he said calmly. By February 1996, with funding again from Ray Williams, Key College was fully equipped and operational.

Min was, at first, sceptical about how it would work. They had a school and two teachers, but no kids. Their first two students soon arrived: one from the refuge at Marrickville, and the other from another refuge down the road. Then word seemed to spread like wildfire. Very soon they were teaching classes of around eight kids a day, all surprisingly eager to learn. By following a special program of study in addition to completing life skills courses, the students were able to obtain their School Certificates, and were later able to study for the HSC too. The first of the annual presentations of School Certificates and Certificates of Achievement proved an incredibly emotional occasion not only for the kids, but also the teachers, Father Chris, the few parents who came along and the Board of Studies officials who attended. "You are my heroes, my heroes," Father Chris told the kids. "You are showing incredible strength in overcoming incredible adversity." There was even a glint of a tear in the eyes of the officials.

While she had to admit Father Chris was doing great work, Min confesses that she didn't warm to him at first. He was nothing like she'd imagined. She thought he'd have a natural geniality about him and an openness that would draw her in. He didn't. Instead, he seemed a bit hard-edged and guarded. "But knowing the kind of things he deals with every day, I suppose that's served him well," she says.

Father Chris's personal assistant Judy Gorton felt much the same when she first met him at her job interview. "I thought he was a bit standoffish," she says. "He wasn't what I expected. But now I realise that it was just because he's so shy. It takes a while to get to know him." It could also be difficult to reconcile the image of a saint that some people had with the reality of a hot-headed, short-fused man who was always so impatient to make things happen. Judy remembers vividly the shock on people's faces during a rodeo where Father Chris was having trouble controlling a high-spirited horse. "This bloody horse!" he shouted in frustration. A murmur of surprise immediately went round the crowd. "Father Chris swears!" they muttered in disbelief. "But he's an ordinary person too, he's not a saint," she told the people closest to her in the throng. It was just his passion for his mission and absolute determination to see it through that usually took so many onlookers' breath away. "He just knocks down walls to get things happening," says radio host Alan Jones, who is another admirer. "He's a goer, and it all springs from a simple idealism."

Spreading the word further afield about streetkids, the problems they faced and the courage with which they were tackling them, all remained urgent priorities for Father Chris. In Sydney in October 1996, Father Chris organised a sponsored walk for kids, Walk A Mile In My Shoes. The aim was to give others a sense of what it might be like to live on the streets permanently. He was joined by schoolkids from across the State, as well as a few streetkids themselves. The event was given greater poignancy by the release a few days before of an international study conducted by the Bread For The World organisation which found that the poverty rate for Australian children was, at 14 per cent, worse than any other developed nation except the US.

Beyond Sydney, Father Chris decided to try a daring experiment: a cattle drive. A group of kids would travel on horseback, camping overnight, herding 50-odd head of cattle along an old outback stock route. Father Chris had always believed in the power of the countryside to rejuvenate kids. Lots of boys grew up playing cowboys, after all, and now he wanted to set a few of the boys at Better Homes Farm a major challenge. If they succeeded, he reasoned, the sense of pride and achievement they would feel would be worth far more than any classroom lessons. And if they failed, well, he would just try his hardest to make sure that didn't happen. Moss Vale horse trainer John Urquhart, who'd been teaching the kids at Better Homes to ride, and his wife Jill volunteered to be chaperones. Father Chris gratefully accepted their offer. In March 1996, after appealing to those living along the route to donate cattle for the cause, the couple set off from Echuca, bound for Wagga Wagga, in southern NSW. With them was their son Matthew, 19, six boys from the farm, six horses, a caravan and 55 head of cattle, all being seen off on their journey by a big crowd of cheering locals.

None of the boys from the farm had ever ridden a horse before, none had ever slept under the stars in the bush, and all had immense problems. One was a 15-year-old who'd been making a living servicing paedophiles since running away from home at the age of nine. Two of the others had been charged with offences involving violence. What's more, a camera crew from ABC TV's *Australian Story* was going to film the journey. The potential for disaster was massive. But Father Chris felt he really didn't have much choice if he wanted to continue helping these boys. Despite bringing in caravans to supplement accommodation at Better Homes Farm, he still didn't have enough beds to cope with demand. The cattle drive was a way of keeping the boys on the program when there wasn't any room for them elsewhere.

Father Chris need not have worried; the inaugural cattle drive was an astonishing success. Along the way, locals donated more cows and welcomed the kids into their homes. Other boys from the farm rotated shifts with the six boys at various points so they too could share the experience. During the last four weeks, locals covered the entire running costs of the cattle drive — providing legs of lamb, fruit and sponge cakes for the kids, offering the use of their washing machines, telling them to drop in for showers, visiting their campsites to give free haircuts and putting aside hay for the animals. The boys played in the local football teams as they passed through, helped farmers harvest rice crops, and visited dairy farms and piggeries.

By the time the group arrived at their destination three months later, led into town by Father Chris on horseback, they were followed by several hundred people cheering them on, and they had collected 180 cows to sell off to raise funds for *Youth*. The people of Wagga donated food for a town barbecue and trophies were given out to everyone who had taken part. The first cow that had been donated for the drive and had led the herd along, was sent back to Better Homes Farm. The boys said it had been one of the best experiences of their lives. "It's the best break I've ever had," said Dave, 15. And from Ron, 16: "You can get your head together out here." A third even got a job along the way as a farmhand in country Victoria. John Urquhart was delighted. "The kids have had rejection most of their lives," he said. "But meeting country folk, finding kindness and goodwill, they've learned to trust a bit. They found it difficult believing that strangers could be so giving. For them, that's a big start." The next drive started from Corowa on the Murray River, in southern NSW, the following September and finished at Goulburn on the southern tablelands. Two drives a year were held for the next three years.

Back home after the first cattle drive, there was fresh hope that the shortage of beds at Better Homes wouldn't last too long. Matt and Fiona Handbury had bought another 49 hectares of land opposite Better Homes and lent it to *Youth*. The Property Industry Foundation, the charity arm of the property industry, then offered to build a 10-bedroom home, worth $600,000, on the new property with all materials and labour being supplied free by its member companies. The building would be filmed by the *Better Homes and Gardens* television show, an offshoot of the magazine. It was the perfect mix: new land, new beds, and publicity.

Chapter 16

MAKING MORE ENEMIES

WORKING ON the streets one day, Father Chris was approached by Mike, a bedraggled 16-year-old in dirty jeans and a torn red sweatshirt. "Farvs," he gasped. "Please help me. My mate's been taken away. I think he's in trouble." Father Chris handed him a cup of hot sugary tea from the food van, and then sat down beside him on a park bench and asked him to explain.

Mike had been working as a prostitute for about a year. He told Father Chris about a middle-aged man who was a regular around the dark streets by the notorious Wall in Darlinghurst. The man picked up young kids, took them to his flat, drugged them and then sexually assaulted them. This had happened to Mike when he first arrived on the streets. The man had given him a drink when they arrived at his unit, and then raped and bashed the boy, before driving him, still bleary-eyed and disoriented, back to Kings Cross. After that, Mike had always kept a wary eye open for the man. It wasn't enough, however. A few nights later, he had been terrified when the man crept up on him from

behind, seized him by the arm and ordered him to go back
to his flat with him again. If he didn't, or if he tried to tell
anyone about it, threatened the man, he would be found
dead the next day. Mike went with the man that time, and a
few times after that whenever he had been too slow to get
out of the man's way.

"But now," he stammered, "he's got my mate. He's only
13. He's too young to go through that." Father Chris
asked Mike if he would be prepared to tell his story to the
police. Mike cast his eyes to the ground. "I'll think about
it," he mumbled. Father Chris went back to the food van
and continued serving drinks and hot dogs to other kids.
Half an hour later, Mike came back. "No, Farvs," he
whispered. "I know you'll be ashamed of me, but I can't.
I'm scared. I've been off heroin for eight weeks and just
the thought of testifying makes me want to have a shot."
Father Chris nodded. "It's OK," he said. "I understand."
And he did. It was too much to ask of a boy with his kind
of background, and his associated fears of authority.

Father Chris reserved his anger for the paedophiles who
so openly preyed on young boys, and the laws that
allowed it to happen. "As we walk through the streets, the
paedophiles laugh at us," he says. "We can't do anything
about them. They warn the kids not to talk to youth
workers. They beat them. They lure them with drugs and
money which become a trap. I know kids they've given
hotshots to — heroin laced and contaminated which
causes overdose and death — just because the children
have asked for help. We are powerless to protect them. It's
hard for them to stand up to any adult, let alone ones so
evil and abusive."

When the 1996 Wood Royal Commission turned its attention to the grim world of paedophilia, Father Chris was ready to fight for the kids. He'd seen those men ruin so many young lives and he desperately hoped the inquiry would expose them. He was still seething over the deaths of kids like Sid, 14, who'd stayed on and off at Marrickville for two years. Sid had seemed happy at the refuge, but found it hard to make friends. Whenever one of the kids said they needed a pack of cigarettes, Sid would volunteer to run down the street to fetch one. With parents who hadn't wanted him and a string of disastrous foster home placements, Sid, lonely and desperate to please, quickly became prey for paedophiles on the streets of Sydney. Early one morning, Sid died of an overdose that most assumed was deliberate.

Sid was perhaps typical of many victims of paedophiles. Lacking in any kind of self-esteem he'd willingly go with anyone who offered him money or the slightest sign of affection. In the end, he simply couldn't cope with being so used and abused. Father Chris knew many, many kids on the streets like Sid. One night, as Father Chris drove off in the food van near Sydney's Central Station, he glanced in the rear-vision mirror and saw a man pile a whole bunch of young kids who'd just been eating at the van into his car, presumably to take them back to his place. He was furious but knew he was unable to do anything about it. Another kid, whom he knew from Better Homes, had been taken back to a seemingly kindly stranger's house and had been raped there by several men. He was only nine years old at the time. The experience left the boy unable to communicate, he knew only how to touch people in a sexual way and was completely incapable of trust. "These kids never, ever recover," says Father Chris angrily. Through his experience working with streetkids, Father Chris has learned that within two days of being on the streets, most kids have been raped; within six, most are on drugs. If no one helps them, many are dead by the age of 22. Father Chris has also long suspected that many kids have actually been murdered because they tried to report paedophiles who abused them. After all, who would notice when a streetkid went missing?

In the days before he was due to take the stand at the Royal Commission, Father Chris appeared in newspaper articles talking about the importance of the inquiry, and his personal determination to beat the scourge of paedophilia. One of the kids he knew well, Matthew, rang him after reading his comments in the press. Matthew was a real success story. He'd been with Father Chris for six years, three at Boys' Town and three at Marrickville. He'd moved out of the refuge in 1994, taken a job with a solicitor's firm and had been thriving ever since. He now lived with his girlfriend and baby son, Christopher. Father Chris had always had a real soft spot for him, since he was a kid who'd been through so much, and seemed now to be triumphing against such overwhelming odds.

That day, however, Matthew's voice was tense. "Farvs," he said over the phone, "don't you realise how dangerous paedophiles can be? *Please* be careful!" Father Chris smiled to hear Matthew's concern, but he wanted to make the young man understand why he was taking a stand. "If anyone wanted to hurt Christopher, you'd want to protect him, wouldn't you?" he asked. Matthew agreed. "I'd die for him!" he said. "So," replied Father Chris, "I have to put my life on the line for the kids that I look after." Not only was the priest happy to give his life for the cause, he also fervently believed that everyone else should feel exactly the same way. "The Royal Commission is merely highlighting the type of abuse we've been protesting against for years," he said later. "It will come and go, but kids will continue to be abused until we, as a broad-based community, say, 'No more. These kids are *our* responsibility.'"

On 30 October 1996, Father Chris finally went before the Royal Commission to make his submission. His words caused a storm. He talked about how investigators seemed intent on naming "big" name suspects, but claimed that the victims of paedophilia weren't being treated with anything near the same degree of urgency. "Services to young people at risk have been cut more and more," he told the inquiry. "DOCS have left their District Officers with little support and resources." To illustrate his point, he revealed that two children, both in the care of DOCS, had been living with paedophiles in the full knowledge of the department. One boy, a State ward, had been residing at the home of a "sugar daddy" who plied him with food, cigarettes and money. When the boy happened to be arrested on an unrelated matter, Father Chris took him out of custody and introduced him to the cattle drive program. Another boy, this time a 14-year-old State ward, was discovered to be living with a 24-year-old male "lover". He remained there until Father Chris gave him a place on the farm.

"DOCS and the Minister do not take these cases seriously enough and we, as a society, do not give our young people the protection they need," said Father Chris. "The District Officers should not be made accountable for these incidents, as they are out there working hard but have no resources and, more importantly, no voice. If they speak out, they are sacked."

The next day, Father Chris received a phone call from DOCS senior manager David Sherlock asking for details of the boys and promised that none of his staff would be scapegoated. Father Chris faxed him the details immediately. He didn't even receive any acknowledgment that the fax had arrived. That afternoon, however, NSW Community Services Minister Ron Dyer launched a scathing attack on Father Chris in Parliament, claiming that the priest had refused to pass the information to the Department. "This year I have had two meetings with Father Riley and at neither of them has he felt it necessary to raise directly with me any of his alleged concerns in terms of providing facts or details of individual cases," he said. "The Government has a solid commitment to streetkids and State wards." When Father Chris later met with one of the directors of the Department, she told him that his allegations about the two boys were followed up and substantiated. The Minister, however, did nothing to retract his remarks or set the record straight. Today, Dyer says he doesn't see his words as having been an attack on the priest. "I think Father Riley is being a bit precious in seeing it that way," he says. "I don't want to attack him, but I don't think I was attacking him."

The affair began what Father Chris saw as a mini-war

of attrition waged by the Department against him at the time. The potential for conflict is always obvious. On one side is a Government department often hamstrung by a lack of cash, and sometimes with a dispirited staff working 9 a.m. to 5 p.m. who always have to observe strict rules and procedures. On the other is a solitary priest, happy to work 24 hours a day, doggedly determined to help whichever kids come his way, free to make up his own programs and processes as circumstances dictate, and protected, to some extent, by his public reputation as a courageous lone ranger. For some DOCS workers, Father Chris must be as frustrating as the apparent intransigence of the DOCS' system is to him. "He has a clear idea of what is best, and doesn't let anyone get in his way," says one of his great supporters, media personality Prue MacSween. "He can be absolutely bloody-minded about it."

Tragically, this time, Father Chris believes the Department went on to use the cases of another two boys in a misdirected attempt to get back at him. One was a 10-year-old State ward whom DOCS had pleaded with Father Chris to take to his farm. Father Chris argued that his program wasn't set up to cater for such a young boy, but DOCS said they had nowhere else for him to go. Finally Father Chris agreed to take him. Five days later, the boy left the farm, but DOCS then got back in touch, saying that if the farm didn't take him back, he would have to stay at a Juvenile Justice centre. Unwilling to see the kid put into custody with much more hardened young offenders, Father Chris eventually placed him on the cattle drive. There he settled down quickly and responded to the family atmosphere. A few weeks later, however, DOCS contacted Father Chris to say they had found a suitable foster family for the boy — even though he'd previously been considered unsuitable for a foster placement because he was so wild. Then they said they had another institution lined up to accept him, one which had previously indicated it was not prepared to take him. When the boy was told he had to leave the cattle drive, he became distressed and pleaded to be allowed to stay where he was. Father Chris sympathised. He believed this was simply a personal attack on him, that while DOCS workers at the coal face of working with kids were eager to use his services, suddenly those in charge had decreed he be avoided.

Extraordinary scenes followed at the cattle drive campsite when DOCS officers arrived to take the boy away. He refused to go. The DOCS workers then called the police, but they refused to help. Finally, they gave up and left. DOCS later took the matter to court and, in what the priest saw as complete vindication, the presiding judge eventually bailed the boy back to the care of *Youth*. From that point on, the boy made wonderful progress. He'd found safety and no longer lived in fear of being moved on. Only once did he lose control again, and that was when he was taken to hospital. As a nurse tried to give him an injection, he screamed and struggled. It turned out his mother had overdosed on heroin and the boy had been terrified of needles ever since. The rest of his background remained somewhat of a mystery until a year later, when Father Chris mentioned the boy during a mass in a small country town. After the service, a woman approached

Father Chris and asked if he would tell her the name of the boy. When he told her, she nodded. He was the same boy she'd fought for permission to foster when he was two years old because his grandfather had been sexually assaulting him from the time he was a baby.

Father Chris's next clash with DOCS came over a 16-year-old State ward being held in custody for murder. DOCS wanted him to remain in custody, but Father Chris, who knew about the boy's background, felt he'd be far better off at Better Homes Farm. It was a tragic case. The boy and his sister were born to an alcoholic mother whose profound neglect led to both children being placed with a foster family. There, things went from bad to worse. Both were sexually abused and treated badly, with punishments including being deprived of food for 24-hour periods. Possibly as a result of the abuse, the boy developed an eating disorder known as pica, where he ate everything he could get his hands on, including snails, dirt, concrete and faeces. Later moved to an institution, the boy was again physically abused until he ran away onto the streets. Finally, he was picked up by a man, a Sydney City Mission worker, who took him back to his house where he drugged and raped him. When the man tried to rape him a second time, the boy seized a carving knife from the kitchen and repeatedly stabbed him until his attacker lay dying on the floor.

DOCS failed to turn up to the boy's hearing in the Supreme Court, and Father Chris discussed the teenager's circumstances with his Legal Aid barrister and great friend Sue Kluss. She felt Father Chris should take him back to the farm, so the priest applied for bail. The judge agreed.

When the DOCS worker in charge of the boy returned from Melbourne the following week, she was furious. She insisted the Department had a plan for the boy, which included custody and possibly later a foster family — a family, however, who had taken the child before and then given him back. DOCS challenged the bail application, and lost. Father Chris was bewildered by DOCS' determination to keep the boy in a detention centre, particularly since an Ombudsman's report had just described the centres as inappropriately staffed, with substandard accommodation, inadequate food, and few programs in place to rehabilitate young offenders. Eventually, the boy ended up staying at the farm for his full three years of bail. During his time there, Father Chris gently encouraged him to reflect on a quote from the great American writer Ernest Hemingway: "Life breaks everybody, but then some become strong at the broken places."

When the boy's case finally came to court, there was yet another sensation in store. After the jury found the boy not guilty of murder, but guilty of manslaughter, the boy was put on a four-year good behaviour bond, a punishment highly unusual for the severity of the offence. Moreover, the judge, Justice Robert Hulme, slammed DOCS in his judgment. "My views are coloured in part by what I regard as an appalling performance by one Government department during the best part of 20 years," he said. He added that he was most impressed by the teenager's progress under the care of *Youth*. Father Chris later invited the judge to the next presentation evening he held for all the kids taking part in his programs. The judge was happy to accept. "It was a truly exceptional sentence for an offence like manslaughter," says Sue Kluss today. "But the judge was so impressed by the work Father Chris had done with the boy, he just gave him the bond. Father Chris helps people who have nowhere else to go, no one else to care. He's had such an impact on so many people's lives."

There was enormous publicity over the case and the subsequent release of the boy. Many onlookers were baffled by the outcome. Broadcaster Mike Willesee was one of them. Unaware of the terrible circumstances of the crime, he remembers grumbling about how someone who kills a man in cold blood should be punished as a murderer, and how judges were becoming ridiculously soft. A few weeks later, Father Chris invited Mike to a barbecue at Better Homes Farm, after the pair met at a function. The priest introduced the broadcaster to a young man and then left them to chat. The young man was the kid he'd been complaining about. "I found him charming and completely gentle," says Mike. Afterwards, Mike found Father Chris and asked him questions about the boy. Mike was startled by how the priest's demeanour changed from that of the quiet, unassuming man he was slowly getting to know, to a man full of passion and fury about the injustices the kid had faced. "Father Chris said he had been before the judge and told him how the boy had been a victim of the State all his life," says Mike. "Every time the boy was put in foster care he was raped and given drugs. He was brought up believing the only thing anyone wanted him for was his body. When this last man had got him drunk and raped him, he took

216 Mean Streets Kind Heart

everything out on him. I was very impressed by Father Riley's stand. How many priests would have read all the records and jumped up in court and persuaded a judge to change his mind about someone? I thought there was something very special about this guy."

It's an opinion shared by Barbara Holborow, the high-profile Children's Court magistrate who, after 12 years, resigned out of frustration that the Government was doing so little for children. Often, on a Friday afternoon, a child who'd been picked up by police and had nowhere to stay would be brought to her court. Sometimes, the only option would be to put the child in custody. Then she heard about a priest who was providing beds to streetkids. Late one Friday afternoon, she was growing desperate for somewhere to place a child who seemed to have no one to turn to, and she thought she'd ring Father Chris. He was there within a few minutes. That phone call was the beginning of a strong friendship founded on mutual admiration and a shared concern for the welfare of kids. "Chris focused on education, on firm boundaries drawn with love, and on treating each child's needs separately," says Barbara, the author of the best-selling book *Kids: Loving for Life*. "As a result, he seems to have a wonderful relationship with kids. He's straight with them, by God he's straight with them, and they really respect him for it. They'll try it on with him, and tease him about his clothes, but they'll stop short of rudeness. He really cares, and I admire him so much for that."

Father Chris invited Barbara to Better Homes Farm at Canyonleigh so she could take a closer look at what he was doing. When she walked in and sat down, a kid came over to her, put his arms around her and asked, "Do you remember me?" Desperately, she tried. Whenever she made a child a ward of the State, she'd always sit them on her knee, give them a cuddly toy and whisper in their ears, "Travel well." So she asked this boy if she'd perhaps given him a hug when they'd last met. "Yes," he replied, "when I was four years old." Then he burst into tears and, still hanging around her neck, cried and cried and cried. Barbara looked over to Father Chris, who shrugged helplessly. Both Barbara and Father Chris had learnt early on that if you treated these kids with kindness, they'd never forget it.

For each, helping kids had become their mission in life. Barbara has her charity, Hope For Children, whereby experienced mothers help out new mums who are struggling with their kids. She thinks it shameful, though, that the Government gives no money to her cause, and very little money to Father Chris, despite all the good they are doing. "Children have such a low priority in society because they don't vote," she says. "But I like the way Chris doesn't sit back and wait for things to change, he's a real doer. He's devoted and very practical."

The only point they disagree on is Father Chris's conviction that there are no bad kids. "Codswallop!" says Barbara. "There are some kids who will never change. I don't know whether it's chemical, hormonal or psychological, but I believe some are just born bad. I wish I could believe it wasn't true, but I'm glad he can. He's got his faith." The pair are back on safer territory on the subject of DOCS. Barbara bemoans the fact that you no longer see a DOCS worker sitting in a gutter smoking with the kids; they all now seem to be so remote.

The Department itself seemed remote too for Father Chris, and their relationship hit a new low when he made press headlines with his attack on DOCS for its decision to take a 15-year-old State ward out of a *Youth* centre because it didn't want to pay for his place. When Opposition Community Services spokesperson Patricia Forsythe revealed that the kid, as a result, was forced to sleep on a police station bench, the public was outraged. DOCS was quick to try to smooth things over this time, and returned the boy to the care of *Youth*.

But Father Chris wasn't appeased. Just the year before, he'd taken on two other State wards who'd spent almost a month in motels under the supervision of a freelance youth worker because DOCS didn't have anywhere else for them to go. That worker was paid, for his time, $5000 more than Father Chris received to look after a kid for a whole year. Father Chris had begged Ron Dyer on a number of occasions for funding, but the Minister remained unmoved, responding that he, the politician, "lived in the real world", a world in which he himself "had to go to Government and ask for funding," — and had been told they had none. Father Chris was enraged by Dyer's words. The Minister should get up off his seat and look down on the streets, he said angrily. "When did you last have to bury someone who had died from a drug overdose? When did you last cut down a kid who was trying to hang themselves? When did you last comfort someone who had been told they had AIDS and would die? *This* is the real world. And you should be fighting for the marginalised and disadvantaged."

The relationship with DOCS is today largely positive. Many staff work closely with *Youth* and provide great help and support. There are now even specified contacts within DOCS for *Youth*, an area director, Jill Heberte, and one of her staff, Trish Mackey.

Yet the anger has never completely left Father Chris. So totally dedicated to the welfare of kids, he struggles to understand other people's priorities. He resents public money being spent on things he views as far less deserving causes — such as the $1.3 billion on the Sydney Olympics, the $5 million on rescuing British yachtsman Tony Bullimore, and the millions spent on landscaping at Sydney's Domain. "Our kids are hurt, abused and murdered, but no resources are allocated," he says. "At the same time, Government can find money for anything they choose, but why don't our kids get the same support? We will be judged as a society by the way we look after our kids, those who are the most powerless and dependent in our community. The number of kids who are homeless is increasing and we have to keep opening new programs. I often wonder how long we can keep fundraising to support our work. Every time I come across new kids in our system, I make new commitments to help, but how can we keep going?"

There was no shortage of those, too. In just the next couple of weeks, Father Chris was asked to help get 14-year-old Kim out of custody — a boy who'd had 29 placements in the past three years — after he tried to commit suicide by drinking bleach and detergent. Father Chris took Kim to the farm, even though the boy protested that he didn't deserve the chance because perhaps he hadn't been abused badly enough. The priest shook his head. Kim had been beaten by his mother to the point of having his jaw broken and being burnt with an iron so savagely, he still had a clear scar from the imprint. Father Chris reassured Kim that he'd earned his place.

Generally a pretty mild-mannered man, it was only when Father Chris saw injustice that he was roused to the attack. Then, he became completely fearless. Prime Minister John Howard became a target when he started talking about cutting the Young Homeless Allowance, the welfare payment for streetkids, to force them back home. Father Chris was seething. "John Howard models his idea of a family on his own," he announced. "He would probably find it difficult to believe that other families are not safe for kids. We are not talking about kids who have left home because they don't like Mum and Dad's rules; we are talking about kids who have left because their homes are too dangerous for them to stay. We are getting children as young as eight who need our help, and yet John Howard is saying, 'Let's take the Young Homeless Allowance away from these kids and make them go back home.'"

A little later Father Chris was in DOCS' bad books again when he criticised them publicly for not arguing forcefully enough for bail whenever their charges got into trouble with the courts. For regular children, their parents would put up a strong defence. State wards, Father Chris claimed, often had no one, and so were put into custody for petty offences when DOCS had nowhere else to place them. Research findings backed up his stand. A NSW Community Services Commission report in 1997 found that State wards were an astonishing 15 times more likely than other kids to enter a juvenile justice centre. Official

NSW Department of Juvenile Justice figures showed there were 450 young people in the State's detention centres, and Father Chris argued in the press that many of them were being locked up for trivial matters, first offences or welfare issues. One time, one of his kids who stole a chocolate bar, and another who stole a jumper, were both sent to juvenile justice centres.

Another 12-year-old kid was locked up with older children after a first offence of breaking into a car and stealing a handbag. "The Government is keen to lock kids up," he says. "They say the public demands we lock kids up."

But Father Chris just couldn't understand the logic. Kids at Better Homes were showing great progress and generally staying well out of trouble. In addition, over 1999/2000 it cost Juvenile Justice $167,170 to keep a child over a year, compared to the $55,000 it cost to send a child to *Youth*, a figure that includes full secondary schooling costs. The fact that DOCS so often refused to pay for a child to stay at his farm, he felt, was less bloody-mindedness, and more the contamination of logic, and simple human compassion, by the eagerness of successive governments to win votes in the law-and-order debate. Whatever the cost.

It's little wonder then that in every election, as a matter of principle, Father Chris has voted for the side that wasn't in power. They might always be better, he reasoned. And, besides, he felt far more comfortable on the side of the underdog.

Chapter 17

LOATHING THE LIMELIGHT

H E WAS only 11 years old, but already Sam had committed 137 crimes and been the subject of 162 police intelligence reports. Bailed to the safekeeping of Better Homes Farm on a further 17 criminal charges, he'd been taken into Sydney one night to watch a State of Origin rugby league match — and had run off halfway through. His disappearance made headlines in all the newspapers. The public outrage was palpable. What was this young thug, this solo crime wave, doing being taken to a match and allowed to wander off, when he was fast becoming one of Australia's Most Wanted?

Father Chris navigated the storm calmly. The group of boys he'd brought to the match from the farm had enjoyed their evening at the match, he said, and had even met star player Julian O'Neill before the kick-off. Sam had been doing well at the farm and was working hard to get his life back on track. He was an entrenched runaway, but since he'd been under Father Chris's care, the gaps between his disappearances were growing much longer. He'd simply been dazzled by the bright lights of the city. When he was found and brought back, he'd obviously not be allowed on that kind of trip again. The priest appealed for the public not to brand Sam as some kind of violent criminal and sensationalise the case to the point where the boy would be in danger of becoming a political football. Moreover, he insisted that custody was in no way a better option. "We've still got a chance of breaking this kid's cycle," he said. "He'd only get worse and worse if he were gaoled."

Indeed, three days later, Sam rang Father Chris in tears, saying he knew he'd stuffed up and would probably never be allowed back on the farm. When he was finally recaptured — after one failed attempt when he was put in the back seat of a police car and then escaped through the door on the other side — he was taken to children's court and remanded in custody. Father Chris, however, was determined. He went before the magistrate and begged that he be given another chance to help the boy. One of his greatest supporters, Colleen McIntosh, remembers his angst at the time. "He always felt for every one of those kids, even the impossible ones," she says. "I remember him saying that time though, that he didn't know if he'd cope with the boy. Everyone else wanted to hang him from a tree. But Father Chris stuck by him, even though he kept running away to Kings Cross, and Father Chris would go off and bring him back." His instinct proved right. By the next year, Sam was taking lessons at the farm three days a week, attending the local school nearby the other two days, and going back to his family every weekend. He was a completely different boy. His mum, Tracey, was overjoyed. "We have our son back," she said, "And he has his childhood back."

It was exactly the kind of happy ending Father Chris longed to be able to give so many kids locked up in custody, kids who, he was convinced, were slowly becoming more and more brutalised by a system that would let them out one day, angry, bitter and bent on revenge. With successive reports both nationally and for individual states showing how little rehabilitation was going on inside those detention centres and adult gaols — where so many kids ended up — he knew that it would be impossible to stop those kids graduating on to more and more serious crimes each time. Even NSW Department of Juvenile Justice head Ken Buttram admitted, "It's in detention where contaminating influences re-orient children towards crime."

Instead, Father Chris decided he wanted to make more farm places available for kids who needed help; and an alternative to detention. Better Homes Farm was already hopelessly overcrowded, with some kids forced to sleep on bedding on the floor or in caravans, while others were sent on the cattle drives, even through bitterly cold weather, just to keep them on the program when there was no more room at the farm. The McIntoshes came to his rescue. Seeing how well the kids were doing out in the country, and tremendously admiring of Father Chris's work and passion for the cause, they gave him the funds to buy a 49-hectare rural property at Sutton Forest, 30 km away from Better Homes Farm at Canyonleigh. "I think it's ideal to get the kids away from the city," says Colleen.

"They're away from temptation, they have fresh air, good food and an education. And Father Chris is a wonderful teacher."

Father Chris wanted to call the new farm by their name, but they asked him not to. They didn't particularly want the acknowledgment. Instead, they reached a compromise and it was named Mark David Farm, after the 13-year-old son the couple had lost to cancer in 1970. "Mark went and stayed with a cousin once, who showed him a pig farm," says Colleen. "At 12, he said that's where he wanted to be when he grew up. He wanted to live on a farm and have 10 kids. Ten kids is what Mark David Farm takes. We're just doing for other kids what we can't do for him."

At the farm's opening ceremony on 17 February 1997, Father Chris made a speech about how the plight of the State's homeless children was now at crisis point. The week before, he'd had to employ five extra staff to take kids out on a wilderness program because he had no beds for them. The Governor-General Sir William Deane echoed his concerns. "Some intolerant people may say these young people have somehow failed society," he said in his speech at the ceremony. "The more tolerant and compassionate among us would say it is society that has failed them." David McIntosh, begged by Father Chris not to make a speech about what a saviour the priest was, had to tear up his written notes at the last minute. Instead he had the brainwave of talking about the movie he'd seen on television the previous night — about what a difference one inherently good person can make to a lot of people's lives when they give themselves a second chance. It was

It's a Wonderful Life where an angel shows a suicidal Jimmy Stewart how much poorer his world would be without him. "It turned out to be quite appropriate," he says, smiling.

Among Mark David Farm's first residents was a 13-year-old called Jack. He ran away from home at age nine, started using drugs, and then began stealing to pay for the habit. Sent to a detention centre at the tender age of 12, where he was locked up with boys a great deal older, Father Chris came to his rescue. Jack blossomed at the farm. With little education to speak of, he managed instead to learn lots of life skills, including answering phones, driving a tractor, and tending the horses. He'd even started to become ambitious. He wanted, when he was old enough, to train as a motor mechanic.

David and Colleen were regular visitors to the farm, and were frequently amazed by how well Father Chris dealt with the young residents. "He knew exactly how to handle the kids," says David. "Once down on the farm, one of the kids threw a tantrum and stormed off, saying he was leaving. He started walking down the track, and Father Chris let him go. An hour later, sure enough, he came back."

Mark David Farm quickly became known as a place that could turn young lives around. One of the farm's early managers, Stewart Willey, said that their success had a lot to do with the atmosphere. Designed as a working farm, the kids were encouraged to get involved in helping with the farm's main project of breeding miniature horses. "The relationships with the horses are often very similar to human relationships," he says. "It involves trust and empathy which is very valuable to learn for kids like these. Our program was a very nurturing one, and that really helped." Jamie, 15, was another of the early entrants. A skilled burglar and car thief, he was taken out of a juvenile remand centre by Father Chris, and brought to the farm where he was assessed as a young man "dead-set angry with everyone and everything". His stay nearly turned to tragedy on his second day there when he drove a motorcyle on the farm too fast, and crashed headfirst into a tree. He was airlifted to hospital with a head injury and badly broken thigh to spend five days in intensive care and a further eight weeks in the ward. He healed both physically and psychologically at pretty much the same time. Three months later, full of praise for everyone who'd helped him, he was doing well at school and fired with plans for studying mechanical engineering at TAFE. "That was never a possibility before," he said. "I would have been in Long Bay before I was 20."

John, 18, a graduate of Better Homes Farm after a two-year stay, often worked at Mark David as the caretaker. He managed to get his diploma in horse husbandry and began to help out with the cattle drives too. He planned to study more, and stay in the area. "Now I'm off to America to get my Master Farrier Certificate in Kentucky, then I reckon I'll come back and be a farrier in business," he told Father Chris. Father Chris was eager to help him. He'd recoup the cost of the course by asking John to shoe the farm's horses for free for a couple of years, he said. "My philosophy is that it's better to pour $5000 or $10,000 into a kid for a couple of years to help him get his life on track, than spend $80,000 a year to keep him in a detention centre." John indeed repaid the investment. While in the US, he enlisted in the American Navy, but later returned to work with Father Chris on his projects. "He's definitely one of the greatest men I've ever met," said John. "My stay with him was the happiest time of my life. Nearly all my dreams have come true thanks to Farvs."

In John, Father Chris also invested some of his own hopes. The young man became one of his best youth workers and the start of the dream that, one day, maybe the priest would have dozens of former streetkids running his projects for the new generations coming through. He offered special apprenticeships to the kids on his projects if they wanted to train as youth workers, and a number of them took him up on it. But it was a tough ask. Some of the most promising kids, once they'd faced the demons of their past and got their lives back in order, wanted to start life afresh elsewhere, without the constant reminder of their troubled childhoods. He could hardly blame them. Even John was struggling with the concept of a full-time career on the farms. While he was extremely good at the work, and related wonderfully to the residents, the pressures sometimes got to him, and he'd take off. Each time, Father Chris was understanding. "He's always so willing and works so hard, sometimes the staff can load work onto him too much, and he can't cope," he says. "But I hope it works out. He's so keen and passionate about what he does." And, one day, who knows? John may even prove to be the successor he so obviously needs.

The next project Father Chris embarked on was Francis Farm at Wahgunyah, on the Victorian side of the Murray, near Wodonga, a beautiful property donated by Maggie Fitzgibbon, the stage and television star who became a legend in London's West End. Retired and living in country Victoria, she had read a magazine article about Father Chris's work and wanted to help. The farm was earmarked ultimately for girls, but a specially built cottage by the main house with six beds was filled immediately by the overflow of boys from the other three farms. Five boys started out there, going to local schools or courses at the TAFE college while living at the farm as a family, doing chores around the house, planting a vegetable garden, re-fencing the property and caring for the 19 head of cattle. They also helped out neighbouring farmers and sought part-time work in the local community. In their time out, they'd go swimming and horseriding, and received regular visits from Maggie, who would drop by for a chat. "It's satisfying to see the boys becoming more settled but naturally there are setbacks along the way," she said after the opening in May 1997. "This is giving them an opportunity to have a second go and change their way of life."

With the number of *Youth Off The Streets* programs expanding so rapidly, Father Chris's work was fast capturing the public's imagination. Later that same year, on a trip back to Cabramatta to play basketball with the kids, he was approached by Mike Munro, host of the Nine Network's television show *This Is Your Life*, with his familiar big red book. Father Chris's look of horror, replayed on the show, was not the usual display of polite modesty; it was pure, unadulterated dismay. Off camera, he pleaded with Mike Munro not to make him go through with it. Mike, who'd done a number of stories on Father Chris's work already for *A Current Affair*, told him that it would be a great program, he'd enjoy the experience and, what's more, he was bound to raise extra funds for the kids with the additional public exposure of his cause. That last comment hit Father Chris's weak spot. He admitted the idea of more money for his kids was very attractive, but he was still extremely reluctant to take part. "In all the shows we've done, we've only had two other people who were as reluctant to take part," says Mike. "There was [golfer] Greg Norman who's lived overseas so long, he didn't know who the hell I was, and then there was [marathon runner] Pat Farmer. Chris was like Pat. They're both incredibly modest men. We only got Chris because we promised to give the charity a plug at the end with how people could donate." There was also one additional complication. The day before, Father Chris had bailed out of custody a 12-year-old kid who was facing a murder charge. Bail was conditional on the boy being under Father Chris's immediate care 24 hours a day. So he came along too and had a wonderful time riding in the show's stretch limo, watching a television program being made, and being treated like royalty.

Father Chris, however, hated being the star of the show. Ironically, for a priest so regularly in the news, he has always loathed personal publicity, only speaking out or agreeing to interviews when he felt it might be of benefit to the kids or when he particularly needed more funds. Even in the preparation of this biography, he implored that the book be about his work rather than him. Anyone who wonders whether his modesty is false need only watch the *This Is Your Life* episode. Father Chris sits, stands and smiles his way through the entire program looking as if he'd quite happily shrivel up and die. Sir William happened to be out of town when the program was recorded so he agreed instead to just tape a message to be played on the show. He admits he was relieved not to have to make an appearance and witness, first-hand, Father Chris's discomfort. "Every time those big doors opened at the back of the studio, he looked as if he was trying very hard not to bolt out through them," says Sir William. "Yes, he was very uncomfortable being the focus," says Mike. "If he could avoid ever doing media, he would, but he knows he needs the media to raise funds for his work, so he sees it as a necessary evil." Father Chris's only genuine smile came when Collingwood bounded on to the stage.

The worst moment, however, was yet to come. A photo was flashed up on the wall of Matthew, the reformed heroin addict Father Chris had developed such an attachment to over six years as his carer; he was one of the first boys he'd taken in at the refuge and the same kid who had called Father Chris to warn him about how dangerous paedophiles could be. At that time, Matthew was working at a city law firm and living with his girlfriend and their baby son. Afterwards, however, his relationship with his girlfriend had broken down and Matthew had battled through the courts to win custody of their son. He finally got it, but had to take the boy to his mum's house every day at 6 a.m. so he could go to work, then he would pick him up after work every afternoon. It was an enormous battle for such a young man. Eventually, exhausted by the routine, Matthew sadly agreed to give the little boy back to his girlfriend. She then moved to the country so it became virtually impossible for him to see his son regularly. "His family was the world to him," says Father Chris today. "It was everything." Matthew, in his early 20s, overdosed on heroin in 1997. His funeral at St Patrick's Church in the city was packed with mourners, the law firm where he worked closed down for the day and Father Chris struggled to retain his composure throughout the service he conducted. "It was terrible to see Father like that," says his personal assistant Judy Gorton. "Everyone felt sad about Matthew but they then felt even worse to see how hard his death had hit Father. I was willing him to make it through, thinking, 'Please don't crack'. All the other kids were there too, looking like stunned mullets." When *This Is Your Life* ran the picture of Matthew, Father Chris couldn't speak, so choked was he, all over again, with emotion and pain.

Chapter 18

FARMING OUT FAMILY AND FRIENDS

THAT *THIS IS YOUR LIFE* show was one of the few times in many years that Father Chris's whole family had come together, and the first time in a long while that Father Chris had seen many of his friends. His work had taken over his life so totally, there simply wasn't room left for anyone else. The kids came first, second and third. "There's no way he could do the work he does and have a life beyond," says one of his great admirers, the Reverend Bill Crews of Sydney's Ashfield Uniting Church, who also has a name for helping the disadvantaged. "He works so hard, he doesn't have any time for himself. I think he's wonderful."

Father Chris had remained close to his mother, Mavis, despite the fact she never would convert from the Anglican church and wouldn't let him baptise her. "I'm good enough as I am, thank you," she would tell her son firmly. In some ways, though, the regular lifestyles of his family were as foreign to him as the organised chaos of his own life was to them. Looking at his parents, he couldn't even imagine living like them. "They're together 24 hours a day!" he says in amazement. "He goes outside to sweep up the leaves, and she goes to watch him. It's incredible." For a confirmed loner who shudders at the thought of spending a whole day in the company of another person, it was a complete mystery. He was so different to them in other ways too. The pair never celebrated birthdays, and they never told the rest of the family if they were sick. On his father Kevin's 70th birthday, a few of their children went to visit him, only to discover he was in hospital. When he came out, one of his daughters-in-law, Sally, happened to ask how he was. He cut the conversation stone dead. "We don't talk about sickness in this family," he told her curtly. She burst into tears. Father Chris later asked his dad to apologise to her. "She's not a Riley," he told him. "She doesn't understand how we operate."

Of all his siblings, his sister Helen is perhaps the closest. When her two daughters grew up, she left office work, went back to college and is now also teaching. She calls him regularly, and they catch up occasionally. She's still amazed by the work he's doing. "He hated being on *This Is Your Life*," she says. "He still doesn't like being in the public eye, but he feels he has to do it for the kids. It's only when he's got something to say that he has to say it. Sometimes I still can't believe how this person who is so shy has ended up doing what he is doing, where he has to talk to people so much, and be in the public eye. I do worry about him." Greg also calls his brother sometimes, but usually ends up having to leave a message. "We get on well when we see each other, though," says the army stalwart. "I joke that he saves people, and I kill 'em."

Mike Munro, when researching Father Chris for the show, was astonished to find out how rarely Father Chris saw his family. He organised to have a nephew that the priest had never met before brought on stage. "I thought, 'Oh God!'," says Mike. "He spends his life looking after streetkids yet he hardly gets to see his own family." Father Chris's uncle, Geoff Riley, understands. "He's got boundless energy, but he's devoted to those kids," he says. "He does the work of Jesus, more than other people, including other priests, and he doesn't have time for anything else."

Father Chris has lost touch with most of his friends over the years too, rarely having time to return their phone messages. So when he does make an effort, it seems all the more special. John McAvoy, a television producer at *60 Minutes*, became friendly with Father Chris after doing stories on his work. He then asked Father Chris if he would marry him and his fiancée, journalist Tara Brown. To his delight, Father Chris even turned up for the wedding rehearsal too. But his work was never far away. "He'd come direct from the police station where he'd been dealing with one of his boys who was just about to be charged with murder," says John. "He's such a workaholic, he gives everything to those kids, and you can see how much they adore him." Other old friends, seeing him for the first time in years on *This Is Your Life*, were shocked by how he'd changed from a whippet-slim sports-loving whirlwind to a man who had aged terribly and become overweight from spending so many hours sitting in the back of a car working, snatching junkfood only where and when he could. "I saw the physical change in him," says Tim Cox, the school captain of Chadstone when Father Chris had taught there 14 years before. "I thought, how long can he keep going at that pace?"

While his friends in the media always tried to help, there were others who looked on disapprovingly. Many felt it was wrong that a priest be so eager to court publicity, and some felt he might be taking advantage of his clerical collar to do so. One was Geoff George, the current principal of Boys' Town at Engadine who, although he has never met Father Chris, has strong views on him. "He has played his collar to the nth degree," says Geoff, a former Marist brother. "It's Father Chris Riley. It's unambiguous. He's maximised the use of his clerics. I don't always agree with that. The image that sticks in my mind is of him riding his horse in his collar on a cattle drive. What does a normal person wear in the middle of nowhere on horseback? He seems to have done that very, very deliberately ... He doesn't come across as Salesian at all. It isn't 'Father Chris Riley, Salesian'. It's Father Chris Riley."

While *This Is Your Life* raised some money for Father Chris's cause — with one viewer offering to pay for a leg operation on the limping Collingwood (she'd been kicked by a horse the previous day) — mostly what it gave him was more work. "The main thing I got out of it was lots and lots of extra kids," he told Mike Munro ruefully a few weeks later.

Thankfully, the building of the 10-bedroom farm on the stretch of land over the road from Better Homes was going well, with contributions of labour, building materials, furnishings, financial assistance and expertise from more than 200 companies. The kids from Better

Homes pitched in to help as labourers. One, Brian, 14, ended up juggling two offers of apprenticeships as a result. The farm was designed around the kids' needs with large, open communal areas, and the bedrooms giving each child private space. This time there were murmurs of concern from the local community about having two farms in the neighbourhood. There were even rumours circulating that some of the kids had been involved in three attacks on locals who lived near the farm, and that a staff member had also been injured. They were all completely untrue. What was true, however, was that an incident had occurred on the school bus after one of Father Chris's kids pulled a girl's hair or swore at her. As concern in the town increased, a community meeting was called. Around 100 locals turned up. As they began heatedly to debate the issues, Father Chris pleaded for understanding. "These kids aren't *my* kids," he told the assembled throng. "They belong to everyone. The whole community should be taking responsibility for these kids." The mother of the girl on the school bus stood up. "They're not *my* kids," she said angrily, "and I don't want them anywhere near me." Father Chris felt his temper rising too. "I just can't help it sometimes," he says. "I get so angry and aggressive because I feel that these kids need to have a voice." When finally Father Chris outlined his plans for the new farm, two-thirds of the people present voted in his favour. What's more, many volunteered to help with the building work.

The farm was named Foundation House and was opened in October 1997, with Sir William once again doing the honours. "If you look around at the *Youth Off*

The Streets centres, I think you'll be surprised how many foundation stones I must have unveiled," he says today. "Chris used to think it was helpful to have the Governor-General opening things. It encouraged a few people to come and lend their support. As a result, Helen and I got to know a lot of the kids fairly closely." This time 400 people turned up for the ceremony. In his speech Sir William dubbed Father Chris "Australia's new Mel Gibson", jibing him gently about his appearance on TV. Father Chris smiled weakly back. Never foregoing the chance to make a point about the lack of Government support for youth, however, he recovered in time to thank everyone involved for donating the house and land and labelled it a sad indictment that it was yet another place started without a cent of public money. "It's a tribute to the NSW and Australian communities that once again," he said, "we open a house without any Government help whatsoever and provide for people who, I have to say, are the State's responsibility, as the majority of young people here are State wards."

Kris was one, an angry young man who had stayed at a number of *Youth* programs before finally settling down at Foundation House, where he lived for 14 months. When he first arrived, he hated it. He loathed the country and longed to be back in the city. These days, he's moved permanently to the country, and wouldn't entertain the thought of returning to the city again. "Living at the farm opened up a whole lot of opportunities for me," says Kris, now 21, and working as a woodcutter in the Riverina. "I screwed Farvs about, but he's a good bloke and always made allowances for me. He was strict, but. He just doesn't want to give up on you." Kris studied, rode horses, played basketball for a team that never won a single game, and looked after the two wombats, the kangaroo and the emu that lived on the property. "If Farvs hadn't come along, I guess I would be back in Sydney and probably dead and buried by now. That farm made me."

Gradually, Father Chris was putting comprehensive programs in place at all of the farms, to make sure each centre upheld the same *Youth* philosophy. The thinking behind each program was based on the "Something is right" model. Too many programs elsewhere, he believed, were predicated on a "Something is wrong" model, approaching young people as problems, and dealing with them as if they were dysfunctional, sick or needing treatment and therapy. He believed this attitude only compounded their difficulties. Father Chris's approach was all about focusing on kids' strengths and "wellness" as opposed to weakness and pathology. *Youth's* challenge, he laid out, was to foster the self-actualisation of their residents, helping them grow and develop, and take back power over their lives. All should be treated equally, everyone's special talents should be recognised and nurtured and, overall, the community feeling, the idea that each person belonged, should be promoted as the highest priority. The kids at the farms had all been rejected over a long period. It was important that, once they'd checked in, they felt safe, secure and valued.

Father Chris drew up the *Youth* charter with frequent reference to the Burdekin Report, taking both its recommendations and its criticisms of the existing structure of the social welfare system as his starting point.

Chief among Burdekin's concerns had been the fact that most refuges tended to accept only the easy cases, those young people who needed the least support and would be unlikely to disrupt the smooth running of the centres. Father Chris, on the other hand, was determined to offer options for the most difficult cases. Interestingly, he combined Burdekin's proposals with his own Salesian order's thinking about how best to deal with youth, that old Don Bosco Preventive System. This process gave him clear principles to guide his work. Frequently, he referred back to Don Bosco's sayings, for example "Familiarity brings affection, and affection brings confidence"; "When you are angry or agitated never give corrections or reproofs ... wait until you have cooled down"; "The greatest happiness for a child is to know that they are loved"; "The honey of charity sweetens the bitterness of correction, a public shaming should be the last resort"; and, perhaps most importantly, "Instruction and a kind, patient, long-suffering attitude are the only means of educating".

Looking after animals was also given real priority at each of the farms. With research showing that pets have a great therapeutic effect on people, particularly on abused children, Father Chris felt it was important that the kids be given responsibility for tending animals. Connection with adults could sometimes feel threatening to these young people. Nurturing an animal always proved a good starting point to opening them up, and making them feel needed and important. It seemed to be working well. Andrew, for instance, a withdrawn, solitary child, was paired with a small Palomino jumping horse. He wrote an essay about him. "Show Boat has three white socks and a white blaze," he wrote. "When I jump him, I have a sense of determination to win by jumping with the right methods. I don't let my mind wander. I must keep my concentration and discipline very high. Show Boat and me, we are a team together. We trust each other. If he gets spooked or nervous, I try to assure him everything is all right, which gives him confidence. I spend every single spare moment I have with him. He's the best animal I've ever worked with. When I was at the Dalton Show, someone offered me $8000 for him. I thought to myself, I wouldn't sell him for a million dollars. If Father sold him, I'd probably steal him back."

The founding of a proper school for the kids on the farms was a major step forward. The kids had always received some education, either at the local schools or some one-on-one teaching by Father Chris and another teacher employed to help. Gradually, the lessons spread from a tiny office at the back of Better Homes Farm to a demountable classroom parked outside. Finally, late in 1997, three demountables were installed and an independent school was established for the kids from all of the farms to travel to each day. It was named Matthew Hogan School, in remembrance of the boy who had recently died from a drug overdose, the same boy whose photograph had affected Father Chris so deeply when it was shown during *This Is Your Life*. The school really took off after a husband-and-wife team joined Father Chris, made up of a fellow Salesian priest who had taught under him at Boys' Town, and the female member of staff for whom he'd subsequently given up the priesthood.

They'd become great friends with Father Chris at Boys' Town, and had stayed friends throughout the controversy that accompanied their departure. "He had been really supportive at the time, and had been the only one who was," says Adele Sims who now with her husband, the former priest Laurie, has two children. "That really set him apart from the others." At first, they'd struggled to get on their feet. Father Chris, in his last year at Boys' Town, had found out how tough they were doing it, and offered to help. "We didn't have anything, so he gave us whatever he had," recounts Laurie. "One day, he just said we could have his stipend, which was $11,000 at the time for the year. He just gave it to us. I have no idea how he managed to live without it." With Adele and Laurie both teaching at Matthew Hogan School, the place really began to fire.

When the kids weren't studying, youth workers at the farms were encouraged to actively participate in recreational activities organised by either staff or the young people. They were told to make themselves available to chat with the kids. Whenever there was a problem, they were instructed to take the young person aside to talk to them, rather than doing it in front of the others. And when they were forced to criticise, it had to be done in a positive way, Father Chris decreed. Meal times were occasions for the group to sit together, talk and share.

While the kids were always supported, they were also made to feel responsible and accountable for their actions. They were regularly drug tested, and were rewarded for good behaviour via a points system for completing set jobs and tasks, improving their conduct or volunteering to do extra work. Two hundred points, for instance, entitled them to ride the motorbikes on the farm, 350 points gave them gift vouchers for music, 400 points meant a gift voucher for clothes. They had to earn at least 50 points to go on an outing to a McDonald's, a trip into town, or tickets to a sports game. Conversely, breaking house rules or failing to do chores involved losing points, and a fine of $5 out of their $105 weekly welfare payments. Any display of violence or intimidation toward another resident or staff member resulted in a one-week time-out period. Continual bad behaviour could mean exclusion from the program. Father Chris was still unfailing in his readiness, in the first instance, to take the side of the kids. If one of them swore at a staff member, for example, he'd want to know whether the abuse was provoked by that person failing to follow an established procedure. The staff member might have shouted back at a kid, for instance, which had escalated the situation. That objective assessment could prove enormously frustrating for staff, but it always gave the kids great confidence that they were worth taking seriously, and that they would be protected. Too many people in the past had ignored what they had to say, the priest reasoned. He wasn't going to continue that kind of mistreatment.

Father Chris, however, was far from a soft touch. He was very tough on the kids when necessary, and they respected him for it. If they absconded from a farm and were picked up by the police, he might take his time about picking them up from the station, to teach them a lesson. He also had a very well-honed instinct for when a kid might be trying to take him for a ride. His personal assistant Judy Gorton says it's formidable to see the priest in action. "He can read people, especially kids," she says. "He won't let the kids manipulate him. One boy who was trying to see him, he made him wait. He won't be forced. I remember another time two kids came to see me and Father happened to be here," she says. "We were chatting and he walked into the room. Immediately, he said to them they were using drugs and what on earth were they doing here when they were using. He didn't want to see them until they were clean. I hadn't had a clue." David McIntosh says that at an opening where the *Youth* choir sang, there was a bit of a hiccup, and Father Chris grew angry when someone praised them. "No," he said, "they can do that properly. They don't need people's sympathy, and to have done that was unprofessional. They should know better." The next time they appeared, they were note-perfect.

If a kid at one of the centres hit a staff member, Father Chris would review the situation. Ideally, he'd hope the two sides could be brought together again for a period of calm negotiation, to work out exactly what went wrong. Sometimes, he'd review the situation and come down on the side of the kid. However, if he was satisfied that the kid's action was totally unprovoked, and they couldn't reach a satisfactory agreement, he'd have no hesitation in giving the kid time-out, maybe a week away from the farm to reflect on their behaviour. "The kids tend not to swear at me or disobey me, but I know very well what hell the staff can go through," he says. "One boy said one of the female staff had grabbed his arm and pushed him. I said, 'Dream on'. He just looked at me. I said I knew it wasn't true, that I knew him too well, and he had a problem with women and would scream at them and abuse them. This woman was really calm and caring. He would have cornered her and shouted at her when he lost his temper, and she would have tried to get past him."

No one was perfect. Father Chris, very occasionally, lost it with the kids too. Always though, he'd be overwhelmed by a sense of shame and contrition afterwards. "It could be very hard with these kids. Everyone gets cranky with them from time to time. I went into one kid's bedroom the other day and he'd smashed all the walls. I was furious, I told him off and really got stuck into him. Afterwards, I realised I'd failed heavily. He was one of the most abused kids I'd ever encountered, someone who's lucky to be alive. I hurt him that day saying those things to him, but in other ways it did him good to be treated normally."

It was exhausting work for all the staff on the farms, surrounded by often difficult kids and isolated from anyone else. Father Chris did his best to help, but he knew some of them were struggling. Once, he took all the kids from Better Homes Farm up to the Gold Coast for a three-day holiday to give the workers a break. Even though it wasn't terribly relaxing for him, he had a great time watching the kids excitedly rush from activity to activity, racing back to him to report on each new discovery. They spent the evenings at the malls watching street entertainers. "The young should be allowed to be kids," he wrote in his diary. "Their lives should be fun. Every kid should experience the excitement of rides, the beauty of dolphins flying through the air, of tigers rolling in play with their trainers, a place of warmth and safety. These kids are not so difficult. They are just lost, and waiting to be reclaimed." Even far away from the realities of life back home, Father Chris still tried to keep in touch with those kids he knew were having a tough time on their own. He gave one boy a call in gaol, knowing he was terrified after being raped by two other inmates. And he wondered about Jenny, a 17-year-old girl who had fled to Queensland from Sydney after falling out with her pimp when she said she was too sick to work, and reneging on a debt to drug dealers. One of the dealers had caught her, leaving her with four broken ribs, two blackened eyes and bruises all over her body. She was hoping to be able to disappear in another State. He peered closely at every young woman he saw in the crowds at the mall, always searching for Jenny.

On Father Chris's return, he found the farm programs working so well, there were calls from people all over the country eager for him to set up similar projects elsewhere. Often these callers had farms but couldn't raise enough in donations to pay for the staff to run them, or for facilities for the kids. Every time someone approached Father Chris, he'd be encouraging, but he wouldn't rush to set up a farm for them. He had to be sure it would work, long-term. Francis Farm in the Victorian countryside, for instance, didn't work as well as had been hoped. "It eventually closed because we had no referrals there, it was in the wrong place," he says. "At one stage we had only two kids there, yet we were pouring a lot of money into it, money we could have made better use of elsewhere. So, in the end, if something's not working, we move on. *Youth* originally came out of need. If *Youth* wasn't there, these kids would have no one. I wanted it always to remain responsive to need. I've always been fairly pragmatic about that. We have waiting lists for the other boys' farms, so they have to be our priority. Keeping one program running that wasn't helping enough kids meant that I couldn't set up other programs that might help more."

It was a similar story with Vera Loblay House in Crows Nest, a two-storey Victorian house opened as an eight-bed refuge for young women. Donated by the Loblay family and funded by Rotary clubs and other community groups, it was opened in November 1996 by Sir William for young women aged 14 to 18, providing a safe place for them to live with access to education and job opportunities. Money was always tight, and Father Chris battled to find corporate sponsors and appealed for funds for office equipment. Yet the place soon hit problems of its own. "It was just too close to the city," says Father Chris. "We discovered that some of the older girls were taking the younger girls over the Harbour Bridge to work as prostitutes. We learned from the experience, though. We learned never to open those type of long-term programs in the city. It's too dangerous."

One of the biggest success stories continued to be those cattle drives. They still took place along the southern stock routes, with different kids joining and leaving every day, to fit in with school, college or work commitments. Whenever the cattle grew tired, youth workers would take the kids off into the bush on wilderness programs. Whenever it rained, they'd all squeeze into the small caravan that always accompanied them on the drives. At the country towns along the way, they continued to receive a hero's welcome, with many of the kids invited back to people's homes for a roast dinner, a hot bath and a chat by the fireside, feeling a lot like extended family. Locals along the route remained generous with schoolchildren organising fetes to raise money and holding whip rounds at churches, while farmers donated all the cows and horses they could afford.

Sometimes, the drives would end with a big rodeo and an urgent call would go out for a change of clothes for the kids. Many didn't have more than the outfits they stood up in, and these were pretty scruffy and threadbare after all that time on the road. Val O'Keefe, the receptionist at Murdoch Magazines, was often Father Chris's first port of call. "Once, they'd been away up north for eight weeks and Tamworth put on a rodeo for them," she says. "Father Chris needed the kids decked out in decent gear. They were frozen, and only had what they stood up in. I'd ring up RM Williams and Just Jeans and use all the contacts we had through our magazines *Men's Health* and *marie claire*. We'd then deck them out in moleskins, boots and shirts so they looked like normal kids. A lot of the companies were wonderful about doing that. Father Chris was well-known, and everyone wanted to help. Matt [Handbury] would never mind us using the company letterhead either, and the name always helped too."

They always ended up very happy times. Invariably, the boys relished the sense of freedom they felt under the stars, in the country, with few other people about, sitting yarning around the campfire and sinking into sleep out of pure exhaustion after a hard day's ride. "It's not just cattle and droving," said the head drover John Urquhart. "There's the social interaction between each other, the interaction between them and the folk along the way. It's educating them in social skills, manners and hygiene; that all comes into the big picture of this experience. And halfway through, you see a big change in behaviour and attitude."

Thirteen-year-old Jules was all the proof anyone needed. "I was on the streets and all that," he said, riding his horse just after the cattle drive had set off. "Doing crime, in lock-up. Then I got lucky. Farvs took me. Now look what I've got. I thank Farvs for all this. He's a very good man. He gives you the chance. You don't want to let him down."

But Christmas was fast approaching, and everyone who'd ever had anything to do with streetkids knew what traumas that always heralded.

Chapter 19

A RIGHT ROYAL CHRISTMAS

CHRISTMAS IS always the hardest time of the year for streetkids. The celebrations and excitement going on around them only seem to highlight the fact they don't have a home to go to, or a happy family to share it all with. Father Chris dreads it: he always loses a kid to suicide a day on either side of Christmas. Always. Many of the kids say to the youth workers on the farms, in the refuge or over at Dunlea, "Just don't wake me till it's all over." It's heartbreaking.

In his first few years of working with youngsters, Father Chris had hoped he'd be able to replace their families by surrounding them with people who cared. In later years, he was forced to admit he couldn't. "I've learnt the importance of family, I know that kids need a family," he says. "And if they don't have one, then they've already lost their most important possession."

In the run-up to Christmas 1997, however, there was an unexpected treat in store. A few days before, Sir William asked Father Chris if he'd like to bring over a bunch of his kids for a Christmas party at Government House in Canberra. The priest was delighted to accept the offer.

The visit was a triumph. The Deanes invited everyone to have a swim first, and the 30-odd kids all dived, jumped, or water-bombed their way into the pool, unintentionally catching Sir William more than once. He just laughed to see them having such a wonderful time. When one of their young guests confessed he'd forgotten his swimmers, Lady Helen even lent him an old pair from the Governor-General's wardrobe. Of course, they were much too big, even when tied at the top with one of Sir William's old neckties to keep them on, but the kid was round-eyed at having been given a pair of swimmers of such lofty origin. One wag immediately asked Lady Helen if she had any more swimmers to give out. She did. Another kid told Sir William, "This is the flashest place I've ever been into." Smiling, Sir William replied, "Me too."

The couple then laid on a sumptuous buffet, in a ritual that quickly became an annual event for *Youth Off The Streets* kids, either at Government House or at Admiralty House in Sydney. That first occasion went so well, no one could resist repeating it. Adults there were taken aback by how respectfully the kids conducted themselves. "No one pushed, nobody shoved, nobody spoke out of place," says David McIntosh. "You couldn't find 30 kids better behaved." After lunch on that first visit, Sir William took them all on a tour of the house. Colleen McIntosh says he was careful to explain to them the significance of the place. "He was saying, 'This doesn't belong to us. This beautiful place, this furniture belongs to the people of

Australia, to you all.' Then this young lad at the back says, 'Right, where's my room?' Sir William tried to keep a straight face but he broke up."

Sitting down in the lounge room afterwards, Sir William and Lady Helen handed every child an envelope containing $40. It was a carefully thought-out plan. "When Chris takes them in, they are often introverted, resentful, very difficult to communicate with," Sir William says. "He builds up their self-esteem to the point where they then start thinking of someone else. At the Christmas parties, I'd give them an envelope with a small amount of money inside, and I would say to them that I would like them to consider spending half of it on somebody other than themselves who might need it more than them, or someone they loved and respected." Sometimes they'd give that money to the kids who hadn't been able to come, but often they'd turn round and give it straight to Chris. Colleen felt a lump in her throat when she saw that. "It was wonderful to see how much faith and respect and gratitude they had for Chris," she says. "It was always very moving."

Each year, Sir William and Lady Helen would receive a stack of mail from the kids, thanking them for the day, for the gift, and writing about what it had meant to them. "It was extraordinary the things we got from the most unexpected of the kids," says Sir William, shaking his head. "The ones who would most likely just grunt at you in the early days, would write beautifully about what they'd done with the money. Some were very, very sad letters."

At the end of the day, many of the kids didn't want to leave. With a lot of the smaller kids drawn to Lady Helen, chatting and playing with her, she was often very close to tears when they left. Some begged the Deanes to adopt them. "We both found that very moving," says Sir William. "The couple of times that happened, we made a point of staying in personal contact with them to the extent that we could. There were many occasions where I think Helen was more than close to tears, but never in front of any of the kids."

A few days later, on Christmas Day itself, there was more excitement in store. Over at Matt Handbury's Murdoch Magazines, the staff had decided to lay on a day the kids wouldn't forget. The company chef cooked turkeys in the big ovens used for testing the magazine recipes, the staff at *Family Circle* baked cakes and Christmas puddings, and the food writer for their books division organised the menus. They set up tables in the park behind their offices at Ultimo and laid out a magnificent Christmas dinner for all the kids from every one of Father Chris's projects. "I think some of those kids had never had a Christmas dinner in their lives before," says receptionist Val O'Keefe, who became the "fixer" for *Youth* until she retired from Murdoch Magazines at Christmas 2001, remaining, however, an enthusiastic volunteer. "Everyone would be happy to give up their Christmas for them. There'd be presents for the kids too. We'd have collections, we had a Christmas tree in the front office for donations, and we'd pass on a lot of the stuff that all magazines are sent, like cosmetics for the girls and clothes for the boys. We'd always be sending boxes of magazines up to the farms and having raffles."

A couple of months later, Matt Handbury offered *Youth* the top floor of his company's building to use as office space, since the front room of the Marrickville refuge was becoming impossibly cramped. Gratefully, they took it. The move meant the start of even closer relations between the magazine staff, *Youth* and the kids. Some of the staff took on kids for work experience during the year, and happily helped out with favours. A boy who dreamed of becoming a model was treated to a photo shoot by a *Men's Health* photographer. Food left over in the test kitchens was used to feed students at Key College in Surry Hills. The *Youth* logo was redesigned by magazine artists. Furniture and furnishings for the new farms was often found by the *Better Homes and Gardens* magazine team. The company chef advised on meals at the farms. Many staff became volunteers — part of an ever-expanding group of willing helpers who did tasks as varied as overseeing audits, interviewing staff, cooking meals at the Marrickville refuge, working on the food van, helping out at the cattle drives, fundraising, decorating and giving kids haircuts.

That steady stream of good deeds and good people eager to help played a huge role in reassuring the kids about their own value as individuals, and teaching them that not all adults were out to get them. Father Chris believes that very often this kind of generosity is what's helped keep them alive. "Many of these kids have lost the desire to live," he says. "They've given up the dream of living a normal life, and see themselves as either deathbound, or gaolbound. They've lost the ability to have an education and therefore there's no point in planning a future. They have no friends. Even within their own little groups, they don't survive very long together. They're so socially destroyed, they can't connect with people very well at all. They've lost their trust in adults to a large extent, because the majority have been sexually assaulted. They've lost their innocence. They've lost their trust in people they should have been able to trust — family members or close friends or someone respectable in the local community."

While volunteers such as those at Murdoch Magazines have helped some of the kids slowly regain their faith in the outside world, Father Chris still believes we have a long way to go in learning how to relate to young people. We're so busy getting on with our own lives that we become isolated from the next generation, ignoring their needs and, sometimes, we are even afraid of them. The media, for example, is full of stories of violent youth, of kids going on "the rampage". The many good, positive things done by young people are commonly ignored. "In order to help kids, adults must lose their fear of kids and the isolating individualism which separates us from each other," says Father Chris. "I suppose my biggest push in terms of philosophy goes back to the North American Indians' way of raising kids. They believe the only reason adults exist is to look after children, and that we're all relatives, basically. In this country, we as a nation have to say, 'Not only are we biologically connected to *our* kids, but to every young person we encounter.' The biggest breakdown in this country, even more than marriage breakdown, occurs between adults and kids. Those relationships are so fragile. I think kids feel very much alone, and adults are intimidated, so in the end, there's no relationship. It's like the teacher in [the 1996] Dunblane [school gym massacre] who put her body between her children and a bullet. She died for those kids. I think we as adults have to do that every day. Until we are prepared to die for our kids, the abuse is going to go on."

Adults taking responsibility for the next generation's welfare was only ever going to be half the story. The other half lay in picking up the pieces of the kids whose lives had already been shattered by those who were supposed to care for them. Father Chris knew that some kids would gradually turn, with the passage of time, from abused to abuser. He was trying to work out ways of trying to help them, and to break the cycle before more kids were damaged by those who had been hurt themselves. It was ridiculous, he felt, that while the Royal Commission in 1996 had highlighted the abuse of children to an extraordinary extent, all the attention and funds made available had been poured into further inquiries and trying to catch the perpetrators. Few resources were ever devoted to helping the victims or to developing preventative programs for the future. Research had found that early intervention was the only effective strategy for preventing paedophilia. Why weren't people organising programs for that?

Father Chris resolved to try. He'd come across kids as young as 11 raping victims as little as three year olds, often in the same household. Moreover, statistics showed that 80 per cent of paedophiles had been sex offenders as children — a quarter of these had started before the age of 12 — behaviour often triggered as a result of having been victims themselves. And the only way to halt their

progression to abusing other kids, was to give them help
— as early as possible. By mid-1997, there were 120
juvenile sex offenders in NSW, but not a single residential
program operating in the country to help them, only State-
based individual counselling services. When it was known
that, on average, each paedophile who started young
would have 200 different victims over a lifetime, offending
against a number of those victims many times, it was vital
that they be stopped.

On the subject of adult paedophiles, Father Chris is
adamant: the perpetrators should be locked up for life.
"I'm not saying make their lives hell, or bring back capital
punishment, I'm saying lock them up for life because they
will reoffend," he says. On the subject of priests who have
abused children, he is just as hardline. "I don't care if they
are priests, if they are guilty they should be given long or
permanent custodial sentences if that is the only solution
to stopping the problem," he says. "The diocese has been
rocked by [clergy] sex scandals and no doubt it has badly
affected the faith of victims and their relatives."

Where young sex offenders are concerned, Father Chris
feels that there is real hope that they can be helped so they
won't develop into the paedophiles of the future. Father
Chris had experience in dealing with child sex offenders: he
had been looking after a 12-year-old boy who'd raped a
five-year-old girl when he was 11 and another 12-year-old
boy who'd admitted to fantasies about abusing other
smaller kids. "Kids like these need specialist help and if
they don't get it, they'll go on to sexually assault hundreds
of kids and commit thousands of offences," he says. "The
younger we can get them the better. It's absolutely no good

parents covering for them, or police not wanting to take action. We have to treat them as early as possible."

Spurred on by the release of the report on paedophilia by NSW Police Royal Commissioner Justice James Wood and a NSW Child Protection Council report which revealed that 31.6 per cent of child victims had been abused by kids under 16, Father Chris set up Australia's first residential treatment program for juvenile sex offenders on 22 September 1997. Costing $600,000 per year, the Milestones Program began with four 12 to 15-year-olds living with a team of youth workers and counsellors at an undisclosed location in western Sydney for between nine and 12 months of intensive therapy. The aims of the program were to allow, and to encourage, adolescents to take full responsibility for their behaviour; to identify and understand the pattern of abuse; and for the kids to learn how to interrupt the cycle and control themselves in order to prevent it from happening again. They also had to face up to the abuse they'd usually suffered themselves as children and their own family situations, as well as try to develop empathy for, and awareness of, their victims. Strategies were developed to prevent each child from relapsing, along with ways of making restitution and reparation to their victims and the community. Importantly, they were also being taught good relationship and communication skills so they might develop much more positive outlooks towards other people, and understand the limits of appropriate behaviour. The program also offered help for bewildered parents. They were reassured that their sons (they were nearly always male) were by no means alone in committing sexual offences and that, while it wasn't known why some teenagers offended and others didn't, the experts were learning all the time about what contributed to sexually abusive thoughts and behaviour, and how to help them control their impulses. Father Chris ardently hoped that similar programs might be set up in other States, indeed he publicly called for them to do so.

Father Chris's denunciation of adult paedophiles at the Royal Commission as well as public declarations that he would stop kids from being victimised by them, followed by the Milestones Program, won the priest plenty of enemies as well as fans. This came as little surprise to Father Chris. In the past, as his public profile continued to rise, so did the number of death threats he received on both his mobile phone and his answering machine at home. Sometimes they'd be from parents, often drug-addicted, who were angry that he had taken over from them in looking after their kids. Now, however, the number of threats spiralled. He tended to laugh them off, and certainly the thought of being intimidated by them never seems to have crossed his mind. "He isn't a man who would be put off by things like that," says Prue MacSween. "He's far too courageous — and determined."

Even when those death threats came at the most inopportune moments, Father Chris's enthusiasm for his mission failed to be dampened. In January 1998, Father Chris was nominated as Australian of the Year, with the award eventually going to Olympic athlete Cathy Freeman. Just as he was entering the hall for the ceremony at which he was to receive one of five Australian Achiever Awards his phone rang.

On the other end was a caller repeating the now familiar words that he'd soon be killed if he continued his campaign against paedophiles. Father Chris shrugged, and hung up. "I thought, 'Oh yeah, God's keeping me humble'," he laughed afterwards. "Just when I might be getting too proud, He kicks me in the guts. It made me remember that the Award, after all, wasn't so important in the scheme of things."

Chapter 20

A Cash Crisis Bites

WHEN FATHER Chris first started teaching, drugs were virtually unknown. Now, they'd changed everything. With so many young people trying drugs early in life, the stakes had risen so much higher. It would take most kids abusing alcohol a long time to kill themselves. With drugs it could be instant, and often was. According to a 1997 National Drug and Alcohol Research Centre study, 70 people died from drug overdoses in 1979. By 1995, that annual toll had reached 550. The slow damage drugs caused was often cataclysmic too. It was estimated in 1997 that 100,000 Australians were regularly using heroin, 8000 — mainly young people — were in gaol because of drug-related crime, and 70 per cent of the total prison population were drug-dependent. Father Chris came to hate the power that drugs held over so many people. He could work so hard with a kid at getting his or her life back in order but there was always the danger that they'd turn back to drugs for help to get through a rough patch.

"When you see some of these kids, they are beautiful, bright, funny, sharp kids who are ready to take on the world," he says. "Then the very next day they could be back using, and it's just devastating to see how quickly their lives can come undone."

David was a tragic case. He was staying at the refuge at Marrickville when Father Chris approached some friends to ask if they'd employ the boy in their company so he could take his forklift truck licence test. They agreed and, after David gained his licence, they offered him a permanent job. David soon formed a close relationship with the office manager, Bob, who took the 18-year-old under his wing. Bob became friendly with the boy's probation officer too and, whenever David failed to turn up for an appointment, Bob would yell out, in front of everyone, "David! Why didn't you see your probation officer last night?" He would often good-naturedly tease David that he hoped a judge would put him in gaol if he didn't do exactly as he was told. David occasionally got his own back, though. Under pressure from Bob to supply a tax file number, David eventually insisted he'd managed to get a beaut: 1–2–3–4–5–6–7. Bob wouldn't believe him at first, but David was so persuasive, saying that *someone* had to get that number, that he convinced Bob to accept it. And then the tax department rang, to ask, "What's this 1–2–3–4–5–6–7 about?"

Sadly, Bob contracted cancer and died soon after. David was heartbroken. Outside the church, before the funeral, he seemed agitated, and said he wanted to do something for Bob. He entered the church a little later holding a single flower and then, as the entire congregation held their breath, walked up the aisle, knelt down by the casket and placed it carefully on the ground underneath. As he turned and walked back out, there wasn't a dry eye in the house.

David moved on to another job and had a baby with his girlfriend but, sadly, his past came back to haunt him. Early in 2002, he died of a drug overdose. "Whenever anything like that happens, Chris takes it on himself," says the employer who doesn't want to be named. "He says maybe he should have done something differently. He takes it very hard."

"There have been many terribly tragic disappointments where kids have been unable to cope without drugs," says Sir William. "After going through some *Youth* programs, and in some cases, having seemed to have exorcised their demons, there have been young people who have gone on to commit suicide. But *Youth* can only do so much. Chris can turn their lives around, but when they leave the programs they may come up against the terrible plight of youth unemployment in this country, or face overwhelming pressures, and some of them fail to cope."

Some of the drug deaths of Father Chris's kids were, of course, accidental overdoses. For a kid who's been off heroin for a while, taking the same dose as he or she may have taken in the past can prove fatal. Many drugs sold were also contaminated. In order to slow the tide of young drug deaths, many experts working with drug-takers in the area were talking harm minimisation — concentrating on keeping users safe and healthy rather than making it more difficult to buy drugs — decriminalising drugs, running experimental trials providing heroin to registered addicts and providing safe shooting galleries for users. Father Chris was adamantly against all of these approaches. He maintained his argument that a far more effective strategy was to give kids a safe environment, with people who genuinely cared about their welfare, so they wouldn't *need* to resort to drugs to feel better. He believed this passionately. "If you ask any of the kids whether heroin should be made more easily available, I'm sure the majority will say, 'No way'," says Father Chris. "They'll say, 'It's destroying my life, I need to be helped off it, rather than it being made easier for me to use.'

"Drug use, in my kids' cases, is a symptom of abuse. We are not resolving any of the pain kids go through. The real fix is to heal the brokenness, make kids feel like they belong and are valued, hold them close to us when we feel like pushing them away, offer them employment and give them futures. We don't want to get caught up with 'quick fixes' and 'political correctness' or be held captive by those who have a vested interest in these 'trendy' options." While Father Chris's stance was well-liked in the heartland of his older, conservative, Catholic supporters, it wasn't particularly popular among other organisations that helped kids with drug problems. Wesley Noffs, for instance, the director of the Ted Noffs Foundation, says that Father Chris's outspoken stand drove a wedge between the priest and many of the others striving to help kids. "He put a lot of people's noses out of joint with things he said and did like that," says Wesley. "We had philosophical differences."

At the other end of the spectrum, an increasing number of people were calling for the NSW Government to introduce custodial sentences for drug addicts. Every expert in the field agreed this time that this would be a travesty. "We know that locking up kids doesn't work," sighs Father Chris. "It's the easiest way to deal with juvenile crime, and the Government would be seen to be doing its job, but that's no way to break the cycle. There's no rehabilitation inside, no drug counselling. It's not a real, long-term solution." One of Father Chris's most potent arguments in calling for the parents to be punished, rather than their children, has always been to quote some of the chilling stories of the kids he'd had in his care. Little wonder, he'd say, that boys like 18-year-old Corey ended up on heroin. His mother started him on drugs at 13, injecting him with amphetamines — giving him Hepatitis C along with the dose — and then started sending him out to steal to support her drug habit. Unable to read or write because his family was always moving around the Central Coast so he never went to school, the most devastating blow, however, was yet to come. He was later told that his uncle, his mother's brother, was really his father.

It was no surprise either that boys such as 13-year-old Jim also became heroin addicts. Father Chris had pulled out the 50-page report on Jim many times. It revealed the boy's abusive childhood, including being slapped severely by his mother, having his head cracked against his younger brother's by his drunken father, and then being whipped with electrical cords. The abuse only got worse: his father progressed to holding Jim's head underwater, belting him if he cried and at any time Jim's father would forcibly have sex with his wife in front of the children. She left a few times, but always came back, terrified that her husband would carry out his threats to shoot her. Finally, he began sexually assaulting Jim.

Treating those drug-dependent young people was obviously a far better option than punishing them, but most parents who stumbled into the world of drugs for the first time via a son or daughter with problems were always astonished to discover how few detox beds there were for kids in this country. In February 1999 entertainer Normie Rowe, whose daughter had been a heroin addict, wrote a passionate feature for a newspaper about how shocked he was to learn that the previous year there were only 21 places for juvenile detox, evaluation and referral in the whole of Australia — and they were all in NSW.

The Dunlea Drug and Alcohol Centre for Adolescents had been relocated from its home in Campbelltown when the lease ran out in late 1999, to a new premises on the site of a Marist Sisters' convent at Merrylands, in Sydney's west. The demand for places there, at the refuge and at the farms was escalating, with daily waiting lists of at least 30 kids, but Father Chris was struggling to cope on the resources he had available. He sent some of the boys off on a new cattle drive to help them get away from drugs, as an alternative to sitting around Sydney waiting for beds to become available. At some points during the drive, the boys were sleeping on the ground in a Bathurst winter of minus six degrees. "They were so cold, yet they never gave up," says Father Chris. "Those kids who embraced this journey are among the most courageous I've ever seen. They were so committed to getting their lives together.

They then travelled to Maitland for a warmer climate but, sadly, they were met by days of rain. As they sat in their saddles, travelling the long paddocks, rain soaked through them and flu took hold. One ended up in hospital for four days. I felt ashamed that I couldn't take better care of my kids. I could find no room or no home except the freezing and wet backroads of NSW. So many empty buildings and homes, so few with so much, and yet these kids live in poverty."

That cash crisis dragged on. Every time Sir William saw Father Chris, the first question he'd ask was, "How are the finances?"

"I think I got on his nerves," smiles Sir William. "But he's always had such great difficulty, to put it mildly, in saying 'No' when there's a young person in need he wants to help." Television journalist Mike Munro was startled to hear Father Chris confess one day to him that even while *Youth*, at the time, was an organisation with a turnover of $2 million, it never had more than $50,000 spare in the bank. At first, Father Chris's projects had been funded via private money. Later, he'd discovered that his organisation was entitled to receive money from DOCS for allocating places on his programs for kids who were referred by the Department. When he started requesting contributions, however, suddenly DOCS wasn't as keen to use his services. The Department referred fewer kids to Father Chris's programs, saying they couldn't afford it. He had no idea why they thought, in those circumstances, that he could.

Even when the Department did refer kids to Father Chris's programs and made a commitment to pay for them, they didn't always deliver on their financial obligations. But when *Youth* funds got extremely low, he insisted on it. DOCS and Juvenile Justice, he claimed, had reneged on their promise to pay *Youth* to take care of five young people who they had referred to the service. In a strongly worded letter to Community Services Minister The Hon Faye Lo Po in February 1999, he demanded the $60,000 he said his organisation was owed. Among that group of kids was the 11-year-old who'd been dubbed the mini-crime wave. He'd ended up staying at Better Homes Farm for two years before returning to his mum — at a cost of $23,410. Another resident was a 12-year-old who, before being cared for by *Youth*, had been virtually starved over a two-week period, mutilated his own arm and had been working with an adult gang. A third child, aged 12, had been taken in by Father Chris after his mother was taken to gaol and he was discovered to be in the care of his heroin-addicted dad in a suspected drug-dealing den under police surveillance. The Minister called an urgent meeting between Father Chris and DOCS Director-General Carmel Niland, and *Youth* received their money.

Father Chris continued pulling out all stops to raise money. A CD was released, *One Hope One Dream* by Christian band Graeme Swords and Friends, featuring 13 songs about life as a young person in today's society. A second book of poetry and artworks, *Streetlights 2*, was published. One of the poems was written by a streetkid who was in gaol at the time, as a plea for understanding of the plight of those living on the streets. It started:

I'll write you a poem from the heart,
And sit back and see if you tear it apart.
I once was in love, now in pain,
Sitting in gaol, rotting again.

The author was released from prison shortly after penning this poem. He walked to a railway station and threw himself to his death in front of an oncoming train. His words had been a final attempt to explain his life to people before he'd resolved to die.

Another rodeo was held at the end of the 1998 cattle drive, which raised around $10,000. Even more important than the money, however, was the way the locals applauded feverishly every time a kid managed to stay on an animal's back for more than a few seconds. One of the organisers, Tony Hallam, was glowing in his praise. "You meet these kids and realise they've never had a chance, and some of them are the sorts of kids that you'd keep and feed yourself if you had the money," he said.

Father Chris appealed for donations from everywhere. He experienced some successes — and some bitter disappointments when pledges of cash sometimes never materialised into the real thing. But he tried everything.

He helped organise a $150-a-head "Guess Who's Coming To Dinner" function where celebrities are seated among paying guests to raise funds. He found plenty of willing stars, including newsreader Jessica Rowe, swimmer Shelley Taylor-Smith, rugby great David Campese, TV personality Kim Kilby and TV host Andrew Daddo. Country music star Gina Jeffries performed at the launch of *Youth's* new Benefactors Program, and John Brown, emeritus chair of the Tourism Taskforce, brought up to eight the number of scholarships he was offering kids to allow them to finish their education. "He's a remarkable man," he says of Father Chris. "He picks up all the worst cases and turns them around with love, affection and discipline. He makes a marvellous contribution to society. I wanted to nominate him for Father of the Year, but the organisers wouldn't accept the nomination." At the annual dinner of John's Sport and Tourism Youth Foundation, businessman Solomon Lew bought Father Chris his regular gift of 10 tickets in the big $500-a-ticket raffle, with $60,000 worth of prizes. The priest ended up the most popular winner of the night. Those winnings were a big financial boost, as he sold many of the prizes to raise money for *Youth* — and gave one, a luxury train trip to Cairns, to his parents.

For the kids, free activities proved the best. Once, 29 of them went over to the Singleton army base for a week of activities. Soldiers and kids eyed each other warily at first but, over their stay, the kids learnt how to cope with new challenges and the soldiers began to see beneath the tough exteriors of the kids. At the farewell, Father Chris saw tears well in the eyes of both sides.

The Australian women's hockey team, on their arrival back in the country from the Commonwealth Games, dropped in and played a game of hockey against the kids at Key College. Father Chris was grateful. "They must have been exhausted from the gruelling tournament and a long plane trip, and yet here they are, running around the park with a group of streetkids," he remarked. A few people looked at him sideways — he looked far more tired than anyone else.

The day after his ordination, Father Chris said his first official mass.
He invited many of his students from Rupertswood and encouraged the
congregation to clap in time to the music. It was one of the most informal
services anyone there had ever seen.

i make the vow
forever to be
chaste

TOP: Following his first official mass, Father Chris was given a party by family and friends to celebrate his ordination. ABOVE: Father Chris's first job as a priest was at a school in Chadstone; he worked hard, in his own inimitable style, to make mass lively. LEFT: Bishop John Kelly lays his hands on Chris's head during his ordination ceremony at Oakleigh's Sacred Heart Church in 1982.

Photo by Michelle Darlington

TOP: Father Chris chats to a couple of residents at one of his farms, with Collingwood ever watchful by his side. BOTTOM: In 1997 Father Chris was the reluctant star of *This Is Your Life*. For a man who sees so little of his family, this is a rare picture of Father Chris with all of his siblings. FROM LEFT TO RIGHT: Peter, Wayne, Father Chris, Helen and Greg.

Photo by Andrew Taylor / The Sydney Morning Herald

ABOVE: Father Chris's faithful companion, Collingwood, followed him everywhere. The Great Dane was happy to give anyone a nudge out of the way in a bid to stand close to her master — even the wife of the Australian Governor-General, Lady Deane, at the opening of Mark David Farm.

LEFT: The cattle drives: a daring experiment that involved Father Chris putting a number of kids to work herding cattle along old stock routes through the countryside. They were a huge success.

LEFT: Father Chris where he's at his happiest — teaching the kids from his farms all over the Southern Highlands at his Matthew Hogan School.
BELOW: Australian Governor-General Sir William Deane is the Patron of *Youth Off The Streets*. Sir William is a wonderful supporter of Father Chris and the kids. Every Christmas, he made it a tradition to invite a number of Father Chris's kids to his official residence in either Canberra or Sydney for a fun-filled day of swimming, eating and socialising.

Photo by Valerie Martin

Photo by Frank Violi/News Limited

Photo by Judy Gorton

Father Chris alongside his great friend, Australian Governor-General Sir William Deane, with Lady Deane, during a boat ride in Canberra that followed Sir William's retirement as Governor-General. He and Lady Deane remain patrons of *Youth Off The Streets*.

Photo by Michael Perini/News Limited

Photo by Michael Perini/News Limited

ABOVE: Father Chris during one of his greatest challenges — a trip to war-torn East Timor to help children orphaned by the years of bloody conflict. It was to be a life-changing experience for everyone involved. RIGHT: Father Chris and the boys he took to East Timor on their service learning project. They ended up taking over the running of one of the orphanages while they were there.

There are not many quiet moments when Father Chris can take a break from his work, but when he does — seen here during a few minutes snatched at Better Homes Farm — Woods is always by his side.

The Property Industry Foundation also invited Father Chris and a group of kids on to one of the yachts in their inaugural sailing regatta. At the age of 45, it was the first time he'd ever been on a boat or, in the borrowed windcheater, dressed in white. The kids, however, ever resourceful, adapted quickly, and even managed to help the boat sail in second in their division. "I remember he got so excited to see their happiness," says Judy Gorton. "It's so obvious how much he cares for all the kids, and they see that."

Despite his ongoing financial troubles, Father Chris always felt he was being given the strength to keep going by the courage shown by the kids around him. One boy at the farm was devastated when his father launched custody proceedings to try to take him back. Eventually, with the priest's encouragement, the boy wrote his own letter to the Family Law Court to be read out during the proceedings. "Dad used to pick me up and throw us at the wall and smash our heads together," he wrote. "Dad used to get us to watch blue movies. Dad put us in a sheet and threw us down the stairs. Dad touched me on the penis. Dad took me to the police station and I jumped out of the van that was going 60 kph. Dad covered us with a pillow on our faces until we almost suffocated. Dad used to hurt my mum. I don't want my dad to know where I'm living. I don't want my dad to have my phone number. I don't want to see my dad. I don't want no one [sic] to know where I'm living but my mum."

There was a real need to raise more money quickly, because Father Chris desperately wanted to open a girls' farm. The rate of young women committing violent crimes had more than trebled in the five years to 1997, according to the NSW Bureau of Crime, Statistics and Research, with the reasons attributed to rising homelessness, drug addiction and abuse. Research at the State's main juvenile detention centre, Yasmar, supported these findings. It found that more than 90 per cent of girls currently remanded there had been sexually abused, and 80 per cent had drug and/or alcohol problems.

In early February 1999, the aim of establishing a farm for girls assumed a new urgency. Staff at Dunlea called to tell Father Chris that an 18-year-old girl called Remy had turned up, once more, in a distressed state. She'd been raped yet again by a friend of her parents, suffering vaginal bleeding and hurting badly. She was led to a bedroom by staff. Soon after, there was a crash. Staff ran back to discover she'd smashed a window and was trying to slash her wrists. They talked to her, calmed her down and then faxed Father Chris in the southern highlands to tell him how she seemed. He immediately resolved to open the farm. He told his *Youth* board of directors he'd be stopping the cattle drives to pay for it, and asked Dunlea to care for her until he could have her moved. But he couldn't get the farm opened quickly enough for Remy. A few weeks later, she was discovered dead in the back streets of Kings Cross, after a massive heroin overdose. Father Chris was shattered. At her funeral he hailed the young woman a hero. She'd endured seven years of sexual assault by a friend of her parents in order to protect her twin sister. She knew if she had left home permanently that the perpetrator would have moved on to her sister, who, even today, lives unaware of the sacrifice Remy made. Soon after, Father Chris opened a girls' farm off a dirt track at Marulan, near Goulburn, and named it Lois House, after one of *Youth's* greatest benefactors.

In the face of seemingly insurmountable problems, Father Chris always remembered young people like Remy as his champions. Someone once asked him what was needed to do his job. "All you need is the guts to get up again the next day and try again," he'd replied. "That's all you need. That's what these kids do."

Sometimes the circumstances of his kids plainly appalled him, and he wondered how on earth they managed to keep going. Twelve-year-old Adam, for instance, who often scowled and growled like a feral animal, was a mystery to Father Chris. Adam often spoke of suicide and was very definite in his plan not to be alive 10 years on. The only positive experience he could ever recall was visiting his paternal grandmother on a farm with his father, where he made friends with the animals. The rest of the time, he confessed, he felt totally unloved and wished he could be a fish that could spit poison at people.

Mike, 15, was another boy who tore at Father Chris's heart. Never good at schoolwork, he grew up with a brother who was always putting him down: telling him he was a low-life, and that everyone hated him. "Why don't you go and kill yourself?" he would say. "No one will miss you, kid." Father Chris took Mike to the farm and discovered he loved to work on bikes, cars, mowers and anything with a motor. "He's not stupid," the priest told the others. "If he really put his mind into something, I know he would succeed at it. But at present he thinks he is no good for anything because he's so used to people putting him down." Father Chris similarly came close to tears the day he received a letter from Christopher, a boy others had labelled as hopeless. "I am just writing you this letter to thank you for turning my life around," it said. "I am doing excellent at my TAFE course and at school I am doing good some time too. My mum and dad said to say hello. They love me more now thanks to you Farvs. Now I am building a vegetable garden and looking after a chicken because that's my responsibility. When I leave, I want a good job and to support myself. Thank-you Farvs for helping me."

In order to raise more money to keep his projects going, Father Chris organised a fundraising day in April 1999 at Luna Park in Sydney. The kids loved it, and *Youth* managed to make a healthy return. The highlight for everyone was the sight of a little five-year-old handing over his birthday money to Father Chris "to help streetkids".

Two of the kids who'd come along were from the new Lois House farm, two girls aged 16 and 19. They had a wonderful time wandering through the crowds, savouring the excitement and going on the rides. Life had just seemed to turn the corner for the 16-year-old. A former heroin addict, she'd been studying at Key College and had been making enough progess to be allowed to move up to the farm. On the wall of her new bedroom, she tacked up her goals: "To finish Year 11 and stay in stable accommodation and maybe even make my way back into mainstream school. I also want to get a part-time job and stay off the drugs." There, she met the older girl, another former addict. The two girls struck up a firm friendship. At Luna Park, in front of the big wheel, they caught Father Chris so they could have a happy snap taken with him. It was the last time they would ever be photographed.

On the drive back to the farm with two youth workers, the Toyota Landcruiser ran off the road and slammed into a tree on an isolated stretch of road in the southern highlands. The two girls, together with a 45-year-old youth worker were all killed. Father Chris received a call in the middle of the night from a neighbour saying there'd been a bad accident on the road, and he thought his kids may have been involved. He raced down there at 160 kph, and arrived at the same time as the police and ambulance.

Everyone at *Youth* was devastated by the three deaths. A memorial service was held at Better Homes Farm, with more than 100 people coming along to pay their respects. "The two girls had made the commitment to themselves and to me to leave drugs behind and make something of themselves," Father Chris told the crowd, his voice cracking. "They had all hope before them." He then took the rest of the kids aside and told them he wouldn't be around for a little while. They'd be able to call him on the phone if they needed him, but they wouldn't see him. A few of the kids touched him gently on the shoulder. A few days later, Father Chris conducted the funeral service for the younger teenager. She had loved balloons so, at the end of the ceremony, a big bunch were cut free to float through the sky — straight to Heaven. And then Father Chris disappeared, locking himself alone in his house to grieve.

"It was a terrible time for him," says Judy Gorton. "He was so sad. You could hear the sorrow, and the strain, in his voice. He was desolate. I think he felt that somehow it was his fault. He'd arranged the event at Luna Park, so he was to blame for their deaths. Of course, he wasn't. But he always takes it hard losing kids. He thinks of them as *his* kids. And they are, they're *his* kids. He loves them as if they are his own." Everyone worried that he might never recover from the tragedy.

Chapter 21

THE COURAGE TO EXPECT GREATNESS

W HEN FATHER Chris finally emerged from his self-imposed exile after two weeks, he seemed to have resolved his grief. It was just as well. There were a lot of problems facing *Youth Off The Streets* and since he ran every aspect of the organisation, he was the one who had to deal with them. Firstly, the grief-stricken husband of the youth worker was said to be thinking about suing *Youth* over the accident. Happily a lawsuit never eventuated. In time, a second house for girls, close by Lois House, was established and named Debra Benson House in memory of the dedicated youth worker.

As always, the cash crisis continued to bite hard. In March 1999, the charity had $400,000 in outstanding debts, and had been unable to pay its food bill for the past six months. Father Chris's phone was on the verge of being disconnected, and the Tax Office was about to take action over an unpaid bill. "It was very difficult there for a while," says Judy Gorton. "Father was saying, 'God will provide', and we were all thinking, 'Hell!'" Fortunately, a mystery benefactor stepped in at the last minute with a $1.6 million donation after hearing of their plight.

"But we were in major trouble, and we knew that donation would only get us off the hook for a while," said Father Chris. "We were so desperate, I was personally selling raffle tickets and I'd never done anything like that before. I was just so determined we weren't going to close down any services. I just kept thinking, 'I'm going to find the money, no matter how I do it'."

One of the difficulties was that he'd come to rely on a handful of very generous benefactors, supplemented by a host of community groups, church congregations and well-wishers running events.

The alternative, having to raise money personally, took up valuable time, and it seemed sometimes ridiculous to Father Chris that he was working so hard for cash that was obviously such a direct investment in the future of Australia. Sir William felt for him. He'd always considered it a problem for a man like Father Chris to even have to thank donors, cap in hand. "For Father Chris to go round saying 'Thank-you' to everyone who gives a few dollars strikes me as slightly nuts for someone who's given his whole life to looking after kids and giving away everything he's got, to live an extraordinarily underprivileged life himself," says Sir William. "For all the time he has to do that, it means time he's unavailable to teach and help the kids in the most direct way he can. From the point of view of the young people, that time would be better spent in a direct relationship with him."

Father Chris's parents formed a committee in Echuca to raise funds for *Youth* and set up a second-hand shop in

June 1999. They were soon raising over $1000 a week. Mavis worked behind the counter and organised the team of volunteers, while Kevin lugged around the furniture they stored in the shop next door. "We'd been retired for four years and felt it was about time we got back to work," says Kevin. But the reality was that they wanted to support their son. Every time they visited him at Canyonleigh, they marvelled at the work he was doing, and how well he coped with his charges. "There might be six kids smashing themselves to pieces and he says, 'Stop!' and they all do," says Kevin. "But he has the knack. He's been given the gift. It's not from us. I wouldn't have the patience with the kids to do what he does. I'd give them a clip around the ear. I tell the kids, 'I'll kick you in the bum if you don't do this'." The shop in Echuca was working so well that soon after second-hand shops were also set up in Singleton and Maitland.

It was obvious, however, that *Youth* couldn't continue limping along from year to year, with Father Chris setting up projects and then scrabbling, hand-to-mouth, to fund them. Patricia Marsland, a former consultant with the Australia Council, development director at the Museum of Contemporary Art and wine company manager, was recruited in May 2000 as the priest's deputy chief executive officer to work on restructuring the charity. When she started looking at the organisation, she was appalled. "They were in major difficulties," she says. "They had a real cash flow crisis." Part of the problem was that it had grown, almost organically, from a simple idea into a huge plate-spinning operation, with Father Chris running from one project to the next, able to do just enough at each to keep it going. "It was a very complex small business, but few people there seemed to be experienced in small business", explains Patricia. "They didn't even have a budget and they seemed to have little idea of what was being spent and what was coming in. Father Chris had been trying to do everything himself. They were heading very quickly for disaster. In time, it would have fallen over."

Patricia introduced a new management structure; a system whereby each of the 17 projects had responsibility for their own budgets and a team of personnel to support them, organising fund-raising — particularly from corporates — as well as supporting Father Chris in his ongoing plans. She also discovered that *Youth* had been undercharging DOCS by 50 per cent for all the kids the Government had placed with them and, as a result, hiked up their prices. Within two years, their assets had doubled, and the annual turnover increased from $3 million to $8.5 million. Today the organisation is also trying to broaden its support base by introducing more partnerships in place of one-off donations.

"The system now is that Father comes in with an idea and we make it happen," says Patricia. "It's all very much still his vision, we just provide the framework for him to operate within, so he can go and fulfil his dreams for the kids. He no longer has to run the day-to-day business. I think he's a fantastic man, an extraordinary man. With the right backing, I think he'll be able to do a hell of a lot more. He hasn't got halfway yet. He's fearless, and he will be even more influential than he is now, a true advocate for kids. His organisation could ensure that there's enough legislation passed to protect kids. He knows more about Australian youth than anyone else in the country. The sky's the limit for him." Patricia still finds it amazing to think that 45,000 streetkids have had contact with his programs since 1991, but that only 30 per cent of the charity's $8 million budget comes from the State Government. "It's outrageous that one of the largest residential programs is mainly privately funded," she says. "It costs $55,000 to feed, clothe and educate each person in *Youth* residential programs. It's much cheaper and, on most occasions, significantly better for the child, than the alternatives. Look at detention, the Director General, David Sherlock, has just noted to me that, in 2000, the daily cost to the community of a child in detention is $167,170 per annum. Our fee to the department is $55,000 and Juvenile Justice say they cannot pay it — even for children where a magistrate's advice is that the child be released to one of our facilities."

Youth grew like Topsy as Father Chris was able to mobilise more and more financial backing for his dream of supporting as many kids as he could who needed help. In the past, the perception of *Youth* within the community service sector was sometimes one of an organisation made up of well-meaning amateurs, rather than a sleek, powerful advocacy. Certainly, Father Chris has always been a great visionary — "A great big picture man but a little thin on the details" as radio host Alan Jones puts it — but his impatience, impulsiveness and eagerness to have everything set up yesterday meant that cracks were appearing in the business that could have, in time, become weaknesses. Now, with better processes and procedures in place, the organisation has become much more stable.

"Father Chris is a very dedicated, committed individual," says recently retired *Youth* board chairman John Bullwinkel, a corporate and investment consultant. "What we are doing is putting a framework around him that can grow with his vision and really support him in his role. We are putting a lot more professionalism around him to handle the business. It's gone from an Op Shop business to a major organisation that is subject to the same corporate governance issues as BHP and Rio Tinto. In the past, the organisation has sailed very close to the wind on a number of occasions, so we're determined to build a structure that will avoid that situation in the future. It's better for us to tap into the corporate sector effectively, than organise lots of dinners, particularly at a time when people are suffering from donation and charity fatigue."

Any change in an organisation, particularly a charitable organisation, can be painful, and *Youth* is no exception. Even today, there's a certain tension between the business gurus and those involved in the core business: caring for kids. Board meetings have become legendary for the often heated exchanges taking place. Mike Willesee, who's now become one of Father Chris's greatest supporters, laughs. "There's a big distance between him and his board," he says, delicately. "They don't understand him, and he doesn't understand them."

However corporatised the charity was becoming, there were always limits to the types of changes Father Chris was willing to endorse. Some charities globally have found that it's far more efficient to sell off buildings given by benefactors and erect cheaper, more efficient, purpose-built centres in their place, banking the profit to meet running costs. Others point out to their supporters that, with any bequest of property, it's imperative that an endowment also be set up to maintain it, since those costs can be phenomenally high, particularly with older buildings or those originally constructed for other purposes. Father Chris would never even consider such options. He's always placed great store on loyalty to those people who helped him set up *Youth* in the beginning. When the bloodletting over HIH's collapse started, for example, he was distressed to see Ray Williams in the firing line, someone who'd always been a kind and generous benefactor. He even wrote to a newspaper's letters page to tell people so. "I know Ray as a genuine and generous human being," he wrote. "What the public need also to know is that when HIH was at its peak, Ray Williams gave millions of dollars to various charities. Over a three year period, he gave us almost $1,000,000 ... What has happened is tragic and people will be made accountable. However, I hope in our quest we don't demonise a basically good man." He never regretted writing that letter, even when he had calls from some of his supporters saying they would never contribute money again as a result.

Today many more fundraising programs are now in place, including the Benefactor Program, providing regular donations via credit cards and direct debits from wages; the Bequest Program, encouraging people to include *Youth* in their wills; and targeted corporate sponsorships, like sponsoring a child's education for a year. Initiatives such as these have meant that Father Chris has been able to continue to expand *Youth*. A new service was set up outside Muswellbrook in the Hunter Valley on a 4.8 hectare property made available on a peppercorn rent by Dartbrook Coal Pty Ltd. It was named Holborow House after retired children's magistrate Barbara Holborow. Designed for younger children, mostly 12-year-olds, Holborow House is big enough to accommodate six kids, who all attend local schools while living in a family atmosphere at the farm and caring for the horses there. Jason was the first resident. He'd left home at the age of 10 unable to cope with family fights, and had ended up in a youth crisis centre. The second was John, a kid who'd started running away from home at the age of five. For both, it was the most stable home they had experienced in their lives. "This is the best place I've ever lived," Jason said after his first few months, "because they don't treat you like a little kid or a criminal."

The work of *Youth* was spreading further afield, too. A youth worker travelled to Narromine and Trangie, near Dubbo, to help locals who were organising camps for their kids as well as work experience, town discos, court support and schooling. On the Gold Coast, a new program, Connie's Place, was set up for boys aged between 13 and 17. There was also a new house erected on Mark David Farm by the Property Industry Foundation, who bought four houses from the Olympic Village at Homebush, transported them to Sutton Forest, and transformed them into two 10-bedroom homes. One was named PIF House, after the foundation, and earmarked for training programs for *Youth* workers, and the other became home to Mirvac House, a new program for young sexual offenders following the closure of the Milestones Program. Outside Juvenile Justice, it is the only residential treatment facility for young sexual offenders in the whole of Australia.

The establishment of Mirvac House meant that another dream of Father Chris's had been realised. Help was now available for kids like Marcus who was sexually assaulted by his father, saw the same happen to his sister, was again a victim when his mother's new boyfriend moved in, and then, unsurprisingly, turned sexual offender himself. At 10, he had assaulted two girls, aged five and six. He'd learned that behaviour from adults, Father Chris explains. He could well have thought that it was simply what boys did. The NSW Bureau of Crime Statistics reported that in the year 2000 there were 376 reported assaults by juveniles in the State who were aged between 10 and 17. Of these, 111 were charged, but generally it remains one of the most under-reported assaults because parents are loathe to seek help for, or draw attention to, their children who commit such crimes. Mirvac House offers treatment for eight boys aged 13 to 16.

Nothing seemed to be able to dampen Father Chris's enthusiasm for setting up new projects to help his kids. His fights with the board of *Youth* continued. "They often wanted him, quite understandably, to find the money first, then start the facilities," says Colleen McIntosh. "But he wanted the facilities first, then he'd worry about the money afterwards," says David McIntosh. "He's never seen a reason for *not* doing what he wants to do." That single-mindedness in his quest to do his best for the kids often knew no bounds. In January 2000, Father Chris took the McIntoshes out to the Dunlea site at Merrylands. Walking around the expansive grounds, he told them he was planning to buy it. "Which bit?" asked Colleen. "All of it," he replied, without turning a hair. When he told them the price, they blanched at how low it was. "You'd better get on your knees and pray," said Colleen. "You're diddling those nuns. You are disgusting," she joked. Father Chris had little compunction about the niceties of life when it came to providing for his kids. Two years later, in mid-2002, he set up McIntosh House on that same property, a halfway house project providing mentorship programs to young people.

Getting his message out to the wider community continued to be a top priority for Father Chris too. He held a Permission to Shine Brightly Youth Conference in April 2001, with representation from both international and Australian experts, and a forum for young people on the last day. A few months prior to this, he'd received his second nomination for Australian of the Year. He received his third in 2002.

As word continued to spread there were usually kids lining up for the chance to join one of his programs. Onlookers marvelled at how popular he was with them, and how easily he won over even the toughest, surliest of kids. Judy Gorton recalls the first youth pageant a group of *Youth* kids took part in at Darling Harbour. When Father Chris arrived, a frisson of excitement came over all the kids, thrilled that he'd come to watch them. They all raced over to him and asked the priest to mind their coats, look after their cigarettes, or hold their bags for them while they took part. "So he was standing there with all these plastic bags hanging off his arms and jackets and packets of cigarettes," says Judy. "It was just as if he was their real dad. That's how they treat him. Well, to many of them, he *is* their dad. Things like that are so beautiful to see."

Another quality the kids respond to is Father Chris's sense of fun. In the classroom, he jokes and plays with the kids, offering them chocolates for getting questions right. For many of them, he makes up the most ridiculous nicknames, which they also love. "He's just like a big kid himself," says Rachel, 19, one of Father Chris's big success stories. "At one point, he got hold of a big megaphone and started announcing classes through that. It was mad. He loved that thing."

Rachel's story is typical of many of Father Chris's kids, including her surprise at how tough he was prepared to be. Following problems at home, Rachel started running away. By 15, she had fallen in with a group of homeless people who introduced her to heroin. When she began stealing from her family to support her drug habit, including all of her elder sister's twenty-first birthday presents, she was finally asked to leave home permanently — although her mum, Lorelle, said she'd always be ready to help if Rachel wanted to quit drugs. Life on the streets was hard for Rachel and her boyfriend, who was also using, and he became violent toward her. "My world just spun completely out of control," she says. "It was terrible." One day, she called her mum and begged her for help. Lorelle picked her up and drove her to the country to see Father Chris, someone she'd been told about by a friend. Rachel expected Father Chris to be a kindly, sweet man, eager to help. He wasn't. "He was really hard on me," she says. "I didn't like him. He asked me what would make him believe I wouldn't run off with my boyfriend first chance I had and go back to drugs. He then told me to call him back when I'd had a chance to think about it."

Lorelle was hopeful but she was also at the end of her tether with worry about her youngest daughter and, if Father Chris had refused them, didn't know what she'd do. She'd been driving Rachel around in her car for a week, killing time, waiting for their appointment at the farm. She didn't know if she could do it for much longer. "I think he could see the desperation in my eyes," she says. "Before we went to him, she'd been using more and more, and getting sicker and sicker."

Rachel did call back, but she had to do it five more times before Father Chris eventually returned her call. "I think he was doing that on purpose, to see if I was really keen," she says. Father Chris finally admitted Rachel to Lois House but not long after her boyfriend began calling, pleading with her to come back, and making her feel guilty for all the times he'd bought her drugs. She left Lois House to be with him and quickly ended up in hospital following an overdose. Father Chris gave her a second chance; he sent her to Dunlea, where her boyfriend hung around outside, trying to lure her back. Rachel was strong, stuck with the program, and finally Father Chris allowed her to return to Lois House. She stayed there for two years, and hasn't looked back since. Today she works in one of *Youth*'s offices, is studying journalism at TAFE, and is hoping to go to university.

It's been a long hard slog. "At first, I used to dream I was back on drugs and then I used to wake up in a panic," she says. "Socialising was hard because I felt everyone was against me. I felt people were looking at me thinking I was a drug addict and wondering if I could be trusted. It's been very difficult." She even bumped into that old boyfriend recently at her college. "He said he was clean but he looked as if he'd been using," she says.

As for Father Chris, she's now one of his biggest fans. "I learnt you had to earn his trust, he wouldn't be friends with you straight away," says Rachel. "He'll give you attention if you show that you're doing well. So all the kids run around trying to get Farvs' attention. It's funny to see him now in an office. At school he was really relaxed. In the office, he's much more withdrawn. He relates to kids really well, but I think he doesn't relate to some adults."

Lorelle agrees. He can read kids accurately, guessing what, and how, they're thinking, but adults sometimes seem a mystery to him. "You can see the barriers going up inside him," she says. "I don't know how my life, or Rachel's, would have been without him. To the kids, he gives and gives and gives. Rachel loves him dearly."

Rachel is certainly grateful for the second chance she's had in life, and says she thinks of him as being more like the dad her real one never was. "He always had this saying about having the courage to expect greatness from our kids," she says. "On my nineteenth birthday, he sent me a fax saying, 'You have achieved greatness. Never look back.' Someone said, 'That's a bit extreme'. But I thought about it and thought, 'No it's not'. That was one of my biggest problems: not thinking I could achieve anything. Now I know I can, and he believes in me. Without him, I know I wouldn't be here today."

Chapter 22

REPAIRING THE DAMAGE

L IFE IS PERPETUALLY hard for kids trying to put their lives back together. Often, they are full of good intentions, but falter at the first hurdle. Or second. Or third. Many come along to a farm, or check into Dunlea to detox, but drop out halfway through. Usually, they return to both the streets and the drugs only to realise that the cold, hard reality of their situation bears little relation to the fantasies they build up while going through the miseries of withdrawal, or the dislocation of living in the country. They are then faced with the challenge of persuading Father Chris they are worth another try. He always makes the kids work at it. If they aren't sincere in wanting to change, then he doesn't want to waste his time on them, he reasons. After all, every place one kid takes, means one less chance for every other kid trying to change their life.

Many of the kids write to him, fax him, or phone him begging for another go. Their letters often make heart-wrenching reading. Rosie, who'd been allowed back into

Dunlea, was pretty determined to change. "I want to come back to Lois House when I finish here," she wrote. "I made a very bad decision, believing the drug world had something to offer me but when I got here, it was only a hollow, empty and unsafe place. Using is such a lonely place within myself. I look around now and I know that the drug life doesn't get any better. I want more than I've had in the past. Lois House gives me room to grow and a chance to make those changes. I want to complete my Higher School Certificate this year. I need your help again and I can only promise to try my best. I know, one day, I will be a big success story." Elizabeth, who had absconded from Lois House, was much more direct and to the point. "Please," she wrote. "Please, I want another chance to work my life out. The drugs are just a dead end for me. Sorry for disappointing you."

Tammy also knew that feeling of being torn between the past and a future all too well. She was another who had a false start before she really knuckled down to rebuilding her life. Her early years were tough. Her mother died when she was aged nine and, having never known her father, she was separated from her sister and they were each sent to different aunts. Tammy never settled with the aunt. The woman had three children of her own and Tammy felt she was treated little better than an unpaid skivvy, running around after the kids, cooking, cleaning and washing their clothes. When she turned 15, she walked out and never went back.

At first, she lived with her sister, who had, by this time, a flat of her own and a boyfriend. Soon, however, Tammy fell in with a group of friends who were all smoking heroin. She joined them. Her sister's boyfriend disapproved of Tammy's lifestyle, and said she was no longer welcome to stay. Tammy didn't mind. She'd fallen in love, and went to live at the house of a friend of her new boyfriend, Mick. It didn't last long. She hadn't known Mick was injecting heroin and, when she found out, he persuaded her to try. Before long they were kicked out of the house when he stole his friend's cameras to raise money for drugs. They ended up sleeping on the streets for months, in shop doorways, on pallets out the back of shopping centres and in parks, often shivering under sheets of cardboard to keep warm. Eventually, Tammy got a bed at Marrickville, and a place at Key College. She weaned herself off heroin, and ended her relationship. Mick started hanging outside Key College every day, calling, "Tammy, Tammy, come back!" but she managed to resist. From the refuge, she moved into independent living accommodation, yet had a row with the people running the project. In the end Tammy left and with nowhere else to sleep every night she hunkered down in her sister's car, which her sister would park across the road from her flat.

"I rang Don Bosco House and said, 'I'm really sorry'," Tammy explains. "I asked if I could come back." Eventually, she was allowed to return, but only under strict conditions: that she leave the refuge at 8 a.m. and not come back until 8 p.m., to ensure that she wouldn't hang around all day, doing nothing. It was the turning point she had hoped for. Her results at Key College were among the highest achieved at the college ever, and she started working part-time to try to save some money.

Today, aged 19, she works full-time for *Youth*, is taking extra courses and plans to become a youth worker. "Without Don Bosco, I don't know where I'd be," says the bright, bubbly blonde in a T-shirt enscribed with the word "Angel". "I first met Farvs at Key College and I think he's just a legend. He's excellent. He's so kind and caring and giving. He would give you his last dollar if you needed it. It's amazing what he's done for so many people in just 10 years. He's the patron saint of kids!"

But if the kids ever thought Father Chris was tough on them, leaving them hanging on whenever they came back for help a second time, he was always much tougher on their parents. Once, he was looking after an 11-year-old kid called Jack on one of his programs whose parents were both in gaol. Jack had just revealed to Father Chris that he'd been sexually abused by his older, intellectually handicapped brother. When Jack's father found out, he wrote him a heartfelt letter from his prison cell. "Jack," the letter said, "you told me if I ever came back to gaol, you didn't want to see me again. Well, if you decide that then I understand little mate, as I have let you down time after time. I hope you will forgive me for not being there for you when you needed me. You know I love you more than life itself. So if there is anything you want to talk about, you can, matey. I don't know what's going on but I swear if anyone has hurt you, tell me mate. I love you buddy, so all I want you to know is that I'm here for you." Father Chris was totally unmoved. "The fact is that Jack was obviously not as important to him as crime and drugs were," he said. "A father should be with his son to make sure no one hurts him. That can't be done from a gaol cell." Jack was the tragic victim of two parents who really didn't care enough, believes the priest. By 14, Jack was dead from a heroin overdose.

Father Chris was equally angry with the drug-addicted mother of 15-year-old Monica. She'd started Monica drinking at the age of 14. "It's the best fun!" her mother assured her. Monica had to stay home from school all the time to look after her younger siblings and soon developed a drinking problem, followed a couple of years later, by the same drug addictions as her mum. Her mother had effectively destroyed Monica's life as well as her own.

There were so many cruel, manipulative parents around that sometimes Father Chris just despaired. When he was staying in the shed at the back of the Marrickville refuge one night, there was a banging on his door at 3 a.m. It was a kid called Matt who was staying at the refuge, asking for a counselling session. Father Chris almost turned over and went back to sleep, but the kid sounded desperate. He recalled what one of his Boys' Town mentors, Father Denis Halliday, had always told him, "Don't let one go by". He answered the door and sat with the boy in the kitchen. Matt had always had terrible trouble sleeping and now he wanted to talk about the way he was "raped in his dreams". Gently, the priest quizzed the boy about what exactly he meant. Gradually, the story came out. Matt had been heartened when, at the age of nine, his new stepfather began building Matt his own special bedroom. It was under the house, had no windows and only one point of entry. Soon after it was finished, his stepfather slipped into the room when Matt's mother was out and sexually assaulted him. For Matt, there was no escape, and he felt there was no one to tell. He began running away, establishing a pattern he couldn't break — even at Don Bosco. At the age of 26, he ran away for the final time: he killed himself. At his funeral, his sister approached Father Chris. Her earliest memory of Matt was of him hugging her and whispering in her ear that he adored her, and if anyone ever messed with her, he'd sort them out. She'd never forgotten it. "You know, he would have literally killed to protect anyone he cared about," says Father Chris. "There may be wild kids, but they often have such incredible loyalty to anyone who cares for them. His life had been ruined, but he desperately wanted to make sure hers wasn't."

Far too often, it seemed, these kids could never quite escape a tortured past, no matter how hard they tried. Their history had a terrible way of catching up with them. Sometimes they just couldn't shrug off the dark memories that were haunting them even if, on the surface, everything looked bright. Father Chris was particularly rocked by Danny's case. He was a kid who'd got into the habit of ringing the priest every Christmas Day. Even though the priest had not seen the young man for six years, Danny always remembered to call. This year, he sounded positive. His twin three-year-old daughters were fine and he also had a four-month-old son with the girlfriend he adored. He was then 22, fit and healthy. "Hey, I'm really looking forward to seeing you, Farvs, sometime soon," he said. A week later, his girlfriend rang Father Chris: Danny had hung himself in the garage behind their house. Overwhelmed by a sense of sadness and loss, Father Chris sat at his desk, his head in his hands, still cradling the phone, and wondered if he was, truly, making a difference. The girlfriend, still on the other end of the line, interrupted his thoughts. "He's at peace now, Farvs," she said calmly. "You know, he always wanted to die. There was nothing you could have done," she continued, now tearful. The reasons why were all in Danny's file that Father Chris pulled out that afternoon. Rejected by his mother, the sensitive and intense young man had never really recovered. He'd once said he couldn't love anyone, as his mother had never loved him. At a very early age, she'd kicked him out of the house with the cruel words, "No, I don't love you. I never have. Get out."

Danny had then gone through a long line of institutions and community placements — over 50 since the age of seven — and had been abused in one of these at the age of 12 or 13. He'd been talented at sport, clever with music, intelligent and motivated, but had never recovered from his mother's rejection. Once, Danny had even played Russian roulette. He'd acquired a revolver, put one bullet in the chamber and spun it round. He then put it to his temple and pulled the trigger. When it did not go off, he took it as a sign that he should live. Later, however, when he was arrested, he attempted to hang himself in custody. A previous girlfriend and his best friend had been killed in a car crash and he'd lost another friend to drugs, so Danny had begun to see death as a constant companion.

Sad stories like these helped Father Chris continue to believe so passionately in the essential goodness of kids. They were only corrupted by their parents, or their environment, or the people around them. And it was up to everyone in this country to help them out of the mire. "We need to change the culture of the expectations we have of our kids," says Father Chris. "I believe that the culture of negative labelling needs to be replaced by adults who have the courage to expect greatness from our kids. We must see all kids as kids of promise. We must believe that goodness is in all children. We must develop environments where kids can flourish, learn generosity and have a valuable role to play in society. Kids are not born bad, they are born and learn any badness from us. We must take responsibility for the way they are. And then we have to give them the chance to achieve."

In many cases, this philosophy has been successful. Two kids took up *Youth* youth worker apprenticeships, lots passed their exams, many, many found jobs and some even returned home, stronger and reconciled with their families.

Some of the hardest kids have come good. Even aggressive heroin addict Ben — the boy featured on the TV program *Hinch* for making negative comments about those trying to help him — did well. After his time at Better Homes Farm, Ben stayed away from Sydney and found the perfect job in Adelaide: he became a demolition worker. Today, at the age of 27, he's engaged to be married, he's just got his driver's licence (even though he's been driving for 15 years without one) and has been clean of drugs for eight years. Life is looking good. "I was one of his first kids," says Ben, "and it's all credit to him that I'm still alive. So many of the people I was on the streets with are dead now. If it wasn't for him, I would have joined them. A lot of people tried to help me, and they ended up getting onto drugs and having the same problems as me. But he was very strong-willed. I owe him my life."

Father Chris's strong will, however, has often caused trouble elsewhere. Frequently, Father Chris becomes so wrapped up in the problems of his kids, and so determined to help them, that he refuses to brook any dissent from anyone he sees as getting in his way. He clashes regularly with officials from DOCS and Juvenile Justice.

"He's absolutely fearless," says fellow teacher Adele Sims, in awe. "He's like a bull at a gate. He just goes for it. He gets so fired up." Once a child was killed in a big traffic accident on the Glebe Island Bridge and newspapers and the radio airwaves were filled with people complaining about how long cars were being held up and how much the accident had cost. It was as much as anyone could do to stop him taking a few of the kids from the farms, lining them up on the street and making the point that the child's life was the most important issue at stake.

His obsessive nature can also make him hard on his staff too. With so much focus on the kids, there's not always much time left for anyone else, and sometimes those working with him find that difficult. Some feel he should be giving them more support in jobs that, to be fair, are among the toughest in the child welfare field, particularly when they are so isolated on the farms. Invariably there has been a high turnover of youth workers at his organisation for this very reason. Others baulk at his huge expectations of them. He is dedicated, committed and available for 24 hours every day, and often he can't understand why others aren't too. "It's hard to live up to his standards," says Bernie Eviston, a teacher at Key College. "Being a priest, you'd think he'd have a big understanding of the importance of human connections and family. But no, he wants everything done in five minutes as if you don't have anything else in your life, or families. But he's mellowed a bit now, and the organisation is trying to support us more. But it can be difficult. You feel you shouldn't ask for a pay rise because suddenly you're made to feel part of the charity. That's hard." The teachers at all the schools are paid award wages.

Adds Lois House's Millie Kellett, "He's so very busy, and has a lot of time for children, but not much at all for adults. He does expect a lot of you but that's probably because he gives so much himself." Yet when staff do get as involved in the lives of the kids as he is, it can prove equally problematic. Unlike Father Chris, his staff tend to have problems keeping a balance. One teacher at Matthew Hogan started getting very emotionally involved with her class. When a child ran off one day, she followed him, leaving the rest of the kids alone. "She was a real mess," says Adele. "We had to explain that what we needed at the school was a teacher. The kids have got other supports, care workers, psychologists, social workers. But education is their way off the horrible slippery slope to ruin."

For Father Chris, there were excruciating lows away from work as well. In May 2001, his elder brother Peter was killed in an industrial accident. He fell on to a bed of steaming coals at his workplace and died almost instantly.

The family gathered sadly for the funeral, only the second time they'd been together in years.

Shortly afterwards, Father Chris's constant companion, Collingwood, also died. She was mourned by the kids too — they reckoned she'd probably looked after 40,000 of them in all the time she'd been accompanying her master. In the early days, the kids were tough on her, but she always thought they were playing, so she never retaliated. It would only take one bark from her to stop them running in the house, break up fights and, once, terrify a young thief into handing back the biscuits he'd stolen from the kitchen. Soon after, Father Chris took on a new dog that he named Woods, another black and white Great Dane in the colours of his favourite AFL team Collingwood.

Another cycle that was coming to a close was Sir William Deane's tenure as the Australian Governor-General. With characteristic humility, he decided to forgo a grand exit to share his last vice-regal lunch with Father Chris and the kids. On his final day in the position, in June 2001, he welcomed 27 young people for a last meal of roast beef and chicken, vegetables and home-made ice cream at his residence. Sir William knew the publicity his departure would receive could at least help his favourite charity. His words in his final speech echoed his deeds. "The principle I've been trying to get across to people for my whole time as Governor-General is that the ultimate test of our worth as a nation is how we treat the most vulnerable and disadvantaged of our people," he said.

He didn't forget his usual gifts of money to the kids, either. As he handed out the magic envelopes, he reminded them to give half to someone they loved and admired. Yet even he was stunned by the effect of his words. "To my amazement, most of the kids automatically pulled out half and handed it over to Chris," he says. "He had no hesitation in thanking them profusely and taking it for what he obviously thought was an extraordinarily good cause. While the individual cases are often terribly hard, it's always a great joy to be privileged to be, in a minor way, part of Chris's work. He is an inspiration." Father Chris was equally admiring of the friend who had done so much to make his mission a success. "The great thing this country needs is a champion of social justice, and that is what he has been," he said on Sir William's departure. "I don't think this country has ever had a Governor-General who is so well-loved and respected." The kids presented a gift to Sir William, a man who'd always been so good to them: a framed collage of pictures of the teenagers with their messages of thanks and poems. It now hangs in his home in Canberra.

And with that, Sir William, Lady Helen, Father Chris and all the kids stepped on to a boat to cross Lake Burley Griffin, a journey that would lead to the Governor-General's new role as a private citizen. However, before he departed from public life altogether, he told Father Chris of a decision he and his wife had made. After much soul-searching, he and Lady Helen had resolved to stay on with *Youth* as joint patrons. Father Chris was overjoyed.

Chapter 23

PRIEST MAGIC

WITH 18 different projects operating by the end of 2001, it's hard to imagine how one person can keep on top of everything that is happening at each of them — particularly if that person is stuck at the end of a dirt road in the middle of the southern highlands. But Father Chris, in between doing his regular shifts sleeping over at Foundation House, teaching at Matthew Hogan School, spending time at each of the programs, travelling to the country to raise funds, and occasionally spending an evening at his rented house close by the farms at Canyonleigh, manages to keep a firm grip on the whole empire by phone and fax. Even when he's travelling, he's receiving calls and faxes in the backseat of his 4WD while his driver Ken is at the wheel, dashing off memos, planning new projects, responding to discussion documents, preparing speeches and writing reports on the various kids in his care. Every evening, the person on duty at every centre faxes Father Chris a summary of the day's events: detailing any incidents, discussing the progress of participants, mentioning any staff issues and making a note of upcoming important dates, for example, kids' birthdays. Thus he manages to keep a handle on it all.

That's often a big surprise for the kids involved in any of *Youth Off The Streets'* programs. At Key College, for instance, the kids don't see him very often, but stories about this mysterious "patron saint of kids" abound. In their eyes, he's very much a remote figurehead, an almost mythical person who's all powerful in being able to decide the course of their lives. When he does occasionally drop into their school, and chats to them about how their project on ancient Egypt is going, or whether they're working harder at their maths after scoring only 17 per cent in the last test, they're completely taken aback at how much he knows about their lives. "I'm constantly astounded by his recall about the kids," says Key College's Bernie Eviston. "He'll always find something to say to the kids, as if he knows them well. It can be an awful shock for the kids." By the same token, if he ticks off a kid about their lack of progress, most are too stunned to do anything but solemnly promise to do better.

Among the kids, stories about "Farvs" acquire an almost legendary status. A number of them talk about how, when he's angry, he touches his dog collar. That's how they'll know he's going to swear at a kid, and give them a thorough roasting. The myth seems to have started when Father Chris once attempted to stop a dog fight and was bitten on the finger for his trouble. He had taken off his collar before swearing out loud in pain. Over the years, Father Chris has been mystified at how powerful the gesture of touching his collar has proved. The kids watch out for it. "It's true," insists Sara, 16, at Lois House. "Touching his collar is one thing, seeing him take it off is how you know when you're *really* in trouble." Fellow teacher at the Matthew Hogan School, Adele Sims, laughs. "Chris put his hand up to his collar one day and this kid just took off down the road," she says. "But it can be handy if the kids believe it!"

While they might fear Father Chris at times, the kids always remain enormously fond of him. He's the guy, after all, who's helped them when few others would, who's given them a roof over their heads, the courage to dream and, what's more, personal presents every Christmas and birthday. Many of his staff are surprised by how much significance he places on remembering each kid's birthday. But it's the little things, as he's always insisted, that are the most important. While he is so good at giving, however, he's appallingly bad at receiving. His personal assistant Judy Gorton remembers one year buying him a bottle of his favourite aftershave and a nice towel for his birthday. A few weeks later, she bumped into one of the kids on a sports ground. "Look at what Farvs gave me for my birthday!" he yelled, brandishing that very same towel in delight. It's as much as she can do at times to stop him going into shops and taking back a gift he's been given by a supporter in order to get the refund so he can buy something with it for the children.

There's nowhere better to see Father Chris's relationship with the kids than in his classroom at Matthew Hogan School, doing what he loves best: teaching. The school is little more than a collection of demountables placed next door to Better Homes Farm, linked by a concrete slabbed pathway littered with wombat droppings. All through winter, it's bitterly cold. The 45 or so students travel in from the *Youth* farms every day, with Father Chris always ending up with the toughest kids, a class of around 12 students of assorted ages. They sit shivering at their desks in big jumpers, fleeces, jackets and a colourful range of beanies. The atmosphere, though, is warm. Whether Father Chris is standing at the front of his classroom writing on the whiteboard, wandering through the room reading out words to test the kids on their spelling, or looking over their shoulders as they sit at the bank of computers, completing their maths programs, he is always interacting with his students. "Don't lick *him*, Woods," he says to his dog, as his Great Dane lollops over to a kid who's not paying attention. "You might get germs." He then jokes with a girl who is wearing her sunglasses propped on top of her head, "How well can you see out of them like that?". Another student complains that his computer is on the blink. Father Chris fixes it in an instant and, when the boy asks wide-eyed how on earth he did it, the answer comes without a second's hesitation, "Priest magic".

The kids' laughter is always genuine. Father Chris is tough, but his warmth and humour seem to make the lessons palatable. He employs a reward system that dates back to his early teaching days at Chadstone: chocolates are given out to anyone who correctly spells every word in his spelling tests, while the rest of the class is made to write out every word they misspelt 50 times. "It's only because I care so much for you," he tells one grumbling pupil. The kids are all eager for his attention and keen to please, calling out constantly how well they're doing in the test, asking how much longer is left of the class, some quibbling over the difference in the spellings of the words "bale" and "bail". "I would have thought all you kids would have got that second one right," says Father Chris to a murmur of good-natured accord. A girl yells out that she had to go to court the day before, so that's why she missed out on some of the English lesson. Father Chris teases her, "So why didn't they lock you up?" A boy who's continually asking for permission to go to the toilet is chided for not going before he arrived in class and Father Chris jokes that he'll be buying some nappies next time he goes shopping. "Remind me to put it on the shopping list," he says over his shoulder to another boy, who looks as if his attention is wandering. The boy looks startled to realise it was noticed.

Father Chris is strict, however, when the occasion demands. He snaps at one boy who's telling the other kids that he's going to Goulburn Gaol to visit backpacker killer Ivan Milat. "Don't be ridiculous," the priest says. "If you want attention, Tas, ask for *appropriate* attention." Another boy argues over how many maths problems he has to solve before he can go on his break. He's told quietly to stand outside the classroom. When everyone else is settled into their workbooks, Father Chris leaves the class to speak to the waiting boy. A few people in the class start talking the minute he's outside, but all eye the door gingerly; they stop and look back down at their books as soon as the door opens again. A girl who calls someone a f...ing dickhead is also asked to leave until she learns to moderate her language, and not put others down. During the break one of the boys twists his ankle during a quick game of footy and is then kicked by a couple of others. "It's difficult," Father Chris explains in a whisper. "That boy has offended sexually and is on the Mirvac House program. None of the other kids like boys who've committed those kinds of offences." Back in the classroom, in front of the class, Father Chris is a picture of rage. A hush falls over his students. "Michael belongs here with us," he storms. "He's got a great deal of courage. He's got issues, but he's dealing with them. We don't have people being picked on here. He has a right to feel safe. He has incredible courage and I believe in him a great deal. We don't make victims here. We care for everyone. We all have troubles, and we all deserve respect." The kids all look down at their desks.

During class, the kids often get out of their seats and wander around the room, to pet Woods, who is lolling about at the front of the room, to take a handful of tissues from a cupboard, to pick up a new biro. Many of them have very short attention spans, Father Chris explains later. For those who've been living on the streets for years, it takes a long time to get used to sitting at a desk for half-an-hour at a time. For others with a history of heavy drug addiction, or bad childhood abuse, concentration for more than short periods is now impossible. The lessons are therefore tailored carefully to their needs. School starts early, at 8.30 a.m., with a number of scheduled breaks, and ends early, at 1.50 p.m. This structure is strictly adhered to, since the kids need to know exactly what they're doing every day. The books they're encouraged to read are all, within the constraints of the curriculum, ones they'll be able to relate to most readily. The piles of books on the shelves include the American novel *A Child Called "It"*, Dave Pelzer's moving account of his own childhood as one of California's most severely abused kids, and its sequel *The Lost Boy* about overcoming the odds to survive and thrive. From Australia, there's Margaret Clark's book *Care Factor Zero*, the story of a wild child who comes to terms with her past and, eventually, her future; and Scott Monk's *Raw*, about a tough boy who's sent to a farm on a rehabilitation program — one with which all the kids, unsurprisingly, identify so easily.

Many of Father Chris's English lessons revolve around the kids watching parts of movies on DVD, and then reading the scripts out loud, with each kid playing an individual role. The themes of the films selected are all remarkably similar: triumph in the face of overwhelming adversity. Father Chris's favourites are eminently predictable — *Good Will Hunting*, *Dead Poets Society*, *The Hurricane*, *Finding Forrester*, *Gettysburg*, *Remember the Titans* and *Brubaker*. He believes in trying to inspire the kids via messages from films and books they can relate to.

The kids watch, spellbound, the part of *Brubaker* when Robert Redford, as an inmate at a brutally corrupt US prison, is finally revealed to be the new reforming governor who had gone undercover to seek out injustice. Father Chris then wrings out the moral of the true-life tale for his students. "Individuals *can* change institutions," he tells the class. "Sam, you are a 17-year-old Korean orphan, how can you help change the world?" Sam looks bewildered. "I can't, Farvs," he replies, shifting uncomfortably in his seat. He gets short shrift. "How dare you say that!" Father Chris thunders. "All change starts with just one voice. One of the difficulties of your life is that you've never met your natural parents. If you met them, that might make a huge difference to your life. And then you could help other kids in the same position find their parents." He looks around the room for another candidate. "Ben," he says, finding the perfect one. "You've been to gaol. What was it like? Why can't you ring a journalist at a newspaper and tell them what gaol did to you? They'll write a story that others will read and find out what gaol's like. Other kids won't want to go to gaol. People might realise they need to change the gaol system." He takes a deep breath and looks around the room. "There's no point in just saying that life sucks, or life is hard and you can't do anything about it. That's not true. You *can* change the world and make it better. Every one of you has that power." It's the kind of homily the priest likes to deliver at every opportunity.

At times, Father Chris's vision does tend to look rose-coloured, excessively optimistic and over-simplistic. Yet he works hard at preserving and pushing his beliefs every day in the cold, hard, unforgiving reality of those kids' lives. And, often, they respond. "With some of these kids, it's a long, hard haul," he confides during a lunch break one day, as the kids help themselves to sandwiches, fruit and warm pancakes. "They're tough kids. They play up. One kid couldn't read at all when he first came here but, because he loves the movies, he's now really making great progress with reading the scripts. One boy, who's very, very damaged, said he didn't want to read a book. When

he started on *A Child Called "It"*, however, he just
gobbled it up."

Most of the kids at the school seem to appreciate what
Father Chris is trying to do for them, and many say
they're very happy to give it a go. Jimmy, 15, says he feels
like he's become a much more positive person since he's
been in Father Chris's class, and that he doesn't focus on
the negative half as much. "I realise he's trying to help
me," he says in the break. "Even when he has a go at me,
he's not taking a potshot at me; he wants me to think
about what I'm doing. You know he's always going to be
there for you, even if he's angry or disappointed." Sixteen-
year-old Will feels similarly. "I explain my point of view to
him, and he says, 'Yeah, I understand that, but have you
thought of looking at it like this?' Some people talk about
Farvs as a modern-day saint. I don't know about that, but
he is so modest, he's a bit of an inspiration. He's very
forgiving. I'm finding this a life-changing kind of place.
You have to put in the effort, but hopefully it'll be worth
it." Joe has been converted into a fan too. "Farvs?" he
says. "He gives you a real second chance. He's as cool as."

Teacher Adele is amazed at how effective that second
chance often is. She says some of the kids arrive at the
school after having failed year after year after year at their
regular schools but they still, somehow, manage to turn
around and achieve either their School Certificate or their
HSC. A few, of course, do fall through the cracks, and
sometimes she finds that hard. "They'll get halfway
through the first term, then they're gone," she says. "I'll
look at Chris and say, 'What's the point?' But then he'll
say, 'They might have learnt 20 new words to take with

them.' When you look at it from that perspective, then nothing is a loss. But the hardest part of the job is when Chris is really struggling. He might walk in and say he doesn't want to do it any more. Then we're all on a downer. We rely so much on his support and strength all the time." The kids do too. "Oh, they love him and they're always so keen to win him over," says Adele. "They really respond to his firmness and fairness. He'll take their crap, and still be there."

After school, all the kids are ferried back to their farms, for sport, outings, service programs — for example visiting the elderly in a local old folks' home — chores, projects, sessions with a psychologist on topics such as anger management, or group meetings together aimed at cultivating an atmosphere of trust between each other, mutual support, motivation, and an overwhelmingly positive peer culture.

Lately Father Chris has been doing double-shifts at Foundation House across the dirt track from Better Homes Farm, because of staff shortages. He drives a few of "his" kids back there from school while the others walk. He then drives a couple of kids into town, 30 km away, for appointments with a doctor and a probation officer, letting them play with Gameboys during the journey as a reward for being good. He drops the boys off and then comes back for a case conference about one kid in his care, reminds two boys who are making toasted sandwiches to clean up their mess, sits in on an anger management group, instructs the kids about their chores for the day and inspects rooms before sitting at the dining table to attend to paperwork. In between all this, he ticks off Woods for trying to nip a workman she's taken a dislike to, who's helping with renovations to the house. Father Chris doesn't much like workmen being at the farm because their presence can be intrusive but he is adamant that all the *Youth* properties be kept up to scratch. If they're allowed to get rundown, then the kids will take less pride in where they live, and run them down further. For similar reasons, he always tries to make sure the kids have the best of everything, including quality furniture, decent clothes and even good manchester. "Giving them good things shows them that we value them," he says. "Then they'll start to value themselves and everyone, and everything, around them."

There are always problems for Father Chris to sort out too. On this particular occasion, he'd been in Sydney the day before, and all hell had broken loose at the farm in his absence. A particularly difficult kid had assaulted a youth worker following an argument, and had fled to Bowral. He'd since been phoning Father Chris, the other teachers, and a variety of staff members, throughout the day to ask if he could be allowed back into Foundation House and the school. Father Chris, who had been working hard to make progress with the boy before this incident, resolutely ignored his pleas. "He's a very charismatic and powerful boy who really psyches people out," he explains. "He's very intelligent, but very manipulative. Once he said I was the only one he hadn't been able to manipulate. But, of course, I couldn't even tell whether that was an attempt to draw me in. He tries to corrupt everyone around him. The other kids, though, have been saying they prefer it now he's gone." He falls quiet for a moment, and a pained expression crosses his face. "I wonder if I keep going with him, whether it'll end up harming the rest. I suppose I can't help everyone, but I find it very hard to let go."

He's also worried about another kid who's becoming increasingly more quiet and detached. His father killed himself, and his mother died of a heroin overdose. He's withdrawn, distrustful and finds it hard to make friends. In the anger management group, when he was asked what he was good at, his response was, "Falling down". Even the retort from the psychologist, "Right, so you must be pretty good at getting up again, then?" fell on stony ground. Then there's 16-year-old Larry, who's smart, funny, and intensely likeable but who has a problem with theft. The other day, he stole mobile phones from a worker at the farm and his visiting DOCS worker. He then stole a clock from Mirvac House. "What the hell would he want with a clock?" asks Father Chris, in despair.

Father Chris is always encouraged by the successes, no matter how small, his kids achieve. One 13-year-old had lost both his parents under traumatic circumstances: his father died of a drug overdose and his mother was murdered in front of him. The psychologist who'd examined him reported that the boy viewed himself as being completely worthless. "The most disturbed of all the children I've encountered in the child protection field" — the psychologist wrote. When the boy arrived at Foundation House, he was considered unpredictable, deeply traumatised and potentially dangerous. Certainly, he proved to be difficult, prone to temper tantrums and sometimes aggressive. However, by the end of his stay at the farm, the worst thing the boy had done was to steal someone's car. Another boy, now 15, is showing similar signs of progress. His mother was a schizophrenic heroin-injector, and he had been born a drug addict. He was taken into care at the age of two weeks. At 12, he was caught dealing drugs in a school playground. He suffered severe mood swings, sometimes resulting in violent outbursts, and a number of foster parents had found him impossible to cope with. Today, at the farm, he says "I kind of think there's no point doing drugs any more. There are better things to do with your life."

In the evening, Father Chris dishes out medication — medicine for a cold for one kid, asthma tablets for another, anti-depressants for a third — sends one boy to his room for five minutes for swearing, tells another he's going to have to start jogging so he won't get fat, then sits down with them all for a meal of braised steak, roast potatoes and vegetables. Over dinner, he talks to them about their day, the excursion they all went on last weekend, tobogganing at the snow, what one of the kids would like to do for his birthday in a week's time and how another boy was feeling about his first day of work experience due to start the next morning. "It's all about *being* with the kids, talking to them, and really listening," he says. After dinner, there's homework, then TV before bed for the kids, while Father Chris catches up on more paperwork, deals with all the messages that were left for him during the day, races back to his house for an hour to pick up his emails, organises someone to take a kid to court the next day, then makes the work experience lad a packed lunch — "The details show that you care", he repeats — and prepares lessons for the next day. At night he dozes, fully clothed, on a couch in his flat at the end of the corridor, behind a glass door through which he can see all of the kids' bedroom doors. "I'm used to it," he says. "I started doing it at Boys' Town and I've never known any different. I guess I haven't had a full proper night's sleep for years."

In the middle of that night, the phone rang. There was trouble at another one of the farms, Lois House.

Chapter 24

THE BLOOD AND THE PRIDE SPILL OVER

CANDY WAS one of the most difficult kids who'd ever been accepted into a *Youth* program. She was "a cutter": a girl who regularly slashed herself with knives, pieces of broken glass or anything else she could lay her hands on in order to damage herself. Psychiatrists call it self-mutilation; youth workers prefer the term self-harm. Either way, it's a tragic syndrome affecting a far greater proportion of our young people than most adults could ever imagine. It's believed today that up to one in every 20 16-year-olds has deliberately injured themselves. Many go on to suicide.

Candy had been accepted into Lois House, but it was proving hard on both staff and the other girls there. The kids found it really distressing whenever she tried to cut herself and, since self-harm is usually intimately related to feelings of complete isolation, misdirected anger and intense self-loathing — commonly a symptom of earlier sexual abuse — Candy often treated staff extremely badly, probably in order to provoke the kind of dislike she felt she deserved. That was immensely challenging for everyone. One worker admitted she found the girl impossible to like, which meant it was also not at all viable for her to work with Candy. Finally, one of the staff who'd previously worked as a nurse, Millie Kellett, moved with Candy from Lois House to Debra Benson House, 30 metres away, which was standing empty at the time. There the pair worked together intensely on Candy's problems.

They were making progress, but when Millie took a couple of weeks out to supervise another *Youth* activity, Candy dropped out and ran away. A crisis was declared. Everyone at Lois House was distraught, they feared for her life. Sexually abused as a baby, and then later in life too, Candy was still very vulnerable. Staff at Lois House alerted Father Chris by phone. There was nothing any of them could do. Millie decided she'd love to push — when funds permitted — to set up a program elsewhere of intensive one-on-one therapy for girls like Candy with such serious problems. "The difficulty is that we're getting more people across the board with serious mental health issues," says Millie. "People get tired and don't know how to heal these kids."

In the meantime, Debra Benson House is being considered for a program for teenage mums and their babies, while Lois House continues looking after up to six girls at a time aged between 12 and 18, in a warm, family atmosphere. The girls' problems are generally similar to those of the boys taken off the streets, sometimes with the added complication of being more vulnerable to the influence of pimps, or other male authority figures. One girl there, for example, was taught to steal at the age of six by one of her elder brothers. That talent then became her lifestyle — stealing to support the family, particularly after her dad died. Helping kids with such ingrained behavioural patterns is a lengthy process. "There are no quick fixes," says Millie. "It often takes at least two years to get a result. You learn to take it slowly. Now she's not stealing from the other kids, so that's a big achievement." When the girls arrive home from school each day, their schedule is similar to that of the boys' with horseriding, chores, trips into town to go swimming or to the gym, working towards their Duke of Edinburgh Awards, community work, schoolwork, talking and TV. Father Chris and some of his kids occasionally visit Lois House for a meal and there are plans for more visits in the future between the farms. "He's got such an amazing energy," says Millie. "He just walks into the room and the kids behave. That can be very hard on the rest of the staff. He's there and the kids are like angels with halos around their heads."

The girls, however, don't always respond to Father Chris like that at first. Skye, 16, who went to Lois House after three years as a heroin addict, says she hated him at first. "I'd never met a priest before, and I thought they'd all be old fuddy-duddies," she says. "I was a real brat to him at first. I really didn't like him. But then he talked to me, and I thought he was the wisest person I'd ever met. He's so witty and quick on the uptake, too. He's unreal, he's so cool." He also seems to have the ability to inspire kids to aspire to any dearly held goal, however unlikely. Sally, for example, despite her background of persistent theft, drug-taking, alcohol abuse and sleeping on the streets, clearly has her own ambitions. "I want to be a police officer," she says. "Why not? I know the law off by heart."

There's a waiting list for girls who want to go to Lois House, which sometimes sparks resentment among those hoping to be referred for a place either from the refuge in Marrickville, or the detox centre at Dunlea. One girl at the refuge sneers when she hears Father Chris's name mentioned. "He's a bastard," she says. "I don't like him." Later it turns out she's one of the girls waiting for a spot. In the meantime, she's forced to hang on at the refuge, with its 16 beds and its average of 10 to 12 kids at any one time. "The kids generally really like it whenever he stops in," says refuge manager Gary Lockhart. "He gets on well with them, and he's got such an air about him, they always jump into line whenever he's around." Those kids at the refuge fall into one of three main categories. Firstly there are the kids who are newly kicked out of home and get picked up on the streets by the police in the early hours of the morning. They, generally, have never stayed in a refuge before, and don't have alcohol or drug problems. They are moved on as soon as possible, before they mix too much with the "hardcore" kids with far bigger problems. Secondly, there are the kids who are out of refuges run by other organisations for only an occasional drug habit. These kids are often referred to Dunlea.

Finally, there's the group for whom the refuge is really set up: youngsters who've been moved around a lot, may have serious substance abuse problems, and have been living mostly on the streets. The refuge offers them a place to stay, meals, counselling, help with applying to other agencies, such as DOCS, for assistance, and practical advice and information about drug or alcohol programs. "Then we'll try to engage them," says Gary. "We'll spend as much time as we can with them and work out what they want to do, and try to do as much positive stuff as we can. We find out what they like to do with their time, and help them do it, things like horseriding, or trips to the movies. Success might be moving into their own place, or totally cleaning up their act, or going on to Dunlea."

At Dunlea, the eight-bed refuge that runs a two-week rapid detox program, the atmosphere is calm and relaxed. A group of four kids sit in a focus group, talking over their problems. Another pair are being taught living skills by youth workers, while a couple of other girls write in their journals. It's always a non-medicated stay: they're all going cold turkey, after a doctor has examined each of them and confirmed that this won't put them in danger. The program aims not only to get them off drugs or alcohol, but also to adequately prepare them to sustain realistic living arrangements and increase their ability to manage their lives effectively. There's also an arts component, where the kids are encouraged to be creative as a way of improving their self-esteem. Some of the poetry and stories they write are heartbreaking.

One child wrote about her eleventh birthday gift from her father: a shot of cocaine. The next morning he injected her with some more before she went to school. That day, by pure coincidence, her class had a lesson about sex, alcohol and drugs. When she realised what her dad had done, she ran away from home and stayed with a friend for two weeks. When she finally returned, he injected her again. And again. On her fourteenth birthday, he asked her what her birthday wish was. She said it was to give up drugs completely. When he tried to inject her, she knocked the needle out of his hand. In a rage, he ordered her two brothers to hold her down while he gave her four shots, one after the other. At 15, she left home again, and was placed at Dunlea. Her essay, however, shows a surprising lack of bitterness towards her father. "At the moment, all I'm thinking about is giving up drugs and getting my life back together," she writes. "My family blames my father for the way I have turned out, but it isn't no one's [sic] fault but my own. I could have said 'No' in the beginning, and I didn't. It was the biggest mistake of my life. When my life is back to the way it used to be, I will try my best to help my father. He has been using drugs for more than 30 years and it isn't long till I lose him. You have only got one father, and no matter how much he has f...ed up, you will never stop loving him."

A 15-year-old writes of how his father shot his mother before turning the gun on himself. The boy then describes being taken in by a half-brother and his wife. His new "mother", bewildered by how she'd inherited a kid who kept throwing up at mealtimes and messing himself, beat him badly. Drugs were the only thing that made him feel good. Pushing them was the only way he could afford them. Eventually, the boy was sent to a detention centre, where, following three suicide attempts, he was prescribed anti-depressants. He's still trying to deal with his confusion. "I love partying and dancing, but I can never see the way that I can party without drugs," he writes.

"This leaves me where I stand now, wanting, and not wanting, to quit."

The success rate at Dunlea is pretty good, with around 40 per cent completing the program. "Often it takes a couple of times before they stop," says one of the youth workers, Denai Smith. "They usually come back a second time, and then they tend to be more determined. The first four days are the worst, then it gets easier. Most of it comes down to problems with the family, verbal abuse, sexual abuse, assault. When they're on drugs, they don't have to think about it for a couple of hours. We show them better ways to cope than drugs. There's always hope. The biggest step for the kids is getting through the front door." Denai says that while she doesn't see much of Father Chris, who visits once a week or once a fortnight, the workers there always know that if there's a big problem, they can phone him. "Some of these kids are only around because of him," says Denai. "He's a very down-to-earth type of guy. That's good because these kids need that authority. It's good for them. He's done excellent work."

While a number of Dunlea's residents have been referred from the refuge, others are sent there by DOCS, Juvenile Justice or they just walk in themselves. Many are encouraged to go there by the volunteers who staff the *Youth* food van, which today supplies 17,000 meals a year to streetkids. Another point of contact is the Streetwalk, which sees other trained volunteers, under the guidance of the program manager, Tong Galiki, walk particular streets at night between 10 p.m. and 3 a.m., checking that kids are all right, helping kids in need and slowly building relationships with those who say they'd prefer to be left alone. "I think often just our presence makes them feel safer," says Tong. "But some of them don't trust anyone. They get used to seeing you around, and gradually they start to open up."

After Dunlea, some move on to McIntosh House next door, the semi-independent living and mentoring program for previously drug-addicted, abused and/or severely disadvantaged kids, from the age of 16. Each resident is supported by a case worker and a mentor from the community to help them start their transition into mainstream society. Eighteen-year-old Jeffrey is among the program's first residents, a youngster who was living on the streets, became a gang member and then started using and selling drugs. After detoxing successfully, he now goes to a new school set up nearby, Chapel School. This was one of the subjects of the Channel Seven television show *Undercover Angels*, in which Olympic swimming star Ian Thorpe directs his female helpers to do good deeds. One week, the television program arranged for the chapel of the old convent on the Merrylands site to be converted into two classrooms to fulfil Father Chris's dream of it working as a much more efficient school. Along the way, Father Chris won another fan. "He does a great job for kids," said Ian. Jeffrey agrees, too. "McIntosh is such a good idea," he says. "Before you go independent, it helps you get a job and settle down. I hope to go part-time to school, and part-time to work."

Over in the bright airy classroom at the city school, Key College, its walls decorated with artwork, Min Bonwick is holding a maths class for a group of kids. On the far wall, they're running their own Archibald contest, and every visitor is asked to vote for their favourite painting. They're all surprisingly good. "These kids are all very bright," says Min. "They just haven't been given the opportunity before to show it. You'll often see them blossoming, in lots of ways."

Around eight pupils come to the school every day to study, some sent in by the refuges, DOCS and Juvenile Justice, while others walk in from the street. On their first day at the school, many of the kids are surprised that it's such a nice place. After the first few days, all the pupils seem to start feeling a sense of ownership for the school, and are protective of everything about it. The school thus rarely has any problems with graffiti, theft or violence. The kids even cut back on their swearing. Often Min and her fellow teacher Bernie Eviston are amazed by how some of the kids, usually with nowhere stable to stay, manage to turn up every day, clean, well-groomed and immaculately dressed, and then sit down and focus on schoolwork, despite horrendous personal and family problems. One boy there had been treated so badly by his mother that he once wrote what he felt about her in his own blood on a wall. Another kid who came in had problems with the word "ticket". She'd grown up thinking "concession" meant exactly the same thing, as her mother had never bought a full price ticket in her life.

Classes at Key College run from 9.15 a.m. to 3.15 p.m., with many of the pupils these days aged around 14, compared to the average age of 16 when the school first started. Sometimes, it can be tough keeping a 14-year-old's attention, so breaks are built into the school day. Today during class, one girl wanders off to work on a song she's writing, another boy rushes into the next room to play the piano and, unfortunately, a third pupil has decided to learn how to play the drums. The noise from next door is deafening. Min simply smiles, her head cocked to one side. "He's getting better, I think," she says, patiently. All pupils are given the choice about whether they want to take exams at the end of the year, and most are pretty successful. But how do you define success for kids who have often missed out completely on two years of schooling? One kid came to Key College for one day, absolutely loved it, and was then locked up in gaol the next day. His visit was a success of sorts, says Min. "It was a day off the streets, and a vision of how life might be one day when he gets out."

Certainly, some of the kids at Key College might later go on to one of the farms, all of which are used to catering for kids with terrible problems. Mark David Farm was closed for two weeks in mid-2002 so the walls could be lined with plywood. "It's a pretty house, but our kids get angry and put their fists through the walls," says Father Chris, matter-of-factly. "Now if the kids hit the wall, it'll break their hand, basically. At least they won't do it again!" Originally, Mark David Farm took boys of varying ages, then they focused on younger boys, today it once again caters for all age groups after it was found the program worked better with a mix of ages.

"Mark David has a sense of tranquillity about it," says manager Ron Brien. "There are the horses, the chooks, the way it's set up. It's very good for the kids' well-being and recovery. We've undergone lots of renovations, like installing shatter-proof glass in the pool room to make it a safer environment. The kids feed the horses, look after the chooks, collect eggs, help prepare tea. Many have been highly involved in drugs, like speed, marijuana and ecstasy, so some can develop paranoia and all sorts of effects. It's fantastic when you see kids moving on and succeeding. But it's very hard work. Father Chris is a huge inspiration there. You look at him doing three shifts in a row and you think, 'I'm doing OK!' He's the one who really keeps everyone going, the commitment he has. He never gives up on any of the kids. It's incredibly inspiring."

At Better Homes, a lot of attention is focused on the horses too. They all tend to be good horses; Father Chris believes in buying fairly expensive horses so if the kids enter shows, they have an excellent chance of winning. "I don't want to have streetkids on dumb old horses," says Father Chris. "I want to make sure they have as good an opportunity of winning as possible." Holborow House, up at Muswellbrook, also has horses for its six kids and staff and links with the local communities are strong, with committees in their nearby towns supporting the farms. In Queensland too, the farm Connie's Place has great backing from its Gold Coast neighbours.

One of the newest programs is Mirvac House, for children who've offended sexually, the only residential treatment facility in Australia for youngsters who've committed those kinds of offences outside Juvenile Justice. Run in line with the philosophy of young people taking responsibility for themselves and for their group, its central premise is that kids are inventive and versatile, with the ability to solve their own problems. And staff encourage them to do so. The six residents are aged between 13 and 16, with a confirmed history of offending, and a willingness to admit to these offences and "own" their problem. They're likely to be kids who might otherwise have slipped through the court system and gone on to re-offend, for example a boy who's abused his little sister but whose parents don't want to involve the police. The kids are expected to stay at Mirvac House for between nine and 16 months. The centre is designed to make sure kids have little opportunity of abusing each other: glass panels in doors ensure the kids can't hide, so they will feel confident they can't be cornered by another child or member of staff, and movement sensors are switched on at night in case one kid tries to slip into another's room. "I believe it can work," says centre manager Jill Smith, one of the 10 staff at Mirvac House. "We've just got to convince the wider community that we can help young people make the change. It's quite a confronting environment here, they can't sidestep issues. We look at attitudes and values about everything: how to interact with other people, dating behaviours, respect for others, setting boundaries." The kids here go to Matthew Hogan School, then come back to Mirvac House to cook meals, do chores, tend the vegetable garden, play basketball, and all the normal things families do at home.

Mirvac House is an ambitious project, primarily funded by *Youth* with $3500 donated weekly per child by DOCS towards the extraordinarily high running costs, and based on the highly successful Starr Commonwealth programs in the US. Founded in 1913, these provide a wide array of services to children, youth and families from locations throughout Michigan and Ohio, from prevention and enrichment to residential treatment. Jill paid her own way to the US to study the Starr Commonwealth sex offenders program. She returned convinced it would also work in Australia — as was Father Chris. "He has really got the courage to have a go at this," she says. "He's a big picture person. He wants to see this work. He even has a vision of Mirvac 2 down the track."

Kids who do well at Mirvac, like the kids who do well at every single one of the programs, all receive certificates and prizes at the annual *Youth* presentation night, the one evening of the year when all the young people from every program come together to celebrate their achievements. From that first event in 1995 at Martin Place, it's now grown in terms of slickness and sophistication. In the early years, Father Chris had to stagger up the escalator of the regular venue, Bankstown Sports Club, with a terrified Collingwood in his arms after she refused to ride beside him. The kids weren't well prepared either. "They turned up in dirty old clothes with lollipops hanging out of their mouths, and baseball caps on backwards," says David McIntosh. "They didn't take the lollipops out of their mouths to talk to us, even when the Governor-General was out front. Father Chris was trying to pat them on the back, and they were all pretending to be tough." Radio host Alan Jones, who volunteers his services as the annual MC of the night, remembers those days well. "God! You'd feel lucky to get out alive," he says. "They were really rough and difficult kids."

Then one year, Colleen McIntosh gave the girls a sewing machine that she rarely used. They decided to make their own dresses for the evening, with the help of Millie at Lois House, who once owned her own fashion label. The boys heard about it and asked Father Chris for money to buy new clothes for the big event. "No," he said. "You'll have to look in the St Vincent de Paul shops." When the night finally arrived, few could believe the transformation. "No one could believe it when they turned up," says Colleen. "They'd changed completely. They looked *amazing*. The girls looked lovely." Barbara Holborow adds that the girls even took the rings out of their noses and lips. "They looked absolutely beautiful," she sighs. "And the boys looked so smart," Colleen smiles, shaking her head. "One boy was in a suit four sizes too big, with the sleeves rolled up and the shoulders falling off him," she says. "Another kid had this bright orange suit on. I'd never *seen* an orange suit before! You could see him glowing in the dark as he walked proudly through the hall to go up onto the stage to pick up his prize." Alan Jones did a double-take when he saw the boy, and said to him, good-naturedly, "Aren't *you* a picture of sartorial splendour!"

Alan is always simply astonished by the kids at the Bankstown event. "Some of the kids can be apprehensive about talking, but I speak to every one of them and I treat them as I find them, there and then. I ask them what they're going to do, and tell them that we're proud of them. Some of them are very funny, some are shy. But they're all kids who've really suffered yet are doing great things: going to university, getting jobs, passing exams. It's all very humbling."

Val O'Keefe, formerly of Murdoch Magazines, says she's usually in tears all through the evening. "I've watched the girls grow into young women, the boys into proud young men. You're so touched, listening to all their stories. A lot of them have had such hideous lives, it's amazing they've even survived. It's absolutely miraculous. And Chris is so totally dedicated, if only he could clone himself."

When the presentation draws to a close, everyone is usually tired, emotional, and utterly uplifted by these smiling, glowing young men and women, all of whom have come so close to losing everything, taking their place on stage, being congratulated and celebrated by everyone who's had a role in turning their lives around. "By the end of the evening, I'm exhausted," says Alan. "But to think that Father Chris is doing this thing every day, day in and day out ... Someone like that just has to be supported."

Father Chris spends these evenings encouraging his kids, smiling at them, applauding their success, and thanking God that he could play a role in helping them. "People can't believe them when they see them," he says, proudly. "They say these kids look like movie stars. They're just gorgeous kids. They're lovely kids, a real joy to be with."

Chapter 25

SAVE ONE CHILD, SAVE THE WORLD

FOR FATHER CHRIS, it was set to be his biggest challenge yet: a trip to war-torn East Timor to help children orphaned by the years of bloody conflict.

But when the five boys from *Youth Off The Streets* first arrived at the orphanage in October 2002, the children there were wary. They watched their visitors curiously, shrinking away when they approached and following their every move wide-eyed. After an hour or so, the boys brought out balls for the youngsters to play with. Suddenly all barriers came crashing down, as everyone piled in together for an impromptu game of soccer through the dusty, war-torn streets of the capital Dili.

Father Chris watched the scene with undisguised pleasure. It wasn't very long ago that those same boys had been living on the streets, wrestling with drug addiction and alcoholism, and involved in crime to support their habits. One had been locked up in gaol. Another had been so closed to the outside world that everyone at *Youth* had despaired he'd ever recover. But here they all were now, yelling and laughing and whooping as they kicked the balls around, passing them to the smaller kids and gently lifting some of the littlies out of scrums and onto their shoulders. "This is even better than I'd hoped," says Father Chris, his grin broad as he watches the Australians and East Timorese mix joyfully together. "These boys have so much love and laughter to give. It's just all about allowing them to have the opportunity to give it." Former Australian Governor-General Sir William Deane smiles at the scene. "It's a marvellous moment when these young people start looking outwards for the first time," he says. "They want to help others and, in doing that, they also heal themselves."

For the past six months, the kids at the *Youth* farms in the southern highlands had been doing everything they could to raise money for three orphanages in East Timor, for their counterparts on the streets of the newly independent tiny nation, brought to its knees by the departing Indonesians. Kids at the farms had been selling raffle tickets, cleaning cars and doing any little odd job they could find to save enough cash to make sizeable donations to the orphanages, which would be used to buy gifts for the children and supply as much food and vital equipment as they could afford. Now, at last, they were in Dili and were receiving a welcome much warmer than they'd ever dared hope. The smiling East Timorese children were now clustered around each of the five boys, pulling at their clothes, eagerly vying for their attention and giggling with excitement.

After a couple of days, the *Youth* kids visited another orphanage two hours away before making the six-hour

back-breaking drive up to Baguia, a village on the slopes
of the country's second tallest mountain, the 7000-metre
Mate Bian. As they bounced over pitted, unmade roads,
children appeared from nowhere to wave and chase the
minibus towards the third orphanage of their tour.
When the visitors finally pulled up in front of the
orphanage, it seemed as though the whole village had
turned out to greet them. It was a massive culture shock
for the boys. They were used to a quiet life in the NSW
countryside, where they'd been studying for their HSC
at the Matthew Hogan School and living at one of the
farms nearby. Despite this, they all agreed that they
loved East Timor. "It's awesome," says Beau, 18. "But it
was a shock to see how little they all had. You see the
houses, the village, the whole environment. It makes you
feel like a king. It made me realise how well off we are
in Australia." Luke, 16, says that he too was often
taken aback by scenes they saw. "They don't have much,
and they've been through such a bad time, and I thought
they were all going to be unhappy," he says. "But they
were smiling and laughing all the time. I couldn't believe
it."

As soon as Father Chris and his kids disembarked from
the minibus, staff at the orphanage vanished, leaving the
six of them to run the place — unable to speak a word of
the local language, and without a clue where anything
was. The number of kids there, many of them orphaned
by the war, multiplied by the day. When Father Chris and
the boys had arrived, there were 50 children aged between
five and 12 under their care; by the time word had spread
about the visitors from Australia, there were more than

150. But the boys mucked in whole-heartedly, playing with the children from sun-up to well past sun-down. "It was just exhausting," says Joe, 18. "You'd be playing games with them all the time. We played soccer, we ran around all day, we went swimming. It was heaps good."

Abel Gutterres, from East Timor's Ministry of Foreign Trade, watched the scenes with amazement. "The boys were so good and patient with the children," he says. "They handled them very well. They were very gentle. It was such an impressive time. The way they approached them and interacted with them ... wonderful. Even after the boys had left, the children were talking about them for weeks afterwards, and I'm sure the *Youth* boys will have found it valuable playing such a role in society. There was so much mutual learning and friendship there. And Father Riley! What an incredible guy! He has so much energy, I couldn't believe it!"

It had long been a dream of Father Chris's to involve his kids in an ambitious service learning project. Over the years, *Youth* kids had become greatly involved in local communities, including fundraising events for other charities and tackling projects that would help the environment. "Service learning is a process of self-discovery too," he says. "Through success in helping others, youth learn to view themselves differently. They recognise they have gifts which are of value to others, which nurtures feelings of pride and positive self-esteem. They then begin to view themselves as capable of facing challenges which they had never before thought were within their reach. I believe these kids have so much to give."

The week the boys spent in East Timor, with patron Sir William, far exceeded Father Chris's wildest expectations. "We didn't include any training for actually running an orphanage!" he says. "But they managed extremely well. I was so impressed. If you could have heard them running around, having so much fun with these kids and calling the former Governor-General 'Willy Deaney' ..." Sir William simply laughed. "This kind of project really gets them thinking about others rather than themselves," Sir William says. "Their self-esteem as a result will go up. It will do wonders for their self-confidence, the travelling as a group and being part of decisions about what's happening, as well as meeting streetkids in Dili and around the country and being able to help them. It's tremendous."

As well as playing constantly with the orphans, the boys took them swimming at a local muddy waterhole and entertained them with magic tricks, party balloons, dances and sporting moves. Soon, the orphans were following the boys everywhere they went. The boys found they could communicate pretty well with the orphans via hand gestures, facial expressions — and lollies. One day, they threw jelly snakes to the kids and watched, aghast, as they fled: they thought the snakes were real. Another day, the boys held drawing and colouring-in competitions, with more lollies as the prizes. Father Chris was forced to intervene: he had to initial each drawing after the boys pointed out that the kids were coming up more than once with the same picture. Even then, the kids at the orphanage continued to outwit the Australians, incorporating Father Chris's signature into their drawing to disguise the fact they'd already collected their lollies. That night, tired after a 6 a.m. start, the boys couldn't understand why the kids were still racing around, singing and dancing at 10.30 p.m. "I think we over-sugared them with lollies," said Father Chris, tiredly. Explains Beau, "We had to go around the corner and hide in the end as they wouldn't go to sleep when we were there."

The experience is proving life-changing for everyone involved. The boys learnt about East Timor's long struggle for independence, met kids who had been forced to do things against their own families by Indonesian troops, and talked to children who had lost limbs during the fighting. They also had a meeting with East Timor's first lady, Melburnian Kirsty Sword Gusmao, the wife of President Xanana Gusmao. By the time the boys came to say their sad goodbyes and hand out the farewell gifts to the East Timorese, it was hard to tell who was the most upset — the children the boys were leaving behind, or the boys themselves. One of the boys continued sobbing in the plane on the way home, so upset was he to be leaving the children behind. "They all built such strong bonds with these kids," says Father Chris. "I was very, very proud." Today, ask Beau, Joe and Luke what they want to do in the future, and they all agree: more charity work. "I'd just like to travel around Third World countries and try to help them, and give as much back as I can," says Beau. "I wouldn't mind travelling and helping other kids either," agrees Joe. "They go through a pretty hard time. Five is pretty young to be an orphan and to be homeless." And, says Luke, "I would like to travel around the world and visit places like East Timor."

Immediately upon their return to Australia the five boys
started saving again in the hope of being able to return and
help once more.

There are always plenty of projects on the go where
Youth kids are given the opportunity to help others. A
group of kids recently went to the Snowies to muster, on
horseback, some wild brumbies and bring them back
down to the *Youth* farms. There, the kids hope to tame
them, train them and sell them off to good homes. That
way, the brumbies, who otherwise would have been
culled, get to live, the kids have the satisfaction of saving
the brumbies from an often painful death, they manage to
raise more funds for future projects, and they learn even
more about relating to animals. The brumbies are perfect
for this. Naturally nervous and skittish, they respond only
to patient kindness, after learning to trust their handler.

Many people have warned Father Chris that some of his
ideas to help his kids are so far-fetched that they are
completely impossible. Frequently, however, they have to
eat their words. "He's got such great vision," says Key
College's Min Bonwick. "He's ridiculous at times. Some of
his ideas are crazy." "But then," says fellow teacher Bernie
Eviston, "some of his crazy ideas work, for instance, Key
College!" Min agrees: "It's amazing what he's done on a
shoestring."

He's rarely put off by either doubts or shortages of
money, either. Min went to the US to take a look at the
Starr Commonwealth program, while Father Chris was
setting up Mirvac House. She was startled by the enormity
of the American program, and also that it was close to all
the facilities of big cities and fabulously resourced — with

psychiatrists, many staff members, and every type of expert only large amounts of money can buy. "And here's Father, trying to do the same thing in the middle of nowhere at the end of an unmade road. And then he can't understand why it's not up and running so quickly, exactly the way the American project is," she says.

Father Chris seems to let little stop him when he has a good idea. In 2001, after the devastation of the NSW bushfires, he established a program for dealing with the kids who were responsible for lighting many of the fires, the Juvenile Fire-setters Intervention Project. He believed that many of the young fire-setters had severe emotional problems and family difficulties, and that some of these kids were lighting fires as a cry for help rather than a clear-headed intention to damage, destroy or kill. Father Chris felt that it was far better to deal with the cause of their problems, rather than merely punishing the kids for the outcomes of their actions. Some of his options for treatment include conferencing, residential placements and therapeutic programs. He was alarmed, however, to hear NSW Premier Bob Carr on radio in January 2002 talking about how it was important to humiliate and lock up these young people instead. Father Chris immediately phoned as many radio stations as he could to publicly attack the Premier's stand, and to try to present the positive alternatives.

"If you're going to put these kids in gaol, you're just going to have to build more gaols the next year. In fact, then you're going to have to build new ones every year," Father Chris said on air. "These kids need treatment programs, not detention centres from which they'll come out even more angry and determined to do more damage. We need to solve the problem, not create new ones. And if we don't act soon, the country will burn every year. Bob Carr is actually setting up the State to be constantly burning. Locking them up solves nothing. One guy I have at one of the projects has been in detention centres on and off since the age of 13. Now he's 18, and is one of the most aggressive kids I've ever had. We should be putting the kids in places where they can heal, rather than punishing them and humiliating them. Kids in the US who are degraded and humiliated are the ones who carry out those schoolyard massacres." According to Father Chris, Bob Carr stopped calling for juvenile fire-setters to be locked up after the priest's own on-air campaign.

Continually expanding *Youth* to help as many kids as he can is always at the forefront of Father Chris's mind. He's now producing drug education kits for distribution around all schools in Australia and has recently set up an industrial arts program at Matthew Hogan School that he'll be studying carefully to quantify its therapeutic effects. He's also trying to get a TV program on air to educate parents about how to bring up kids and show young people that there's always hope despite their problems — that they deserve the best start in life, and as many chances as they need to get it right.

New programs are opening all the time. One of the latest is another farm for girls, located at Mangrove Mountain on NSW's Central Coast. Donated by Mike Willesee, and named Gordana House in honour of his wife, the farm focuses on health issues, holistic medicine, diet and issues like ADHD. "I started thinking about the enormity of Father Chris's work," says Mike when asked about his donation. "How does he achieve it all? How does one man go on to the streets and then find these kids, build homes for them, educate them, get them off drugs, go to court for them, get them out of hospitals? I was extremely impressed. He's so modest and humble, even naïve in lots of ways. I thought, he needs all the help he can get."

Father Chris's greatest ambition is to stamp out child prostitution: to make sure kids are safe from the men who prey on them, humiliate them, use and abuse them. He's dealt with the aftermath of too many kids enslaved as prostitutes. He'll never forget the 13-year-old girl who was locked up in a small flat with several other girls until it was time to go to "work" every day. She was beaten by her pimp if she tried to refuse. Father Chris has learnt that most of the young prostitutes on the street work six or seven nights a week, doing three tricks a night, often including risky and degrading sexual acts, for between $200 and $600 per "client". "But only the pimps get rich," he says. "And then they play terrible games with the children." Lower-class pimps often snatch a kid off the street, throw them in a cheap motel room and then charge clients $15 for 15 minutes in which they let them do anything they want to the kid. Often, that pimp will sell the girl or boy to a more sophisticated pimp who, in comparison, is seen to be "rescuing" the child from a violent life. The new pimp promises these children he will protect and take care of them, encouraging the young boys and girls to yearn for his love and affection. The pimp can then manipulate and psychologically dominate these kids. "Almost all pimps prey on kids who are financially and emotionally vulnerable," says Father Chris. "Often runaways, or kids who have been sexually assaulted."

During a recent trip to Canada, Father Chris experienced first-hand how children are being protected there. He accompanied detectives on a raid of a well-known pick-up spot for child prostitutes in Vancouver. They waited in an unmarked police car until a customer drove up to a girl and lured her into his car. Then they pounced. Legislation enacted in British Columbia means that the authorities have the power to take the child to a safe house and make sure he or she is protected. The men who sexually prey on children are given a choice of either going to court, or taking part in a revolutionary education program, called the Police and the Prostitution Offender Program, or "John School". The program educates offenders about the sex trade, why children are taking part, and the terrible long-term effects it has on the lives of these kids. Established in September 1999, it's a community-driven, self-funding initiative which is aimed at cutting the demand that fuels the child sex trade. So far, not a single man who has attended the program has re-offended. Father Chris would love to see Australia adopt this approach, starting with amending the current legislation. "At the moment, our laws are crazy," he says. "A child protection police officer told me that police have to actually witness the sex act take place before they can move in on the man. That's patently ridiculous. And every night, these officers are forced to stand by while men cruise the streets picking up underaged girls and boys, knowing they can do nothing to protect these children. We have to do something, and soon."

Father Chris realises that the personal price of launching this kind of campaign will be high. Already used to receiving death threats, he knows that these will only become more frequent, and more serious, and there could well be determined attempts to slur his name and discredit his work to distract attention from those engaged in the child sex trade. He is even bracing himself for false allegations of sexual abuse against him in respect of the very children he has done so much to save from that evil. Needless to say, any such allegation would hurt him terribly, but he is adamant that such risks cannot be allowed to deter him from effecting real change.

"You expect those kind of allegations when you start campaigning against things like child prostitution," says Father Chris. "The most difficult thing about being a priest today is that everyone is very quick to believe it, too. I'm the first to say if a priest has been involved in paedophilia, gaol him for life. But then the mud sticks to us all." Father Chris has absolutely no sympathy either with the approach that a child who has been sexually abused by an adult could somehow be regarded as compliant in the offence. "There are too many people who say the kids deserve what they get, and that's ridiculous," he says. "These kids don't have a choice. That approach really epitomises the way paedophiles justify their actions against children. You can't attach the responsibility to the young person."

These days, anyone working with children is vulnerable to accusations of paedophilia — particularly a Catholic priest working with damaged youngsters. Astonishingly, in 29 years of working with kids, Father Chris has only ever had one allegation made against him, in 1999. After being investigated by the police, as all such accusations routinely are, the allegation was immediately dismissed. Father Chris hadn't even been in the same city at the same time as the young man who had made the claim.

The potential for such accusations remains a constant concern for Father Chris. If one person makes a mischievous claim against him that's not so easily refuted, his reputation and — most importantly to him — his work could be destroyed. It's for this reason he often takes elaborate precautions, avoiding ever being alone in a room with a child or, often, even an adult. At a function one evening, when he'd entered the lift to leave the building, a couple of people were startled to see one of his co-workers race over when she saw a woman was also about to get in, so she'd travel with them. Fellow teacher Adele Sims recalls one night when a kid in their care had fallen asleep while his radio continued to play loudly. "Father Chris had to call me to ask me to come with him to go into the room to switch the radio off. He's so very careful all the time."

Some of Father Chris's youngsters, unaware of the difficulties he faces, sometimes feel a bit hurt that he won't put an arm around them, or let them hug him. For some though, the situation has become a bit of a joke. "Yesterday Jemma went up to him in class and tried to give him a hug and it was so funny," says Sally, a resident at Lois House. "He put his hands up immediately in front of him, stepped back and said, 'Back off, Jemma, back off.

Personal space! Personal space!'" she laughs, mimicking Father Chris's reflex actions.

A priest's commitment to celibacy can invite suspicion from some people, and is certainly a topic of curiosity. Even Father Chris's family have tackled him on the issue. His sister Helen challenged him one day, asking where it was written in the Bible that priests couldn't get married. "He said it wasn't in there, and that he couldn't see why they can't get married, but he would never marry," reports Helen. "I asked why. He said, 'It would be unfair to my wife, and any kids we'd have. I just don't have time for them.'" Rather, the significance of a priest's chastity is explained in the Bible as the decision to follow Jesus closely "by choosing an intensely evangelical way of loving God and our neighbour with undivided heart". While Father Chris admits that, at 18, celibacy was a tough option, later it became a positive reality, an inseparable consequence of a greater gift, and such a way of his life that today he never thinks about it. "It never enters my mind," he says. "I'm so guarded and focused, I would never let myself be vulnerable to anyone. I'm very careful about stuff like that. And, having seen all the problems it causes for kids, sometimes I feel very glad not to be involved in that side of life! Even the thought of marriage now terrifies me, my life is so hectic. I couldn't imagine sitting in a car travelling around Australia with the same person all the time. I think, how can people do that? I sometimes make my own coffee and someone will say, 'Gee, you're so selfish why didn't you make me one too?' I have to say, 'Sorry, I'm so used to being alone.'"

He's similarly dismissive of the notion that, as someone who cares so much for children, he's missing out by not having his own. "I reckon I'm as close as, or closer than, most dads are to their sons and daughters. So, no, I don't think I've missed out. I think I'm really lucky. I spend most of my time with kids. Christmas without kids? I can't imagine it. Up until recently, I hadn't been with my own family for 30 years for Christmas, because the kids were too important."

For Christmas 2001 he made a surprise trip to Echuca and when he knocked on his parents' front door he was talking to his mum on his mobile as if he was phoning from the farm. As she opened the door and saw her son she reeled back in shock, then delight. It was the first Christmas since the death of his elder brother Peter. Conducting that funeral, he realised how much he'd lost touch with his family. He was startled to see how packed the church was, and realised he'd had no idea Peter had been so popular. And he hadn't seen Peter's children in 15 years. "I was staggered," he admits. "There were all these people at the funeral, and I didn't know him. We used to sleep in the same bedroom as kids but as we grew up I really only saw him at funerals. I think if I have any regrets in my life, it's just that I don't know my family. I'm now trying harder to spend time with them."

It's difficult, however, with so many demands on his time, and so many people all wanting his attention. It's a fine balancing act. He has to juggle seeing the benefactors of *Youth*, spending time with the kids, placating different interest groups so he'll retain the support of each, reading up on new research about streetkids and treatment programs, seeing the cases that need his personal care, and making sure all of his projects are working the best they can, fine-tuning the charters of each in response to supply and demand. When too few kids came forward for the sex offenders program at Mirvac House, for instance, he re-wrote it in September 2002 to include kids with matters coming before the courts, rather than being aimed only at those with no official proceedings. Reconciling the strictures of his religion with the running of a non-denominational charity is also difficult. At one board meeting, some of the members baulked about the teachers at Key College forwarding to Father Chris information about girls who were undergoing pregnancy terminations. The teachers felt it was important for Father Chris to know all the details of the kids, since the stresses and strain of going through such a major event in their lives was an important factor to consider in their progress. Despite his deeply held opposition to abortion, Father Chris agreed he needed to know.

"He has to consider so many people's opinions, support them all and then come down with the wisdom about how things have to be done," says Adele. "It's all very political. And a lot of people try to own him, because he's single and lives alone. A lot of women try to mother him. He can't stand that. It drives him nuts. He's a very complex man. Sometimes, you think that what you see is what you get, for example, he finds it hard to hide his feelings — when he's embarassed, he flushes red, and when he's angry, you can see it in his eyes — but he tries to be very contained at the same time. Some people might say he seems quite cold and unfeeling, like at the time of the car crash that killed two of his kids and a youth worker. They wouldn't know how distraught he was and how he shut himself away to grieve. But Laurie and I knew him from the days when he was human, rather than an icon. We know that if anything happens to his kids, he's devastated."

While he remains in contact with as many of the kids as he can, it's rare that he stays in touch with adults. He forgets people. He's often just too busy to return calls. Yet contact with his fellow workers and supporters do help sustain him through the difficult times. If he were surrounded only by kids and their problems, he does imagine he could start to become bitter and cynical about human cruelty. "But the knowledge that these kids can be healed sustains you too," he says.

Father Chris believes that one of the greatest problems is other people's cynicism. Many potential employers won't give the kids a chance when they emerge from *Youth* programs, regarding them with mistrust and suspicion. Val O'Keefe, formerly of Murdoch Magazines, agrees. "We employed a lot of the kids here, and never had a single problem with any of them in all that time," she says. "But I know Father Chris finds it hard [to place them in jobs]. I wish more employers would open their hearts to these kids and give them a go."

Some believe Government departments should do a great deal more to help the kids who need it the most, and that Father Chris shouldn't be operating in such a vacuum. DOCS Director-General Dr Neil Shepherd, however, declined to comment for this book, as did Juvenile Justice Director-General David Sherlock, the man with whom Father Chris had earlier clashed in his previous position at DOCS over kids being placed with paedophiles.

Father Chris has plenty of support elsewhere, though. Sir William Deane is unflinching in his admiration. "He's one of the country's top professionals in dealing with kids," he says. Politicians also regularly phone Father Chris, seeking his advice before they speak out on youth issues. Fellow youth campaigners Wesley Noffs and Reverend Bill Crews are also, in the main, fans. Wesley, of the Ted Noffs foundation, says that, apart from the way Father Chris rejects the "harm minimisation" approach in favour of total abstinence, he likes him very much for what he says about kids. "I have a great deal of respect for Chris Riley," he says. "I do admire him for the effort he's put in and his tenacity, the way he sticks with it. I think he does a lot of things that [my late father] Ted would have done. It might not be what I consider to be the right way, but I'm a much more conservative person. He's put a lot of people's noses out of joint, particularly in Government departments, by the things he's said and done, but the experience of observing my father at work has shown me that sometimes you have to do that to get things done. And people can be jealous when you're successful." Reverend Bill Crews of the Ashfield Uniting Church agrees. "Always when you do this kind of work, you're going to win both your admirers and your detractors," he says. "You have to get up the noses of people in authority to get anything done. I've been there too. Everyone has enemies. There is a lot of jealousy because he's got a high profile, and if you criticise someone like Chris, it makes you as big as him."

Father Chris's friends in the media are solid admirers too. *A Current Affair*'s Mike Munro says he should be made Australian of the Year every year. "He's the patron saint of kids," he says, "as tough as nails with a heart as big as Australia. A truly inspiring man." Radio 2GB's Alan Jones is in awe of Father Chris and his cause. "He's got to be supported," says Alan. "He says he's going to open up a new program and everyone shudders and worries where the money's going to come from. But he always seems to find it. And helping these kids is only just touching the bottom of a gigantic ocean. Adults have created their problems, they've introduced these kids into a dysfunctional environment, and you'd hope there's a much greater awareness about the plight of streetkids since Father Chris started the *Youth* program."

Father Chris hopes this too. Sure, he's had thousands of failures, he says. There've been thousands of kids he hasn't been able to reach. But along with them have been many who have gone on to live lives in which they find happiness, they have learned to love, and they know what it is like to be loved. "We are showing people they can succeed if they're given the chance. They have the courage to try again, and we have to have the courage to let them. We've got to have the courage to demand greatness from our kids."

Always, for Father Chris, when it comes to his kids, there is hope. It is the one constant. No matter how bad the circumstances are or how grim a child's prognosis may be,

Father Chris always looks for the positives, celebrating even the smallest of wins with his kids. One day, a young man with a long criminal record, newly arrived at the farm, was boasting to some other kids that he was about to steal a vehicle and make his escape. Father Chris came out of the house to see a ring of youngsters around his car. "He might steal a car," one of them said, "but he's not going to steal *your* car, Farvs." Another evening, he fell asleep in a chair at one of the farms, exhausted after driving all over the country in search of another youngster, he hadn't slept for 36 hours. He sensed someone next to him, and half-opened one eye to see a boy, one of the most hard-bitten and aggressive he'd ever taken on, tenderly covering him with a blanket. "I thought, 'Wow!'" he smiles. "I'm so lucky to have these kids."

The biggest worry about Father Chris's work from onlookers seems to be how *Youth* would cope if something happened to its founder and CEO. The head of the Salesian order in Australia, Father Ian Murdoch, asks, "How is he going to make sure that the work he started has continuity and permanence beyond his own lifetime?" With all the structural changes that have taken place within the organisation, however, his deputy Patricia Marsland is confident it would not only survive, but continue to thrive. His staff, too, seem relaxed. "There's a support structure now in place if he dies," says Lois House's Millie Kellett. "We'll still go on. He's learning to delegate more all the time." As for Father Chris, he says he's far too busy working out what he can do about kids now, to worry about what might happen later. "My vision extends only to the next kid," he says.

"I picked up a phrase once from the movie *Schindler's List*, 'He who saves a single life saves the world entire'. I've adapted it to 'If you save one child, you save the world'. That's my focus. One kid at a time. And if they put on my tombstone that I saved one kid, then that would be more than enough for me."

POSTSCRIPT

YOUTH OFF THE STREETS now has more than 20 projects in operation:

- The five boys' farms — Better Homes Farm, Foundation House, Mark David Farm, Holborow House and Connie's Place;
- Two girls' farms — Lois House and Debra Benson House — with a third, Gordana House at Mangrove Mountain on the NSW Central Coast to come online;
- The Don Bosco House refuge;
- The three street outreach projects comprising the food van, street walk and a project in Airds;
- The Dunlea detox centre;
- The McIntosh House semi-independent living mentor program;
- The Mirvac House sex offender program;
- The Matthew Hogan, Key College and Chapel schools; and
- The Juvenile Fire-Setters Intervention Project, the Service Learning Character Development Program

and the Early Intervention and Prevention Schools
Program dealing with issues such as drug awareness.

Eighty per cent of *Youth's* $8 million annual running costs
are paid for by private or corporate donations, with the
Government meeting only 30 per cent of funds needed,
mostly via fees for services. Just eight cents of every dollar
donated goes towards administrative costs, and all gifts
are tax-deductible.

Both donations and volunteers are always needed and
anyone wishing to help should contact the *Youth* head
office on telephone (02) 9721 5700 or fax (02) 9721 0695
or see the website, *www.youthoffthestreets.com.au*

Donations can be made in many ways:

- via the Bequest Program, leaving your estate or part
  of the estate to *Youth*;
- through the corporate supporters program — with
  promotional merchandise also available;
- through the payroll deductions scheme donating from
  as little as $5 a week;
- through partnership arrangements; and
- through one-off donations.

Supporters can also sponsor the costs of helping just one
child, contributing towards the $3000 ($250 per month) it
costs for one child's attendance at Key College per year, or
the $2500 for a child at the Matthew Hogan School ($208
per month).

The organisation is also grateful for gifts of

consumables or second-hand goods, particularly furniture, to sell in its second-hand shops, or items that can be auctioned or raffled at fund-raising functions. All contact details are on the website.

Father Chris has donated all his proceeds from this book to *Youth*, and the author, her agent and the publishers have also made substantial contributions.

ACKNOWLEDGMENTS

From Father Chris Riley

I would like firstly to thank my family for the support they have given me throughout my life from Moama, Echuca, Deniliquin, Melbourne, Oakey and Chapel Hill in Queensland to Griffith, and Gippsland.

In setting up *Youth Off The Streets*, I have been supported and helped by literally thousands of people. I thank every one for that fantastic support. But a special thank you to those who believed in my work in the beginning, when I had nothing. Those are: Alan Burns, Jack Spain, Rita Barrie, Gloria Langridge, Clem McNamara, Jean Manual, Elizabeth Willows, Brock Bowen, Jeanette Cudmore, Debbie Wallace and Robert Fitzgerald.

The story of our kids has been presented sensitively, courageously and positively. I thank the media for their great support. Ron Wilson for running the first story on Channel 10 news. Mike Munro who has been outspokenly supportive of all the work we do with kids and for creating the public face of *Youth Off The Streets*. Sally

MacMillan from the *Sunday Telegraph* for the great stories she did in the early days, and Adam Harvey for his recent stories. Many journalists have helped tremendously along the way — thanks!

I thank also my religious congregation for my training and opportunities along the way. My great mentors in Father Wally Cornell, Father Adrian Papworth and Father Denis Halliday. Father Julian Fox for having the courage to allow me to take on this work. And the men who continue to encourage and support me: Father Bob Bossini, Father John Prest, Father Paul Miles, Father John Murphy, Father Bill Edwards, Brother James Hamilton, and Father Oreste Cantamessa.

Thanks to my dedicated and hard-working personal assistants, Judy Gorton and Ken Hill. Their energy enables me still to be able to do so much direct care work with the kids. To all my staff, who work so hard, and to everyone who has been involved as Board members, thanks so much for sharing the vision and pouring in so much of your own personal commitment and your lives.

Thank you to my great friends and patrons, Lady Helen and Sir William Deane. My gratitude also to our great benefactors: Colleen and Dave McIntosh, Gordana and Mike Willesee, Fiona and Matt Handbury, and the Ainsworth family.

Thanks too for the great support from Jill Herberte and Trish Mackey of the Department of Community Services, to barrister Sue Kluss for her fantastic work defending our kids in the courtroom, and to our Ambassador Marie Sutton for all her great fund-raising initiatives.

Finally, thanks to Sue Williams, the author of this biography, for the way she approached sensitive issues and won the respect of all she talked to, and to Selwa Anthony for making it all happen.

ACKNOWLEDGMENTS

From Sue Williams

I'd like to thank, first of all, Father Chris Riley for being such a fascinating subject for a biography. His energy and enthusiasm for his work never ceased to amaze, inspire and, occasionally, daunt and exasperate me. Even when the odds looked stacked so high you could never see over them to the other side, he would still keep on going, absolutely — some might even say bloody-mindedly — focused on the end result. For a biographer, it made it frequently impossible to keep up.

Along the way, he's picked up many supporters who were overwhelmingly generous about sharing with me some of the experiences and insights they've accumulated along the ride. In particular, Father Chris's mum and dad, Mavis and Kevin, were extremely hospitable, while his sister Helen was wonderfully warm towards, and graciously trusting of, a complete stranger. Colleen and David McIntosh were a fabulous source of amazing anecdotes, both happy and sad, about Father Chris, and Sir William Deane was also very helpful — despite his legendary distrust of journalists — as was Barbara Holborow, Mike Munro and Matt Handbury.

A special thank you too to Father Chris's gorgeous personal assistant Judy who, with her infectious laugh, marvellous sense of fun and quick efficiency about supplying even the most obscure of facts, always buoyed me when the going got tough. I'd also like to thank the dedicated staff of the various *Youth Off The Streets* projects who, often in the middle or at the end of a very long day, still found the energy to talk to me remarkably candidly. Some of the young people Father Chris has helped were unfailingly open and honest too about their lives, and very eager to help me in turn, particularly Rachel, Tammy, Kris, Ben and Tom. I salute your courage.

From a personal viewpoint, I'd also like to thank my dear partner Jimmy Thomson who went painstakingly over the manuscript for me, finding problems, suggesting the perfect change every time and encouraging me all the way through.

My agent Selwa Anthony, as always, was a great source of good sense, strength and wisdom. My wonderful friend Jane Anne Lee was tremendously supportive, and a marvellous listener and giver of advice, while my brother Steve Williams was also very generous in his help. From HarperCollins: Helen Littleton, Sally Collings, Vanessa Radnidge, Ali Orman and Melanie Calabretta were all an absolute delight to deal with. And, finally, thanks to my parents, Bill and Edna, who came with me on the roadtrip around Victoria to visit Father Chris's family, friends and foe alike, sharing the driving, hotel bills, adventures, laughs and flasks of cold coffee.